Praise for *Stay Close*

"Cataldi's writing lays her emotions bare . . . she doesn't pull any punches, never shying away from the hard questions or the tough times."
—*The Capital* (Annapolis, Maryland)

"For every drug addict there are at least four people affected, a depressing assertion by some experts that is clearly borne out in this soft-spoken, utterly honest account."
—*Publishers Weekly*

"A spellbinding and anguished story . . . of a mother's deep love."
—*www.ewtn.com* (Eternal Word Television Network)

"Mental-health professionals and parents of addicts could benefit enormously from reading this heartrending story of a mother's struggle with her son's drug addiction. While addiction memoirs proliferate, few wield the power of this one."
—*Library Journal*

"A mother's exceptionally touching, beautifully written story of pain, and ultimately hope. Cataldi writes a deeply honest, moving chronicle of how the natural, normal love of a family can lock everyone into a negative spiral of horrific loss of control."
—Stephanie Brown, Ph.D., director of The Addictions Institute

"*Stay Close* is the poignant and powerful story of one family's struggle to contend with the ravages of addiction in a beloved son and brother. With enormous courage and honesty, Libby Cataldi lays bare the searing family pain as her son descends into a world they cannot fully understand; her fierce efforts to bring him back to health and sanity; and, ultimately, the redemptive power of love, compassion, and a mother's willingness to stay close to her son even during the most harrowing of times."
—Ron Goldblatt, executive director, Association of Independent Maryland Schools

Libby and Jeff, 1978

Stay Close

A Mother's Story of Her Son's Addiction

Libby Cataldi

St. Martin's Griffin

New York

This is a true story, though some names and details have been changed.

www.stmartins.com

Book design by Kathryn Parise

The Library of Congress has cataloged the hardcover edition as follows:

Cataldi, Libby.
    Stay close : a mother's story of her son's addiction / Libby Cataldi. —
1st ed.
      p. cm.
    Includes bibliographical references.
    ISBN 978-0-312-53878-1
    1. Cataldi, Libby. 2. Parents of drug addicts—United States—
Biography. 3. Drug addicts—Family relationships—United States.
I. Title.
    HV5805.C37A3 2009
    362.29'13092—dc22

                               2008044065

ISBN 978-0-312-63839-9 (trade paperback)

First St. Martin's Griffin Edition: August 2010

D 10 9 8 7 6 5

To my firstborn son, Jeff Bratton, who spent over two years, and hundreds of hours, answering my questions, recalling details, and putting into words those of his memories found in this book. Jeff knew that if at any time he wanted the book to stop, I would have stopped it, but he never asked. I've learned from him that life is more fragile than I ever realized, and that the choice of living a sober life takes great courage.

To my younger son, Jeremy Bratton, who chose to break his silence. It hurts to remember or maybe it's easier to try to forget, but Jeremy decided to trust, and to help with the writing.

We've learned to stay close, for it is in the staying close that hope lives.

Again I saw that under the sun the race is not to the swift, nor the battle to the strong, nor bread to the wise, nor riches to the intelligent, nor favor to the men of skill; but time and chance happen to them all.

—Ecclesiastes 9:11,
Ignatius Revised Standard Version Bible

Having had a spiritual awakening as a result of these steps, we tried to carry this message to alcoholics, and to practice these principles in all our affairs.

—Step Twelve, Alcoholics Anonymous

Contents

Stay Close

Prologue

If Love Were the Answer

September 27, 2005

My son is in jail, Miami-Dade County jail. He faces a felony charge for heroin possession and a misdemeanor charge for possession of drug paraphernalia.

This isn't the first time he is in jail; maybe it won't be the last. Addiction invaded our home in 1991. It slithered in and sat down at our dining room table, grew large and fat, fed on our misery, laughing, mocking us with its power. It claimed Jeff when he was just a fourteen-year-old boy. I did everything I could think of to save my son, but in the end I could do nothing, not really, to extricate him or to free our family from addiction's claws. If you love or care about an addict, you know this feeling of helplessness.

My firstborn son, twenty-seven years old, is handsome, elegant even, with large brown eyes and olive skin, a little over six feet tall, and so very smart. A graduate of Boston University with a bachelor's degree in communications, he has worked in Boston, New York City, and Washington, D.C., for some of the most well-known public relations agencies. He could be anything he wanted to be. He is a drug addict.

I'm in Italy and Jeff couldn't make an international call from jail, so he called his father, my former husband, who called me. "He wants me to post bond." Tim sounded incredulous. "I'm done; I told him that he got himself into this mess, he can get himself out. I told him no. In fact, I told him *hell*, no."

Tim did give me the number of the bail bondsman, and I began telephoning to the United States and finally reached the man; he seemed knowledgeable. Jeff's bail had been set at six thousand dollars, high because heroin possession is a third-degree felony charge in Miami-Dade County. Six hundred dollars was needed immediately, 10 percent of the total. Plus, he wanted at least four thousand dollars in cash, since Jeff is not a resident of Florida. "Your son might disappear on us," he explained. "Do you have any property in Florida? Anyone who will take responsibility for your son?"

Anyone to take responsibility? Maybe we took too much responsibility all along. Or maybe we didn't take enough.

It was just last week that I started writing this story. I had returned to Italy after a six-week visit to the States, during which I had spent a lot of time with Jeff, a lot of time laughing and remembering with this child of mine. Jeff had been sober for four months, and he looked good. Eyes shining with charm and confidence, my charismatic son almost skipped as he walked. When I saw him like this, I could have wept. He looked at me, concerned, and said with a little nervous laugh, "Don't cry, Momma, I'm good today. I'm healthy. We're OK."

I'm his mother. Not that this explains anything, really, although it may explain everything about me. I have two children, and my feelings for my sons are inseparable from my being. They are like breath to life, like light to creation, and they are unable to be anything other.

It's my way. Hope for and belief in Jeff resurface even after I swear I will not believe again. It must be like this when they tell a mother her child is dying. Does she accept the sentence or does she hold tight to hope, believing that somehow God, a higher power, some medicine or some surgeon will save her child?

I had tried to quit believing and hoping, but when I saw him this last time, those feelings came rushing back into my bones; I was like a dry sponge soaking up water.

While I was in the States, I asked Jeff how he felt about me telling his story through my eyes. His answer was clear: "Yes, Momma, write the book. Maybe it will help others; maybe it will help even one family."

I asked the same question of Jeremy, my second son, for Jeff's story is also his, a story of brotherly love tangled up with protection, with guilt, with the need to survive. Jer sighed, paused, then nodded his head slowly. "Yeah, Momma, write. It'll hurt like hell, but maybe it will help others; maybe it will help us."

Resolved, then, I packed up ten years' worth of personal journals, diaries of sorts that I had written detailing our family's trial by fire, and carried them with me on the return flight to Italy. They held our story, a long trail of words describing loss and documenting our pain, destruction, despair, and hope.

And so I am writing. I sit before this computer in Italy feeling very far away from my son, knowing that I must write.

What will happen to my son? I don't know. All I do know is that there is no finish line with addiction. Were Jeff to be four months sober or forty years, we will always have to fight against addiction; *he* will always have to fight. But I write today hoping that there will be good news about Jeff, praying to hear his voice on the phone.

Our family has made many mistakes, but maybe in the sharing of our experience we all benefit. I have talked with enough parents and spouses of addicts to know that we can learn from one another.

In our pain, we begin to understand; in our collective stories, we listen to find hope; in our love, we continue to believe.

But we have to know that love is not enough, not with addiction. If love were the answer, Jeff would be healed, he would be fine; he would not be in jail.

Chapter 1

The Boy in the Cape and Cowboy Boots

November 24, 2005, 12:30 A.M. Jeff is twenty-seven years old.

So how do I feel? Like a failure of a mother. Everyone in the field of drug addiction says, "Don't blame yourself. You didn't cause it, you can't cure it; you didn't make him a drug addict." But look deeply into a mother's eyes and tell her that her child is dying and it's not her fault. Sure, it makes sense if it's not your kid. But for a mother to do nothing to stop the pain, to alter its course—is it possible for a mother not to feel guilt, shame, intense hurt? Maybe for some, but I'm not there. I doubt if I ever will be. For me, I think I will wear this like a skin. Maybe I'll forget I have it on sometimes, but it will be forever part of my being, my eyes, my smile, my thoughts—like a breath that catches me short or my heart when it misses a beat. That's it. Jeff is my heart murmur—I have allowed his aches and traumas to damage my heart, and it is beyond repair. Maybe this isn't the case for other parents, and maybe I'm wrong, not healthy. But this is what I feel, this is my heart.

Motherhood wasn't always this way, this battle with addiction, this feeling of failure. How did it all change? I wish I could trace the beginning of Jeff's drug addiction and point to a continuum of events, of specific blips on a chronological graph that cry out the alarm, *danger, drug addict in the making, danger, addiction coming,* like a truck's warning as it backs up. How does one become an addict? How does one become anything? Is it in the genes? Of course that's part of it, but not all. Is it in the upbringing? Life situations? Birth order? Specific events? I have two sons, and they are different. One is an addict; one is not. What is it that has kept Jeremy safe and put Jeff at such risk?

Their early years run through my memory like one of those picture books that you flip quickly with your thumb, the images blending together to tell the story. We lived at the northernmost end of Calvert County, Maryland, a rural tobacco-growing region, a peninsula surrounded on three sides by the waters of the Chesapeake Bay and Patuxent River. Our neighborhood was called Quince View Meadows, and the boys' days were spent there, among the woods and trails. Their memories are filled with the deep greens of the woods at twilight, with the shades of yellow and orange as the light filtered through the leaves, with the laughter of playmates as they raced through the fields, with the crisp smells of autumn and the crunching sounds of leaves as they traipsed up the long driveway home, to their tree fort, to the tire swing that lifted them to the heavens and twirled round and round on the descent.

Jeff, from his earliest years, loved to imagine, to create, and I can trace his childhood through his fantasies. He was Superman, Batman, Spider-Man, and even Aquaman, then He-Man, a kind of invincible superhuman, followed by Luke Skywalker fighting for good against the evil Darth Vader, Indiana Jones on a search for treasures, then a BMX biker taking to the air from the ramps he built with his buddies, and finally a skateboarder leaving the safety of the neighborhood behind as he discovered new frontiers.

Maybe Jeff always wanted to escape reality, live somewhere else. It seemed so harmless then, during his early years. It seemed magical.

When Jeff was just two years old his scarlet Superman cape became part of his daily attire, hanging around his neck and trailing down his small back. He had found an iron-on emblem on the back of a cereal box and asked, "Will you, Mommy? Can you make me a cape, just like Superman, with this on it?" When Jeff donned his homemade cloth, he became Superman and joined the fight for good.

I remember sitting next to two-and-a-half-year-old Jeff as we peered out his bedroom window on the third floor, high above the ground, and always feeling a little afraid that one day he might leap out in the belief that he could fly.

"Jeff, do you think you can fly?"

"Yeah, I know I can."

"Angel, do you know what fantasy is?"

"Yep. It's when things aren't real, like fairy tales."

"And do you know what real is?"

"Uh-huh," he nodded his head slightly up and down, his dark brown hair cut short with long bangs that framed his eyes, intense and innocent, as he studied me quizzically, wondering, I think, what was my problem that I didn't understand this whole flying thing. "Real is true, like what happens, like what we see."

"Great. If fantasy is make-believe and real is what happens, do you really think you can fly?"

"Yep, I know I can fly, because Superman is real and he flies."

And so it went, to the grocery store, to preschool, Jeff wearing his trusty red cape, denim Wrangler jeans, the cordovan cowboy belt with his name embossed on the leather, and the saddleback-colored cowboy boots that my parents had bought for him when we last visited them in Florida. Quite naturally, the National Air and Space

Museum in Washington, D.C., became one of our favorite destinations, since Jeff was enamored with space travel. Once, when he was about three or four, he wore his entire Superman outfit, complete with blue tights, T-shirt emblazoned with the Superman S, navy shorts, cowboy boots, and of course his cape to lead the way to the lunar space module on the first floor to the deep right of the entrance. He stood next to Jeremy and explained in a loud child's voice, unaware of others near us: "Jeremy, Neil Armstrong was the first man who ever walked on the moon, in Apollo 13. The moon has no gravity or air to breathe, so he had to wear a space suit and heavy boots made just for space. He got to the moon from the space ship in this lunar module. OK, now we'll go upstairs to show you the golf club that Neil Armstrong used to hit the ball." Jeremy, just twenty months younger, and who looked like he could have been Jeff's twin—only smaller, and with lighter brown hair and hazel eyes—listened to everything his older brother said as if memorizing each word.

Of course I was proud—proud of them both, my babies. I was a teacher, and that was my life's profession; I was a mother, and my sons were learning together. These were the days when I could love them as openly as I wanted. Which I did.

As Jeff and Jeremy grew older and entered elementary school, their bonds became tighter. They would lie on Jeremy's bed together, looking out his window at the woods beneath, and they would cloud talk, the kind of daydreaming that kids do. Although they were still confined by the borders of Quince View, their days were now filled with leaving home behind. There were other times, too, when Jeff hung out with his friends, and they would hide from Jeremy and his gang because the big guys were just too cool to play with the little ones. Jeff and his buddies built forts in the woods, played basketball at the courts, constructed bicycle ramps, careened through the neighborhood on their two-wheeled horses, and swung between trees on the vines in what they named Vine Jungle. They swam and perfected their cannonball dives in neighbors' pools, hopping between the

Saltas' and the Kesslers'. Winters made frigid playgrounds, with snow blanketing the woods and fields; their world became a crystal wonder as the trees around our home were covered in white, ice dangling from the branches, and almost invisible tracks left on the surface of the snow by the squirrels and birds were the only hint of animal life. The only time we mothers would see the big guys was when they'd appear in one large group at someone's home, ready for grilled cheese sandwiches and glasses of chocolate milk.

It was so easy then.

Later, when Jeff was around ten and in fifth grade, he fell in love with skateboarding. Many of the neighborhood kids tried to balance on the oblong-shaped platform, but most often they would fall to the ground in laughter. The others soon lost interest and left to play basketball or ride bikes, but Jeff loved the sport and stayed, working to master new tricks that he had seen others perform or ones he'd made up.

My older son loved to fly, create, and invent, all positive attributes, but somewhere along the way Jeff lost his desire to use his gifts.

Whatever happened during those years and later, Jeff always protected Jeremy, almost like a father, encouraging him, rescuing him from his childhood mishaps, and listening to his boyish ramblings. When they were in middle school they played on the same soccer team. During one game, a player from the opposing team, a kid who was three years older than Jeremy and outweighed him by at least twenty pounds, was guarding him aggressively, and kept knocking him over, tripping him. Without forewarning Jeff left his position in the center of the field, jogged over to Jeremy's adversary, whispered something in the kid's ear, and then resumed playing. The boy never tripped Jeremy again, and at the end of the game I asked Jeff what had happened. He sighed angrily. "I told the kid, 'You touch my brother one more time and I'll break your fucking nose.'" Jeremy adored his older brother, and he mimicked Jeff's walk, dress, and talk, always watching. "Jeff was like a father to me. I always felt safe when I was with him," Jeremy once told me. They were the Bratton boys. They wrestled, they shared their secrets, they were bonded in friendship and in blood.

The four of us, including Tim, weren't together often. Tim and two partners had started an environmental consulting company in Washington, D.C., and twelve-to-fifteen-hour days became his normal working and commuting schedule; there was also some out-of-town travel. Work was his domain, and he was successful; with two small children, I was happy to make our home my world. Tim's income allowed me to stay home and be a full-time mom, and his absence seemed to be the price of successful entrepreneurship.

We weren't the kind of family that ate together each evening, picnicked, camped, or even played Scrabble. On weekends we were the kind of family that usually ate together only on Sunday evenings, and sometimes we went to church, but usually the boys and I would go alone or not at all. Planned family outings for special days like Mother's Day or Father's Day consisted of brunch and a round of golf. We went on occasional family vacations, planning times of togetherness in advance to fit Tim's work schedule. The boys and I had supper together, and I would prepare Tim's dinner, place it in the microwave for heating when he came home—often as late as 10:00 or 11:00 P.M.—and he would eat in the kitchen alone. By that time the boys had had their baths, had been tucked in, and were sound asleep. If I was still awake I would join him, although I was usually asleep, too. In the mornings the boys might see their dad for a brief hello, but often he would be asleep, or would be busy dressing to go back to work.

Even when Tim was home he was frequently consumed with business; his was the kind of work that was always present, floating in his head, needing attention. I knew that he wanted to be a good father and husband. He was kind, and when we first met and dated in college, I fell in love with his quiet and gentle manner. He was also smart, and when we were young and newly married he'd earned a master's degree in business administration. In addition, he was athletic and had been a long-distance runner, and I thought he would connect with the boys especially through sports, but his intense work schedule dominated his time. I felt sorry for Tim during those years; his physical and emotional absence seemed to keep him apart from his sons. Once, when Jeff was ten years old, he corrected my complaint, "You say that Dad's never home. Dad's home, but when he's home, he's like the cat."

For myself, when both boys were old enough for school, I returned to my teaching career. I had earned a doctorate in education from the University of Pittsburgh, and I was anxious to resume working, to use my degree, to publish educational research of some kind, and to make my mark in my profession. Jeff and Jeremy attended the Calverton School, a small independent day school in our county, and I began working there two days a week. Later I accepted a part-time position at Towson State University as codirector of the Maryland Writing Project, and I taught preparation courses for teachers in secondary education. I was happy with a four-day workweek teaching and a three-day weekend to clean the house, grocery shop, and cook meals for the following week.

Things changed in July 1987 when Jeff was about to enter the fourth grade and Jeremy the second. The Calverton board of trustees dismissed the head of school and the president of the board asked me to accept the position. This offer came out of left field and took both Tim and me by surprise. It was an opportunity to use my degree and to build something substantial. I was tempted; however, my dad, the Italian patriarch, a domineering and successful self-made businessman, warned me, "The school is in grave financial debt. You'll be riding a dead horse. Don't take the job."

I was conflicted. My sons were at the school, the fourth-grade teacher had quit and a replacement was needed, the second-grade teacher was great, and I cared very much for all the teachers at Calverton with whom I had been working for four years. The school was in a sorry way, and with its opening less than two months out, the calendar for the upcoming year wasn't even published. In addition, without my consent, the board had already mailed a letter to the parents announcing my "headship," and parents were calling me at home. I was angry that this dilemma had been forced on me, and to make matters worse, I was under contract to fulfill my upcoming yearlong teaching duties at the university. Also, I reminded myself, I had always stayed home with the boys during the summers, and I cherished our time during those lazy months. On the other hand, my sons were benefiting from their education, from their gifted teachers, and I didn't want to put this at risk. I was happy to be a part of my sons' educational lives. I loved kids and teaching, I thought I could do a good job, so, in the end, I accepted.

Jobs can take over lives, and as Tim's business had taken over his, Calverton began to take over mine. I started my duties as head of school on July 14, and my sons' care for the remainder of the summer was left to Hattie, an older woman who cooked, cleaned, and watched the boys. They still roamed the neighborhood playing with their friends, but with a father whose presence was still unreliable, the boys were now faced with adjusting to a mother who was around less and less.

In September, the school was ready. Veteran teachers were in charge of the fourth and second grades, my sons' classes, and I was satisfied that their education was in good hands. The school opened its doors with renewed optimism, although the serious financial issues loomed.

Each morning the boys and I would now get ready together for the day at Calverton. We'd have breakfast and then pile into the car and travel to school. I cherished those quiet moments when we would talk.

On one of those early mornings, Jeff asked me, "Do you believe in the devil, Mom?"

I wondered where this question was coming from.

"Well, some people believe in the devil, and in the Bible they talk about the devil, but I wouldn't worry about the devil if I were you."

"Do you believe in God?"

"Yes, I believe in God, Jeff."

"Do you believe in heaven?"

"Yeah, I believe in heaven."

"Good, I believe that, too. I believe what you believe."

It was just that easy. He believed because I believed, and Jeremy, who listened quietly from the backseat, probably believed, too.

That was when I could kiss a knee scrape and my mother's magic could make the hurt go away. As Jeff grew older, my power faded.

My dad proved to be correct about the school's desperate situation. It was dying financially, and it demanded long hours from me as I worked to save it from closing, to keep it alive for my sons and all the children, as well as for the dedicated teachers. It took a mighty team effort, the combination of powers of the board of trustees, the staff, the parents, and me. Sacrifice became the name of the game, and maybe because I was the head of school, I felt singularly responsible, and felt the need to work harder than anyone else. I often stayed late working, while the buildings were quiet, returning phone calls to parents, conferring with teachers, or attending the many events and meetings that happen during after-school hours. School became my twenty-four-hour occupation. Even at the grocery store, I was that ever-ready professional woman who was alert and visible, answering parents' questions about their children's grades, playground altercations, and the college application process.

Hattie didn't stay long into the school year; she didn't want to give up every weekday evening from 3:00 P.M., when school ended, until Tim or I came home. I was always scrambling to find someone who would take care of the boys, cook dinner, do laundry, and even help them with their homework. I struggled, juggling work and home responsibilities, because it was important to me that the boys had nutritious meals, regular study periods, and predictable bedtimes. At home I had always been the lead parent, which was a role that suited me well. I was naturally a take-charge woman who had been reared by two high-achieving parents, and especially by a father who was a former Marine Corps drill sergeant who had commanded our family life with mottos like "Speed, accuracy, and results" and "Good, better, best. Never let it rest until your good is better and your better is best." I reveled in the role as primary decision maker for the children during their early years, and Tim was happy to give me control. However, as the boys grew and life's problems became more difficult (as they always do), coupled with the demands of our work, Tim and I had no pattern for coparenting. We weren't prepared for what was to come when our family life began to jump the track and careen off the rails.

Tim and I loved our children and wanted to be a family, united and together, but we spun off in opposite directions. Tim was immersed in building his business and, even though I was with my sons every day, my time was torn between working to save the school and being present for the boys. Sure, Tim and I could have, and probably should have, worked less, spent more time with our sons, established better boundaries, and attended church more frequently. But these are not the causes of Jeff's addiction. Many kids grow up with absent parents, but they are not addicts.

December 3, 2005, 7:30 P.M. Jeff is twenty-seven years old.
I want to blame someone, anyone for my son's addiction, even
me. That would be fine, and I've tried. I was sure that Jeff's
behavior, Jeff's affliction, was Tim's fault. Or mine. I've worn the
yoke of guilt for years; better my fault than Jeff's. The truth is I

still have no one to blame, because I'm sure there is no blame.
After more than ten years and continual heartbreaks, I've come
to realize that an addiction is just that. Folks in the field of drug
treatment call it an allergy. Jeff has the allergy, and we are all
affected.

There were lots of red flags, as psychologists call them, starting
small and growing in intensity, like the smoke that warns of the approaching forest fire. I denied most of them. I noticed, I saw, and
then I dismissed them, talked them away. Tim feels the same and
has said, "We were busy with our professional lives. I made comments, but I didn't question. I didn't realize what was happening until later."

Jeff was in fifth grade when he was caught smoking on the
school grounds. With all the challenges finding reliable child care, I
had decided to keep the boys with me after school until I had finished my work and was ready to leave for the day. While I was
working in my office and Jeremy was in the after-care program, the
music teacher caught Jeff smoking behind the gym. My duality as
both head of school and Jeff's mom maximized my feelings of humiliation, anger, and shame. I removed myself from the situation,
and Tim was called to the school. Other administrators at the school
met, and Jeff received a day of in-school suspension. He was young;
everyone was sorry. Tim shook his head quietly, took Jeffrey home,
and said little. I swung in the other direction and ranted about dis-
honoring the family name, and told him that he was to report to the
school's after-care program until the end of the year.

Tim and I didn't talk together or with Jeff about why he was
smoking, nor about what had happened, and not about how he felt.
This was becoming our pattern. We were growing distant: As Tim became more subdued, I became more forceful and demanding. Tim
and I never yelled or screamed at each other. Instead, we grew silent,
and with time our silence became a fog that filled our home, distorted
our vision, and suffocated us. Jeremy once told me, "When we'd do

something wrong or had a problem, Dad did nothing and you'd over-react. That's one of the reasons we never told you the bad things."

Jeff continued into middle school, ages eleven through thirteen, and the smoking incident was forgotten. He was always a good student, making honor roll and director's list with averages of 3.0 or above. His writing was strong, he led class discussions with ease, and his homework was always completed well because he was conscientious about his assignments and due dates. He dressed with care, wearing either the school uniform of navy or gray slacks, white button-down shirt, and tie, or the casual clothes of soccer shorts, T-shirts, blue jeans, and sneakers. Chores like mowing the lawn and raking leaves were done willingly, and usually without being asked. Jeff played sports and made friends easily with a wide variety of kids throughout the county.

Red flags? Was skateboarding a red flag? I still don't know. At that time it seemed innocent enough and a good outlet for his energy. He was a gifted athlete, and he performed a myriad of tricks on his half pipe, a ramp that we had built in a corner of our driveway for his eleventh birthday. Over time, Jeff constructed his own skateboarding playground, complete with plywood boxes, strips of wood, concrete parking blocks, and jump ramps of all sizes. Kids from around the area came to us to skate, but Jeff was playing at home, and I was comfortable.

Many of his friends who skateboarded were older, kids I didn't know and whose parents I had never met. When I was home I looked through the glass doors or talked with them when they took a break. These brief encounters were just that, a kind of small window of information. Sometimes I spoke with the boys who lived across the street and who spent the most time skating on Jeff's ramp. One was tall, lanky, and a jokester. He'd fall off the skateboard, tumble to the ground, and pretend to be hurt, but like Gumby he'd pop back up, making some silly face or sound. He lived with his mother and brother, whom I didn't know. The other was quieter and said little to me, looking at me obliquely and never meeting my gaze. Although I didn't know his family, I'd heard that his father was a policeman, so I felt pretty confident that he must be a well-behaved kid. Whenever I began probing more deeply about these older boys, Jeff was quick to dismiss my concerns: "They're my friends; they just want to skate. They're good kids; don't worry. We're right here on the driveway. What can happen?"

I agreed. Jeff was eleven years old, active, happy, and close to home. I saw no immediate harm, and even enjoyed shopping for his clothes with brands like Freshjive and Quiksilver, and buying sneakers that were Vision Street Wear and Airwalk high-tops, worn until they had deep holes on the sides from skateboarding tricks. He sported hats that carried the logos of popular skateboard companies like World Industries, SMA (Santa Monica Airlines), and H-Street, and he wore them backward, with the brims turned upward and stickers on the underside of the bill. His shorts were baggy and his shirts hung low over his hips and advertised favorite skateboarders. Hair gel became an important item in his daily routine as he wore his hair clipped short on the sides with the top hanging a little longer and combed just right. *Thrasher* magazine, delivered each month to the house, was devoted to skateboarding and the music culture that surrounded it, heralding skaters like Mike McGill and Jeremy Klein and featuring bands then popular in Los Angeles. At night he and his friends watched skateboarding videos like *The Search for Animal Chin* and *Hocus Pocus* in our family room, and then they'd try out new tricks on the driveway under the lights.

Jeff turned thirteen and our lives took on a new dimension as his horizons broadened. Some of the older boys lived beyond the perimeter of Quince View Meadows, and our sons were not allowed to leave the neighborhood until they were thirteen. The day after Jeff's thirteenth birthday, he was off like a shot, making daily trips to visit those kids who lived within walking distance of our home. They were in high school, and were tougher, more experienced, and

Jeff loved being part of their group. I might have asked, however, why they gravitated to him, why they accepted a middle school child, still in eighth grade, who was two or three years younger, a big difference at that age. Jeff's relationship with these kids has turned out to be one of the real red flags.

Years later I asked Jeff about this time period.

It's hard to say where everything started. Skateboarding, maybe. I adored the sport, and spent a lot of time riding with the older kids across the street. But the older kids were into older stuff. Cooler stuff. Stuff I decided I wanted to do. When I was with them, I thought, "Wow, this is what guys do." They were a total departure from everything on our side of the street and I was fascinated with the sense of adventure attached to their lifestyle. At my age, they seemed fearless. They skipped school, smoked cigarettes and pot, drank beer, and watched pornography. I absorbed it all and imitated where I could. Their entire world was new to me. They listened to music, bands like the Cure, Chameleons, and Bauhaus. They played bass guitars and drum sets, and stayed out all night and drove around in cars. During those years excitement became synonymous with badness. It was cool to do what you wanted and even cooler not to care.

I wanted to believe that all was well. I wanted to believe these older boys were good friends for him and that Jeff was living a life that meshed with all he had been taught. Certainly I now wish we had asked more questions, probed more deeply, and watched more carefully. Tim later reflected, "I didn't question early enough. I knew that Jeff didn't spend enough time with the good kids and that he enjoyed the other kids. Jeff liked to live close to the edge—part of him liked taking risks. It was his personality. By the time we got involved, we were too late."

. . .

Jeff's first arrest happened during the summer between eighth and ninth grades. The mother of one of Jeff's friends was to pick up the boys in front of the movie theater, but they never appeared. Finally, she received a call from the police: The kids were at the station. They had been caught stealing cigarettes. Tim and I went to take custody of our son. The officer simply stared at us from behind the desk, shook his head, and never uttered much of anything except "OK" as he gave us Jeff's personal belongings. He held a little brown envelope in his oversized and calloused hands, squeezed its edges between his fingers with their clipped nails, tipped it, and dumped out what seemed like a hundred safety pins. Swiftly, he handed me Jeff's black torn baseball cap, and I could see all the tiny holes where the safety pins had once been inserted. Moments later Jeff appeared in front of us, ashamed, afraid to speak, head down, glancing at us sideways. He looked small against the cold starkness of the room, his hair cut short, shoulders thin; he was in that time period when kids are about to grow tall, the stage between child and young adult. I felt ripped between two conflicting emotions as I watched my fourteen-year-old son walk through the doors from the holding cell: Part of me wanted to shake him and scream at him, but another part of me ached to hold him, to look into his eyes and ask him, "Why?" But I didn't do either of these things—I turned on my heels and walked away from him.

He slid silently into the backseat as Tim drove. Tim didn't say anything to Jeff in the car that night, nor did he say much later, but I played my usual role and said things I don't even remember.

"What was the most painful thing I've ever said to you?" I asked an older Jeff.

His answer was quick; he knew.

"When you and Dad picked me up from the police station after my arrest, you told me that you wished I weren't your son."

I was stunned into silence, rummaging through my brain trying to remember if I had said those words. How could I have said those words?

"I'm sorry, Jeff. I'm so sorry. Please forgive me." What more was there to say? In anger, we parents say things we don't mean, and our words pierce our children's remembrance like a blade.

I've wondered for many years whether words, actions, or genetic or environmental factors are responsible for Jeff's addiction. In fact, this question of cause has claimed much of my time, and I've spent countless hours reading addiction material and talking with experts about the answer. Why? Because I'd like to blame something or someone for his addiction, because I want to rage and relieve the constant throbbing pain that reminds me every day that my son is an addict. I've searched into our family's history, trying to find some kind of bad blood or alcoholic gene to rail against. He wasn't exposed to drugs at home—Tim and I weren't the kind of parents who had cocktail parties and a cupboard full of liquor, or who used drugs ourselves. I've blamed his addiction on peer pressure. I've wondered if he just liked the drug scene and enjoyed losing control. Maybe he thought real men did these kinds of bad and rebellious things. There's research done by medical doctors that supports the model of addiction as illness, and identifies substance abuse as a chronic and relapsing disease, comparable to diabetes or high blood pressure. I think about cancer: Why does cancer strike one sibling and not the others? Why is Jeffrey an addict and Jeremy isn't? Maybe it's just random.

After all this, I still don't know the answer to the question of cause, but I do know I've finally stopped searching for the answer, because it doesn't really help Jeff. I've redirected my thinking into questions about recovery, about how to support Jeff as he learns to live in sobriety, how to support him through relapse, and how to stay compassionate through the process.

Jeff appeared in front of the juvenile magistrate for his cigarette theft charge, and he carried himself with great ease, took the total blame for the group, and spoke with confidence and maturity. In the end he was assigned community service, and the magistrate admonished him with what proved to be prophetic words: "Young man, the jails are filled with thieves who are the smartest people in there. Be careful. You're smart. Use it in the right way, or I guarantee you, you will be back in front of me, or another judge."

When Jeff left middle school Tim and I applauded Jeff's popularity, his athletic ability, his social skills and good manners, and his grades. We did not see the troubled waters underneath the achievement—the skilled manipulation, the dubious friends, and the premeditated theft. We wanted to believe that our kid was the good kid.

Ninth grade, the beginning of high school, brought a new dimension, a faster pace, and more red flags. I became a detective, smelling Jeff's clothes, hands, whatever, for cigarette odors, or, when doing the laundry, looking in his pockets for remnants of tobacco or, possibly, marijuana. At the same time, I attempted to maintain a mother's air of competence and trust.

Jeff began wearing black concert T-shirts and hanging his baggy jeans so low on his hips that the hems dragged on the ground. His music felt dark, disconnected, and hazy, music that other kids I knew were not listening to, and I remember bands with names like Jesus and Mary Chain, Jane's Addiction, and Pigface. He wore Vans tennis shoes or thick-soled, heavy Doc Martens, and his jewelry became an assortment of leather straps decorating his wrists. Jeff and I talked about these things, my concerns, but I didn't intervene in any significant way. I figured he was just enjoying the passing fads of dress and taste, and besides, what did I know about popular bands?

In ninth grade Jeff joined a weekend school camping trip with some of the high school students. I thought this was great until he was sent home early because he had been caught smoking. The chaperone of the trip, a science teacher at school, called with remorse in his voice. "Lib, Jeff's coming home. Can't stay. Caught smoking with some seniors. I'm sorry." Me, too, I thought. As head of school I respected his decision, but the mother in me wept with conflicting feelings of anger at and protection of Jeff. This time Tim was furious, disgusted, and he stormed into Jeff's room searching through his drawers and closet on a quest to find traces of drugs or cigarettes, determined, I think, to find something, anything. Tim took his anger out on inanimate objects as he yanked Jeff's posters off the walls, rummaged through the clothes in his dresser, and read his journals. He opened shoeboxes in the closet and overturned the stacks of cassette tapes on his desk. When Jeff walked into his bedroom and saw the aftermath of the intrusion, I'm sure he felt violated, but he and Tim were silent to each other, a cold, hard silence. I, as usual, took the parental lead and delivered some form of punishment about the smoking; I don't even remember what it was.

That Thanksgiving, as every year, we traveled to Tim's parents' home in Indiana, Pennsylvania. After the holiday, Jeremy and I returned to Maryland and Jeff stayed on with Tim to hunt deer, a male family tradition. Jeff hated to hunt, hated the cold, hated sitting in a deer stand, waiting, but I thought the time with nature and his dad would be good for him. He and Tim hadn't yet addressed the smoking incident and the searching of his room, and I thought that the quiet time together could be a bonding experience, a time when Tim and Jeff would talk, communicate, really share.

The evening of the second day of hunting, Jeff called. "Momma," he said, "I hate it here." He ended a long complaint with the words "and I'm going to kill myself."

What?! Fighting back the urge to scream with fear, anger, and shock, my mind and heart strained to connect, much like two train cars that jump the track and need to be attached again to be able to function. Jeff had never mentioned suicide before, and I wasn't sure whether he said this for attention, for spite at having to stay behind to hunt, or for help, his desperate cry. I had learned from a school psychologist that if a child has a plan, if a child has really thought out the process of how to kill himself or herself, then there is an immediate and real concern.

"And how will you kill yourself, Jeff?"

"Dad's in the shower and his car keys are on the mantle in the family room. The hunting guns and ammunition are in the car. I'll take the keys and get a gun and shoot myself." His voice sounded shaky but sincere.

"I'm asking you to wait, Jeff. You haven't even seen Jeremy or me to say good-bye. You need to wait." My voice was imploring, struggling to know what to say, my mind racing.

"You just want me to wait. You just don't want me to kill myself. I know." I could hear his head spinning.

Ten minutes after I hung up with Jeff I called back to talk with Tim. He didn't want to discuss the situation while he sat in his parents' kitchen. He was adamant; he would talk with me when he came home. My head was in a whirlwind, and I didn't know what to do. I called a psychologist whom I had been seeing for over a year, and he gave me the name of the head of the adolescent psychology department at the University of Maryland Medical Center and encouraged me to call. "Your son is crying out for help; he's suffering. Do not take this lightly."

When Jeff and Tim arrived home, Tim told me that Jeff had stolen two cartons of cigarettes from his grandfather's grocery store. While Jeff was on restriction from smoking during the camping trip, he stole cigarettes—this time, from his granddad. Jeff explained that he had been afraid because he knew he was in worse trouble than before, and he wept with remorse. He felt overwhelmed with problems, and in his fourteen-year-old mind, suicide was his answer.

I knew Tim and I needed to come together strongly for Jeff, so I asked Tim to talk on the phone with the psychologist. I thought this might help Tim understand Jeff better and provide the foundation on which to build a stronger bond between them. Tim agreed, and I left the bedroom so Tim could talk in privacy. When he hung up I rushed back into the room wanting to know all that was said. He picked up the newspaper and started reading, saying nothing to me. Of course, I pressed him; I was anxious to know what the doctor had said. Tim looked at me absently and replied, "He asked me, 'Does your son need to kill himself to get your attention?'" Tim stopped there. "And what did you say?" I pushed again. Tim continued to read silently and, for reasons I've never understood, he never answered me. We were losing each other, just as we were losing Jeff. Tim closed himself behind a newspaper and Jeff closed himself in his room. And me? Once a week, Jeff and I would leave school early and drive to the hospital in Baltimore, where he talked with the therapist in his office while I sat in the lobby, and the storm continued to build.

The truth of these years of Jeff's early drug use is still a blur to me. While I was concerned about cigarettes Jeff was smoking pot, drinking, and watching pornography.

Meanwhile, Jeremy was watching his brother closely. He was two years younger, in the seventh grade, loved lacrosse and basketball, was a whiz at Nintendo, and looked at life through eyes of youth and innocence. It was only natural that he was confused by much of what he saw. Years later Jeremy and I talked about this time period, and he told me, "I didn't know drugs were bad; I just didn't know. I was naïve, and even when Jeff was high, he never treated me any differently. I was still trying to decide what was right and what was wrong."

It was during these early years that Jeremy learned to keep Jeff's secrets. In fact, he remembers the exact moment that he chose silence, in his mind to solidify brotherhood. He was walking down a neighbor's basement steps to be with Jeff, who was skateboarding with one of his friends on ramps that they had constructed for rainy day practice. The two older boys were listening to the music of a popular rap group at the time called N.W.A., or Niggaz With Attitude. I had forbidden Jeff and Jeremy to listen to this kind of music—songs about death, violence, drugs, and sex—and when Jeff heard Jeremy descending the stairs he ripped the tape out of the player and tossed it under the couch.

"I realized then," Jeremy sighed, "that if I wanted a relationship with my brother, I had to stay silent. I could either not tell you and keep Jeff close or tell you and lose him totally. I never wanted to tell you; I needed Jeff more than I needed you. I wanted to protect him, and I knew that even if he was dying, I couldn't talk. I wanted Jeff's attention and approval. I would have done anything to be part of his life. I had a sense of belonging with Jeff. The silence bonded us."

Jeff entered tenth grade, Jeremy was in eighth, and I had started my sixth year as head of school, yet I still wasn't accomplished at managing my dual roles as mother to Jeff and Jeremy and head of school to 254 children and 42 employees. I remember teachers and parents warning me, their looks of worry and even fear as they asked me, "And how's Jeff?" Some memories smack me, and now I wonder, "Where was I?"

Maybe my ego was in the way, my desire for my sons to look good and thus make me look like the perfect mother. Other kids got into trouble at school, and I disciplined fairly, getting input from other faculty members, listening, I think acutely, to all the issues and trying to lead with integrity and honesty. In fact, there was another smoking incident on a school field trip, but I handled it differently than I had with Jeff. The history teacher sent Anthony back to school before the end of the eighth-grade annual visit to Williamsburg. This brought back memories of how I handled the situation with Jeff, who was then in the ninth grade and was one year older. I waited at school until 8:00 P.M., when another teacher returned with Anthony. I had already called his parents and asked them to come to school.

When Anthony saw me his face registered fear and regret. He and I talked, calmly. I asked him many questions, such as "Can you tell me what happened? Why were you smoking? Do you understand what's happening now and why you had to come back to school from the trip?" We discussed it, Anthony and I, and when I met with his parents I explained that I had assigned him a research paper on the effects of smoking. He wasn't suspended, but he needed to stay home until the rest of the class returned from the off-campus trip. I would leave other punishment to them.

Anthony was well aware that he was in trouble and that I was displeased, but I hadn't told him that I was ashamed of him, or that I was sorry he was in our school, as I had done with Jeff. I felt caught in the gap of being a mother and head of school at the same time.

Near the end of Jeff's tenth-grade year, a senior girl came to me in tears. "Doc, I saw Jeff in a car with one of the biggest drug dealers in Calvert County. I heard Jeff is asking kids to buy him marijuana and other drugs. You've got to do something," she sobbed. "I'm so worried for him."

Immediately I went to get Jeff out of class and took him away with me. While we drove up and down Route 4, I shared my concerns, what I had heard, and explained that other students were worried about him, as was I.

My fifteen-year-old never became defensive (which was perhaps yet another red flag?). He listened and told me all that he wanted me to know, easing my worries.

"I'm OK, Mom. I'm not in any trouble. Trust me."

How many times do we as parents hear these words, "trust me"? I wanted to trust. Sometimes it's easier to not question too deeply. Sometimes it's easier just to believe the sincerity of words offered. Always, it's dangerous to refuse to trust an adolescent.

We returned to campus. He had classes, and I had a school to run.

By the end of tenth grade events hit crescendo pitch. One word tells the story: raves.

Jeff and I often argued about all-day concerts and music festivals he wanted desperately to attend, and I frequently gave in. But now, parties called "raves" were popular in Baltimore, and he pushed hard to go. Raves, he explained to me years later, were like rogue parties, often illegal and held without permits in abandoned warehouses and nightclub venues, and the cops were always shutting them down. In time, after the early nineties, they began appearing as nightclubs.

Tim and I refused to allow him to go to the raves, not because we knew anything about them, but because we felt there was no need for him to travel more than one hour away from home for an all-night party. By that time, however, Jeff was bound and determined to do what he wanted, and he'd spend his entire school week laying careful plans for the weekend, telling us that he was going to a friend's home for an overnight stay, or that he was camping in the field near our home, or a collage of other inventions.

I later found out that these were all ruses so that he could sneak into the city and attend parties with names like Fever, Rise, Remedy, and Buzz. Jeff told me that it was during this time period when he became enraptured with drug use and the party scene.

The raves really opened things up and exposed us to a new world of people, music, and sexuality. This is when things began to get serious.

We started hearing stories from one of the older kids in the county about these underground parties in west Baltimore warehouses. Apparently, DJs spun electronic music and kids from all over the East Coast were there hanging out, getting high, and selling drugs, drugs that we'd only ever heard stories about.

A friend gave us the name of a street in an industrial part of the city, Bayard Street, and we headed there blindly one Friday night. I was fifteen, but Bryan was sixteen and had a license. I remember being nervous, but at that age we were fascinated, more than anything, and filled with curiosity. We found the place and saw immediately that the stories were true. Better, even. Deep bass from the music bumped down the block and a group of kids stood cluttered around an entrance on the side of a brick warehouse. The space sat alongside train tracks that ran to the seaport. Inside it was hot, and dark, and loud, and dotted with lights. The setup was entirely makeshift and smoke seemed to pour from every corner. Kids from all over the region were there, city kids and county kids, from D.C. to New York. So were drugs. We found things like microdots, MDE, Ecstasy, ketamine, PCP, and mescaline. And drugs we already had access to in Calvert, like crystal, coke, and LSD, were there, too. Like a basecoat of paint, everybody was on something, trying to get higher on something else. Raves ended at daybreak and were always followed by after-parties and trips to apartments around the city.

Our only problem was with the parents. We were young and these weekends required elaborate stories about spending nights at friends' homes and all-day trips to museums in D.C. Every parent got a different version, and for a while things worked as planned.

Tim and I argued with Jeff about going to the raves, but his constant pressure, demanding, and cajoling started to wear down our defenses. Before we changed our decision, I asked Tim to go and see for himself what a rave was all about. He refused, didn't want to go. I couldn't blame him really, so I offered to go with him, but his arguments prevailed: "We don't need to go. What will it prove, anyhow?"

In time we relented and gave permission. No, we didn't want him to go, to be out late at parties, but after a while neither Tim nor I were strong enough to say no.

Jeremy later told me, "If you and Dad had communicated, it would have been better for us. If you and Dad had been more involved with Jeff's friends, watched them skate, and discussed the rave scene with them, maybe Jeff would have talked with you. Moms and dads have to be involved in their kids' lives to know what's happening."

I once asked Jeff's best childhood friend, "What would've made the difference with Jeff's drug use? What should we have done differently?" He answered me quietly, with such gentleness, "You should have kept him out of the raves."

January 1, 2006, 12:17 A.M. Jeff is twenty-seven years old.
I need to quit hanging on Jeff's cross. All my angst does nothing for him. If I made mistakes in the past, I need to let go. If some of my mistakes were fatal, I need to let go. It is today 2006, and I can do nothing but support him with my love and affection and strength. My emotional weakness isn't good for anyone, especially Jeff. I pray he finds his courage. I pray I find mine.

During tenth and eleventh grades our life with Jeff continued to be characterized by that juxtaposition of positive and negative. Jeff's troubles came in intermittent gusts, with problems erupting sporadically, taking me by surprise. So much of Jeff's life seemed to be going well, and I wanted to forget our concern about the friends, the raves, and the smoking. He was elected captain of the varsity school soccer team and made the cut for the select team in our county, a traveling group made up of the best players from the three-county region. He continued to get good grades and to complete his work and his assignments. He and his friends would return from a soccer game and they'd sleep at our home. We'd awake the next morning to find boys sprawled all over the family room floor, sound asleep, and I'd cook breakfast for the group. There were good times, and I wanted to hold on to those memories.

At the same time I started hearing things from his teachers, either in conversation with me or overheard as gossip in the hallways, that they suspected something was wrong with Jeff. He seemed inconsistent, sometimes distracted in class, eyes duller than usual, a little slower to hand in his homework or to complete projects. I wanted to scream at all of these people, especially the ones who did not come to me but talked with others behind closed doors and in the parking lot, seeming to relish the details of my kid gone bad.

I remember only one teacher from Jeff's high school years approaching me directly and telling me that he had concerns about Jeff's behavior, and saying he suspected that Jeff was using marijuana or other drugs about which the teacher knew nothing. I listened and nodded while remaining quiet, feeling anxious about whether his conjecture was correct. I could easily have checked his hunch because, theoretically, I had eyes and ears all over the school, teachers and students who could have acted as informants, telling me about Jeff and his actions. However, I never asked, and I don't recall anyone else, except that one teacher, ever specifically connecting Jeff's behavior to drug use. Maybe the other teachers felt hesitant to make these kinds of statements to me because I was head of school. In truth, I didn't want to ask for help. I felt that I could control things, and just as certainly as I was leading the school, I could take care of my son. Failure was not an option for me, nor was admitting my frailties in front of others. I wouldn't even admit my problems to my parents or brothers; I wanted them to think that I was the perfect mother with the perfect family. I wanted to protect Jeff and Jeremy from all harm, from all negative conversation, and I was convinced that I could. I now understand that I had started to isolate myself and my family because of feelings of shame, trying to keep the secret inside the silence.

My administrative assistant told me years later, "You were a role model for the school, the successful head, teacher, wife, parent. . . . You wanted to be perfect in all those roles. I tried to help you and the boys during those years, when you were juggling so much, but it was difficult. You trusted no one completely, so I never really felt your anguish. There were many Monday mornings when you came to school and looked exhausted. You rarely told me what happened; you plastered a smile on your face and acted as though all was well. Within a few days, I'd discover that you and Jeff had another argument about his partying or his weekend activities. You tried to hold everything inside, you didn't want your private life made public, but in our small school community it was almost impossible. Through it all, you ran the school with strength and clarity of purpose."

Convinced that Jeff was a major topic of conversation in the school, I spiraled into a kind of paranoia. I worked even harder; I think I was trying to prove that I was capable, that even if I couldn't control my child I could control the budget, the discipline, and the workings of an effective school. The school's enrollment was growing, we were negotiating the purchase of additional land in order to expand our academic complex, and we were finally financially stable and boasted a strong college preparatory curriculum. As Jeff's mother, I needed to be successful somewhere. Much later I learned that this is a natural response among members of a family dealing with addiction who don't know what to do. I excelled in the world of education and retreated into it, achieving a counterfeit confidence.

As for Jeff, I dragged him to another psychologist and to our family doctor, praying that someone would find the key and help him get himself back on track. Although I didn't seek help from my colleagues, many of whom had direct and daily contact with Jeff, or from my parents or brothers, I felt sure that with the right psychological guidance, conducted out of the sphere of our everyday lives, Jeff would behave according to all the values that I knew we had taught him. I did not consider my child a serious drug user; I thought he might be smoking some pot, but my concerns ended there. In my mind he was a child who had problems, and like many other boys, he was struggling to grow up into manhood.

Jeff's second arrest occurred in eleventh grade on Christmas Eve, after our family had attended Mass and enjoyed a traditional Italian dinner together at home. Jeff was alone in his car driving between friends' homes and was pulled over by the police for not using his turn signal to change lanes. The officers searched his car and found cocaine and ketamine. This time, when Tim and I went to get our son at the police station, I didn't feel anger; I felt deep sadness. I didn't yell. I felt totally alone sitting next to Tim, as though I were a single woman fighting the torrent of problems by myself. Tim and I confiscated Jeff's car and we put him on restriction, again. In short order he had to appear in front of the county magistrate, who gave him community service and ordered him to attend a local drug education program in our county.

Every week like clockwork Jeff and I trudged to this center, and he began group meetings, working with a counselor to address issues of drug and alcohol use. Because this program did not provide education for parents and guarded closely the rights of the client (even though Jeff was a minor), I heard little, was informed about nothing, and waited anxiously each week for the results of Jeff's urinalysis, which they gave to Jeff and not to me. Jeff attended without argument and, when he delivered proudly the negative results of his "pee test," I was lulled into a sense of calm, and I could believe all was well. To those who asked about Jeff's health, I was now quick to respond, "He's fine. His urine tests show no drug use." It was only years later that I learned from Jeff that the meetings put him in contact with the other drug users and distributors in our county. And the negative drug tests? Jeff explained the many ways to get around urine tests, from hiding someone else's clean urine in eyedrop bottles taped to the legs and then substituting one warm urine sample for another, to taking some diuretic that would flush your system clean within a certain period. At the time I hoped that with the monitoring to control him and therapy to teach him how to control himself, Jeff was making progress toward living a drug-free life.

I now understand that I was hiding behind the hope that the drugs were just a passing phase. I told myself that this was that time in a kid's life when he experiments and finds a little trouble, but makes it to the other side knowing better, that time when he tries drugs and alcohol, but doesn't get hooked. I think I always knew that this might have been a cop-out. I was afraid down deep that I was wrong.

Tim later admitted, "I knew Jeff was in trouble, but as parents you want to believe good things about your child. Jeff always had a level of respect with us, a boundary he didn't cross. He disrespected us out of our eyesight. I assumed a lot of things—good school, good kids on his soccer team. Jeff had so many strong qualities. I should have been more forceful, but it's not in my nature."

Jeff explained:

> Throughout my teenage years, the style of our drug use evolved. At first we were experimenters. Drugs brought new experiences and we were excited about feeling differently. Getting high was a game and the process was pretty innocent. We saw the older kids getting high and we wanted to get high, too. They smoked pot and ate acid, so we smoked pot and ate acid.
>
> By the time we were fifteen or sixteen, drug use had become attached to socializing. The weekends were designed to party, and having fun meant getting high. Whatever the event, drugs were part of the plan. It was no longer about soccer games and shopping malls and drinking beer. Everything we did revolved around getting loaded.

No wonder he never wanted to stay home on the weekends. No wonder he and his friends planned weekend campouts. No wonder people were talking about my son. Now it makes sense. The thing that makes no sense is that Tim and I didn't know. I wonder—how was this possible?

At home tensions grew among all of us, and by the end of Jeff's eleventh-grade year Tim and I were at our wit's end. I felt incapable of making Jeff change, and I encouraged Tim to try to intervene with greater intensity, to make a fatherly difference. By this time I was threatening divorce and, in an attempt to save our marriage, I arranged counseling for us, but we only went three times, because we couldn't even coordinate our work schedules around a regular time for sessions.

One early spring evening I invited Tim to walk with me through our neighborhood. In this quiet time, I explained my concerns about Jeff again, and admitted my feelings of powerlessness. Our son was drowning in his own actions, I said, and I pleaded with Tim to take time to talk with Jeff, father to son, man to man. I'm sure Tim wanted to try to make me happy, to try to be a good dad. When we returned to the house, Tim climbed the steps with resolve and entered our study, where Jeff sat at the desk, hunched over the sewing machine, designing new patterns in his jeans.

"Jeff, what do you think of me as a father?" Without any introduction, Tim launched directly into his plan.

Jeff, startled, interrupted in his work, stood up. He was now almost as tall as his father, though thinner, with the same long runner's legs and narrow torso. He hesitated, thought carefully.

"Dad, in terms of you providing for us, you're great. You work hard, have a strong work ethic, and are a good role model for Jeremy and me."

Then a pause—slight, measured.

"But in terms of being a dad, it's too late for me anyhow."

With that Jeff quietly walked out, went into his bedroom, and clicked the door shut. Tim dropped his head, stared at the floor, and sighed, then walked slowly into our bedroom and closed the door. Not another word was spoken.

Our family. We were like four figures in a mobile above a child's crib: We danced and turned alone in our stories, but we were all connected, and the tossing and flailing of one affected us all.

In May of Jeff's eleventh-grade year I was dismayed and stunned to learn that he was using crystal methamphetamine, known simply as crystal meth. A mother at my school called to tell me not only that she had heard this from her own children, but also that she had overheard two mothers discussing Jeff and his problems while they waited in the reception area of a local doctor's office.

That night, when Tim came home from work around 9:30 and entered the bedroom, I was sitting on the edge of our bed, wearing baggy pajama bottoms and a white T-shirt with CALVERTON FIELD DAY written across the front. My heels rested on the bed frame, my elbows were on my knees, and my face was cradled in my hands. I wept as I told him about the mother's phone call and about Jeff using crystal meth. I told him that I was tired and confused and I didn't know what to do to help Jeff, to help us.

I'm sure I hit him out of the blue with the story, and with my sadness. He stood quietly in front of me, five feet and eleven inches, dressed in a suit, his white shirt wrinkled from a long day at work, his tie loosened as if to give him space to breathe. He listened silently, eyes down, never moving. As I wound down I admitted that I didn't know what to do, and that I was exhausted by work, Jeff, the house, and the gossip. I needed him to be strong for us—I needed him to do something. I ended by saying, "For now, I just need you to hold me, please."

Tim nodded his head slightly, up and down, still studying the same spot on the carpet. Pulling at his tie to undo the knot, he walked into the dressing closet. I waited; he would be with me soon. He walked out of the closet, took the two steps into the bathroom, and closed the door. I waited again; he would go to the bathroom and be back. The shower started, the water rushing and whistling as he let it heat up, and I moved to my side of the bed, trying to relax, thinking through the day and all that had happened. Finally, I turned onto my left side, tucked my knees up into my belly, and watched the digital clock mark off minutes, with the steady running of the water in my ears. With each click of the clock, more tears spilled down my left cheek and onto my pillow, where they were silently absorbed. Over one hour had passed when Tim finally opened the bathroom door: The time was 11:01.

I never turned from my side to say anything more; I had said enough. Maybe it felt to Tim as if the water had washed away the pain of the continuing assaults of the drugs, of our shame and my worry, and of the public knowledge of our problems. Without a word, Tim climbed into our bed and turned onto his right side.

Our backs formed parallel lines and I watched the clock while I listened, until his breathing became steady and filled with sleep. Only when I felt sure he was asleep did I sit up in bed. I sobbed, muffling the sounds with my T-shirt. He didn't wake; I knew he wouldn't. Finally, tired and spent, I lay down, resuming my position on my left side. With both of us in it, our bedroom was empty, void. We were two backs facing each other.

The next day, when I confronted Jeff, he admitted his use of crystal meth and told me that our little county had an abundance of the drug for sale. Of course, Jeff had found all the sources. In response to this latest news, I searched for something, anything that might help. My colleague, the science teacher who had sent Jeff home from the ninth-grade camping trip, knew of a program called Outward Bound, an outdoor camping experience for kids. Tim and I leaped at this idea, thinking it would be a good learning opportunity for Jeff, with time away from his friends and our county. We thought this would give him two weeks to reflect on his behavior and work with others, maybe build on his innate leadership skills, away from steady access to drugs. Maybe the staff at the center, people trained to work with teenagers, could make a difference with Jeff. Maybe time away from all of us and our county was what he needed.

Jeff wrote to us from Outward Bound:

July 12, 1997
Mom and Dad,
    This is the most difficult program that I have ever been in. We hike up to ten miles a day over mountains, and two of the hikes were done in the pounding rain. My shoulders and hips are bruised from my heavy pack. My legs hurt and so do my feet. We've climbed high elevations, and many times I didn't think

I'd make it. This is like boot camp. <u>I'm so glad I'm here</u>. It makes me appreciate home and shows me just how much I care about my family!

Give Jeremy my love and tell him that I miss him.

Love,

Jeff

Upon his return, Jeff was lucid and drug free, and said he was committed to remaining clean. It was then that he decided he did not want to return to Calverton for his senior year, but wanted to attend a military academy, a boarding school in Virginia. He had heard about this school from a fellow camper, and he wanted to go. I was incredulous. How could my son not want to graduate from the school where he had been a student since kindergarten, the school to which I had dedicated so many years of my life?

He persisted in expressing his desire, so in late August the four of us visited Randolph-Macon Academy, in my mind just as a lark, but Jeff enrolled himself while we were there. I was stunned. Ten days before the teachers returned to Calverton for the academic year, we registered Jeff in his new school, procured the military uniforms, and negotiated the unfamiliar territory of military life on a school campus.

In September 1995, Jeff left home dressed as a cadet.

In October 1995, after twenty-three years of marriage, Tim and I separated and he moved out of our home. We were a family joined together in love, but Tim and I didn't know how to negotiate life together, let alone a life that included addiction. We started as two, with Jeff we were three, and Jeremy made four, until we disintegrated slowly into ones, four separate players. We had two sons who needed us, and our family problems demanded a full-court press, our total unity and strength. Tim and I weren't that team. We were silent with one another.

Jeff's senior year at Randolph-Macon military academy proved fitful at best, although his first semester seemed trouble free. As was typical, good grades were the norm, and his work ethic was strong and consistent. During parent-teacher conferences the teachers commended Jeff's writing abilities, leadership skills, and scholastic preparation. The second semester started in January, and during this month Jeff was caught smoking in the dormitory, and he served a ten-day suspension. In addition, one of the sergeants called home questioning me about Jeff's history with drug use. He explained that although they had never found drugs on Jeff, he was hanging out with kids who had been expelled recently for selling drugs on campus.

Desperate to learn more, and to become smarter about drugs and drug abuse, I began to study the effects of drugs like cocaine, ketamine, and crystal methamphetamine, the drugs that Jeff had established patterns of using. Ketamine, I learned, was a tranquilizer used by veterinarians for small animals—ketamine hydrochloride, a nonbarbiturate, rapid-acting anesthetic. It was a liquid that could be injected or boiled down into a crystal substance and smoked or snorted. This was a club drug, fashionable at raves. Ketamine, I learned later, had become Jeff's drug of choice.

Jeff came home most weekends, and I was relieved each Sunday night when he returned to the academy. I felt like a sheriff when he was home, wondering where he was, who he was with, and what he was doing. Jeremy was living at home with me, and he and I had settled into a good and comfortable routine, the two of us, but Jeff's presence always brought unease, never any rest.

Jeremy covered well for his brother during those years, as I peppered him with questions about Jeff's activities. Of course Jeremy saw, but what could he do? Not only did he adore his brother, but he also was the younger, and Jeff was supported by all his friends, kids Jeremy liked and looked up to, who were also using drugs. Jeremy couldn't expose the truth about his brother, be disloyal and lose his brother's confidence. Tim and I weren't healthy enough in our own relationship to help Jeremy find a way of telling the truth. Jeremy learned silence, to hold his tongue, and he suffered during these years, first from the constant tension in the house and later from his parents' separation and Jeff's departure, always feeling the need to divide his loyalty between his parents and his brother.

In April 1996, during spring break of Jeremy's sophomore year in high school, he decided to change schools, too. This is not a normal time to leave one school and enter another, but with all of the disruption and tension in our family, he had suffered academically, and was finding it almost impossible to concentrate on his studies, especially algebra II, French III, and chemistry. Jeremy and I had agreed that the military academy would provide the structure and time management skills that he needed. Three quarters of the way through the school year, he joined Jeff.

Jeremy told me later, "I wanted to be with Jeff; I would have followed him to the ends of the earth. Jeff and I had an unspoken bond. I always felt safer with him. As much as I wanted to be his protector, I felt Jeff protected me."

When Jeremy and I arrived on campus, Jeff was waiting. The registrar on duty wanted to assign Jeremy to a unit not with Jeff. Jeff protested.

In a firm voice, the administrator admonished Jeff, "Cadet Bratton, you are not in charge of this procedure."

Jeff bent down over the desk and leaned close to her, speaking quietly but forcefully. "Ma'am, this is my little brother."

She relented, and Jeremy was assigned to Jeff's group, Flight A-1.

The brothers, both away from home, were bonded together by love and secrets.

Shortly afterward, less than a month before Jeff's scheduled graduation in May, suspicions about drugs again became reality. The sergeant at the academy called to tell me that when Jeff and a friend arrived on campus after the weekend, Jeff's car had been searched. They had received an anonymous tip that Jeff and his friend were bringing drugs onto campus to sell to students. Although they found no drugs on Jeff or in his car, the other kid did have drugs on him and was expelled immediately. Since Jeff was the driver and obviously involved on some level, he was suspended for ten days.

This was now Jeff's second round of suspension, and as before he was immediately transferred to the disciplinary unit. While in suspension he was ordered to eat alone, sitting on the edge of his chair, his back straight, as his fork followed a ninety-degree-angle path from his plate to his mouth, eating "at corners." His morning started at 6:00 with physical training (PT), which included running sprints, push-ups, sometimes lifting and carrying rubber tires over his head while jogging, and other physical drills. Another round of PT occurred every afternoon. Much of his day was spent in isolation, completing his academic requirements as he sat in the suspension facility, a small cement building down the hill from the main campus. Two times a day he marched tours for a total of three hours, dressed in military garb and walking in a designated square. Then, on the eighth day of this suspension term, Jeff was caught smoking in the dorm bathroom and received another ten days of lockdown.

That semester Jeff completed thirty days of suspension, determined to make it to the end. Why, I wondered, did he put himself through such torture? Was he in some way trying to punish himself for all the pain he had caused, for all the trouble in which he found himself, for all the hurt that we, his family, had felt? Or was his will so ironclad that he refused to be beaten down by the system?

When I asked him this question, he said, "I don't know. I just knew I had to make it to the end. I knew I had to graduate. I wasn't going to quit."

Jeff was a survivor, and he was smart. He developed his toughness like layers of muscle. He had learned well on the streets, in the classroom, and at home, and with each obstacle he grew stronger, more manipulative, and better able to lie and conspire and deceive.

In May 1996, Jeff graduated. We all attended, including my parents. My dad watched from the bleachers as Jeff and Jeremy marched in military formation by the reviewing stand, one behind the other, both in the line closest to the bleachers. Jeffrey never looked up and kept his eyes straight ahead, but Jeremy, now taller than Jeff, scanned the crowds for his granddad. As the sergeant of Flight A-1 bellowed the order, *eyes right*, Granddad, the old Marine drill sergeant, watched the boys through tears that streamed down his face. In later years my dad would weep many more tears for Jeff, but those would be tears of worry, frustration, anger, and helplessness. On this occasion my dad wept with pride, the old soldier watching his two young bucks march: hup, two, three, four.

Years later, Jeff explained his desire to go to military school.

Following the arrests and the trouble of my eleventh-grade year, I knew that military school would give me the breathing room I wanted. It's not in my nature to be outwardly defiant, but I was determined to do what I wanted on the weekends—and this meant raves, all-night house parties, and car rides to other cities. At seventeen, however, I knew this wouldn't fly at home. My goal became to keep you and Dad out of my day-to-day activities. The move was drastic, but I wanted space. With the rave and drug issues already going on, you were all over me, asking questions and restricting my free time. Military school gave me open weekends and a level of detachment I wouldn't have otherwise had at home.

During the week the regimen was tough; military school can be grueling. But when I left campus on weekend passes, it was accepted that I'd spend most of my time with friends and away from the house. You and Dad were separated and it was hard to keep track of me. Nobody knew exactly where I was and the weekends were entirely mine.

The summer following his graduation from high school, Jeff did not live at our home with Jeremy and me. Jeff and I differ as to how this came about. He says my memory is wrong, not true; however, I remember it this way:

Jeff was in his room, organizing and putting away his belongings. It was at that moment that I decided to lay down some boundaries, and I announced, "If you're staying at home this summer, you'll have a curfew, you can't drink, smoke, stay out all night, or do drugs. Period. Do you hear me?"

I recall him looking at me as if I had two heads, and with a smirk he announced, "You're crazy. I'll do whatever I wanna do."

My head whirled; I was furious. "Then you'll leave," I said. "If you'll not abide by my rules, then you'll have to leave."

"Where will I go?" he asked, mildly amused.

"To your father's." And I exited his room.

This is what I remember, although Jeff's memory is different. He says I told him quite plainly that I didn't think it was a good idea for him to live at home because I didn't trust that his behavior from military school would change, and that I didn't want his problems to disrupt the life I had created for Jeremy and me. Jeff says that I told him to move in with Tim. Whichever of us has the truth of it, I now think that I didn't handle this well. I had finally decided to state clearly my rules, my expectations, but there was little foundation, no work previously done between Jeff and me to support this decision, no inclusion of his dad, of Jeremy, of the family.

Jeff did move out, and he moved into Tim's apartment in Alexandria, Virginia. He stayed there for only a week or two before going on to Baltimore to live with friends: a girl, who became his girlfriend; a young boy, who was a transvestite and drug dealer; and another girl, who was a high-priced professional escort. This was an easy move for Jeff, because he didn't even have to pay rent; there was plenty of money coming into the apartment from the sale of drugs and sex. Jeremy and I continued our lives, and I believed all that time that Jeff was with Tim. During the summer I saw little of Jeff, although we talked occasionally on the phone. He assured me that he was fine, working at a local restaurant and living with Tim. I never questioned this. I never called Tim to ask him how he thought Jeff was doing, and Tim never called me to ask where his son was.

It was only much later, many years later in fact, that Jeff told me a little about his summer in Baltimore.

The party was in full swing that summer. This was 1996 and the scene had just peaked. Between raves, weekly parties, and assorted loft events, we were out almost every night. We were just out of high school and taking full advantage of our freedom. I moved into a brownstone on Holland Street with my girlfriend and our friends from the parties. They were all good kids, just caught up in the scene like everybody else. Other friends had become successful drug dealers, and whatever we wanted was now available without having to look for it. At eighteen, life was fresh and raucous and racing, and besides some minor arrests and fistfights, serious consequences were rare. Baltimore was a reckless stretch, but there was a camaraderie and newness about the period that I remember with real fondness.

Only once did I meet his girlfriend. She and Jeff joined Jeremy and me for an Orioles baseball game at Camden Yards. She was cute, blond, sweet looking, with a wide smile and hazy blue eyes. I knew nothing about her, yet when she looked at me she peered deeply, as if searching for something. Maybe she was trying to decide if I knew who she was or what she and Jeff were doing together. I knew nothing because I asked nothing. That day, when I talked with her and Jeff, I concentrated only on the parts of Jeff that reminded me of the son I had known. I cherished his smile, his language, his elegant mannerisms.

Jeff introduced her to me as a friend who worked as a waitress at a bar in Baltimore. Only later, after the summer ended, did I learn from Jeremy that she was a stripper.

January 3, 2006, 7:30 P.M. *Jeff is twenty-seven years old.*
People tell me to accept. They say that I can keep hoping that he
might recover, but I need to learn to accept. Acceptance. Isn't
that the same thing as saying the words and knowing they are
true? After all these years, it's still hard for me. My guess is it's
hard for every parent of every drug addict and every alcoholic.

In September, Jeff entered Boston University.

Chapter 2

The Three Acts of the Worst
Christmas Ever

The next year and a half proved to be a fragile calm interspersed with disturbing episodes, all leading up to the worst Christmas ever. In the end, even though I wanted to believe that university would be a new beginning for Jeff, that the people, places, and problems of his high school and Baltimore years were over, I reached a turning point when I had to admit that my son was a drug addict.

Jeff settled into Boston University and, at the end of September 1996, all seemed well: Jeff was calling home excited about the city; Jeremy had returned to his friends at the military academy; and I had my hands full with the new school year at Calverton.

With Jeff, however, nothing was easy, and the back-and-forth tug of calm, warning, calm, warning started almost immediately.

Jeff was assigned to Sleeper Hall, a dorm in West Campus, close to his classes, and he and his roommate were a mismatch from the start. His roommate immersed himself in his computer, spoke only when spoken to, and clearly cherished peace and quiet. The inevitable happened. After six weeks Jeff was advised by the housing director that he was to move out of the dorm. Neither Tim nor I ever heard directly from the university, although Jeff, as always, had an explanation. "I did nothing," he told me. "My roommate wanted things quiet, and I had friends in the room. That's normal enough, right? He hated my friends, he hated the noise. His parents complained, and so I got kicked out."

Tim and I were certain that Jeff had broken some rule that could not be overlooked; however, we did not receive any explanation from the housing department. Jeff, always clever, had already located an apartment to rent with another freshman, a minister's son, who had become one of his best friends in Boston. Tim and I were in the midst of divorce proceedings, had problems with work, and didn't have a history of talking through issues and coparenting the boys, so with this convenient solution, we supported Jeff's move into an apartment on Commonwealth Avenue.

Even as I write I am amazed at how naïve I was. Years later Jeff told me that he frequently had girls in his dorm room during the night, and that after multiple warnings from the school, he was kicked off campus.

Jeff started his college career with his typical good grades, earning A's and B's on essays, quizzes, and tests. I visited in late October, and Jeff appeared happy as we strolled the university's campus and he showed me the buildings where he had classes, the football stadium, student union, and library. Jeff flew home for Thanksgiving, so that he, Jeremy, and Tim could make their annual trip to visit Tim's parents' home, but I did not see him during this time. In December, when I picked Jeff up at the Baltimore airport for the Christmas holidays, I was shocked. He was thin, gaunt, his face white, his skin almost transparent; his eyes were dull and lifeless. What had happened to him since I last saw him in October?

Jeff reassured me, as always. "I've been sick, Momma, that's all. I've had the flu, so I haven't eaten much. I know you're worried that I'm using drugs, but don't be. I've changed all that—I'm sober. I've just been ill." I was desperate for Christmas to be pleasant, so while I knew enough to have doubts, I accepted his explanation for the time being. I had asked my mother to join us for the vacation week, hoping that her presence would bring a sense of extended family to our truncated one. On Christmas Day, Mom and I cooked, the house smelled like home, and Tim came around midday so that we could open presents together and enjoy the traditional turkey dinner.

However, I couldn't deny Jeff's diminished physical appearance and his lackluster attitude at dinner. Tim admitted that he, too, saw the thinness in Jeff, but he was not alarmed. I could not agree with him. When I thought about the most recent few years of Jeff's life, a pattern in his health and behavior started to take shape. From periods of drug use I remembered the weight losses, muted smiles, and dwindled energy, so much so that he wouldn't even wrestle with Jeremy. I remembered how his vocabulary languished, as if tiny neurons of his brain's language center were obliterated. This was most obvious during discussions, when he'd start to respond to a question only to stop midsentence as if searching for a word. His eyes would look up and to the left and, after a pause, he'd acknowledge defeat by substituting a banal word for a more sophisticated one that could have expressed his thoughts more clearly. During those times of drug use a kind of curtain seemed to fall between us, as if a cloak of darkness shrouded my son's inner brightness, clouded his life's spark, and eroded his mind's vitality.

Jeremy stayed close to Jeff, as always. Jeremy now towered over him, and the little brother had become the caretaker as they hung out together. Jeremy was now six-feet-four-inches tall, weighed more than two hundred pounds, and above all he was loyal to Jeff. They were brothers, but they were more: Jeff had been Jeremy's father figure growing up, and Jeremy was now faced with the new role of trying to protect Jeff, just as Jeff had always protected him. But how could Jeremy protect Jeff from himself, a hard juxtaposition for a brother, for anyone. This must have been confusing for Jeremy, because he became increasingly agitated with Jeff's behavior and defensive with me, especially when I looked at Jeff with the kind of eyes that said "Where are you, my son? What have you been doing?" or when I offered Jeff the word he needed to complete his thought. My guess is that Jeremy felt insecure and fearful knowing he was losing his brother, and he hung around the house more often than usual. Jeremy's body told of his love: This was his way. I interrogated Jeremy, hoping to corroborate my hunch that Jeff was using drugs again, but Jeremy said nothing, caught in his own internal conflict between betraying his brother or lying to me. Jeremy would continue to protect his brother with his silence.

I've saved two pictures of Jeff from this holiday. In one picture, he and Jeremy are sitting on the redbrick fireplace hearth, side by side, both boys looking directly at the camera. Red-and-white Christmas stockings embroidered with their names are hanging from the mantel behind them. Jeremy's right arm is around his brother's shoulder, and his body leans forward into Jeff's, as though he is ready to guard Jeff from all harm. Jeff is emaciated: His eyes are lifeless; his neck is thin; and his collarbones protrude through his skin—but his smile is still Jeff.

The other picture is one that Jeremy took of Jeff and me as we stood beside the rental box-truck that Jeff packed with his belongings and some things from our home that he wanted for his apartment. A bony and depleted Jeff stands a full head taller than me. Our arms are around each other as we smile into the camera's lens, yet my smile is shadowed with a mother's concern, and my eyes are clouded with fear of the traumas that are yet to come.

That day, at the end of the holiday vacation, the three of us held hands and said a prayer for Jeff's safe return to Boston. Jeff climbed into the truck, and he was gone.

When Jeff returned for the second semester of his freshman year in January 1997, he met a dark-eyed beauty named Sophie. They were the same age, both students at BU, and they were a stunning match, physically and intellectually. Sophie's full mouth spread into a disarming smile, and her long, brown hair framed the edges of her face when she tilted her head down into one of the many books she loved to read. She was compassionate and down-to-earth, bright and articulate, and she loved Jeff dearly. He wanted to be all things to her, and their relationship made things better for him. She offered Jeff the security, the boundaries, the protective haven that, I learned later, kept his use of drugs under some control. With Sophie, Jeff felt comforted; he flourished with her acceptance. With Sophie at his side, we all felt safe.

Jeff ended his freshman year with a nearly 3.0 average, and Tim and I were hopeful for the future. Since he had a yearlong lease on his apartment, he decided to stay in Boston for the summer and work in a clothing store that marketed high fashion, a job that suited him perfectly, since he had panache, elegance, and innate style. I was fine with his decision; Jeremy was home and things were easier with Jeff out of the house. My heart strained to believe that my son could and would live a sober life. Yet, I felt conflicted, because I knew, somehow, despite my many layers of denial, that troubles with drugs continued.

I asked Jeff to outline briefly his freshman year.

Freshman year moved quickly and I made lots of friends on the west side of town. Most were really wholesome, while others had histories like my own. In time I met plenty of people who partied like I did, kids at BU and Northeastern and other local schools who were involved with the party and drug scenes in their home cities. We were young, had little to worry about, and were now free in a new city to do what we wanted. I was using coke and ketamine primarily. Crystal was easy to find, and so were pills like Quaaludes and ruffies. We were drinking a lot, too. I had a diverse group of friends and we'd hang out at Allston bars and house parties.

That year, I met a girl and we started dating. She never supported my drug use, but she didn't outwardly object, either. Not initially, at least. At that point, the drugs were still about having fun. Toward the end of the school year, however, my drug use started to concern some friends, which confused me. I didn't understand how everyone didn't want to get high as I did.

As I reflect on the above words, I feel heavy with regret and sorrow, for although Jeff wrote that his friends began to worry, I know that I was in the dark. I can only assume Tim shared my blindness. Tim and I didn't talk about the important things: the boys and their development, needs, and feelings. When we did talk, our conversations were primarily about money: who would pay for school, for the boys' living expenses, or for clothes.

In September 1997, Jeff began his sophomore year at BU, and Jeremy returned for his senior year at the military academy. One month later, I had a telling dream. Maybe I wasn't as blind as I thought.

> October 2, 1997, 10:20 A.M.
> I dreamed early this morning about my uncle Jim, one of my favorite uncles, who was always kind to me as a child. But in my dream he lost his nose because of cocaine use. I actually awakened in tears with the image of Jeff holding me, and I was saying to Jeff, "Is this what you want for your family?" Obviously the dream is about Jeff and his drug use. I must continue to pray for his survival and health. I wish Jeff's early adolescent years had

been different. *Where were Tim and I? I was in denial; Tim was lost in his own world. What a mess. There were so many mistakes made. I can't do anything about them now, and I have to move on, but I also need to learn from those mistakes. The advantage of knowing history is that we try not to repeat the bad things that went before. Denial comes easily to me. If I deny it, it never happened.*

It seems that while my conscious mind was able to deny the truth about Jeff's drug use, my fears had seeped from my unconscious and entered my dreams. As fate would have it, the very next day I received an e-mail from Jeff:

Last night I was thinking of you. I looked up in the sky and saw one lone star. That's all, just one star. I knew, just then, that you and God were looking out for me. I knew you would always be with me, no matter where you are.

Is it any wonder that I wanted to believe that all was well? Is it any wonder that I continued to assure myself that he'd be OK? I believed that love could conquer all, and with this belief I stayed stuck in illusion.

My friends knew I was struggling, and many offered to help, but I was head of school and it was important for me to appear strong and in control. In my mind, being strong meant that I could take care of myself and my sons, and that I didn't need anyone. I was conflicted, and I didn't know what to do except to work harder, which I did, which changed nothing for Jeff.

During this time I talked with the pastor of our church, a good man and a wise priest. He knew our family; we were longtime members of his congregation, where both boys received their first Holy Communion and confirmation. I told him about Jeff's drug use, and I confessed my feelings of helplessness and vulnerability. He recommended that Jeff start seeing a counselor at college through the student health center and said that he would pray for our family. He also offered to talk with Jeff if Jeff would talk with him. He cared, as so many seemed to care. But Jeff's problems increased.

Then came that Christmas of 1997, when our past and current problems swelled together and collided. This marked our third winter holiday season as a separated family. Jeff, a sophomore in college, came home from Boston; Jeremy, a senior in high school, returned from the military academy; and I promised myself that Christmas would be at home this year, but different. I talked with the boys, and together we planned a Christmas Eve celebration with old friends and neighbors, many of whom were like uncles and aunts to the boys and had known them since they were born. When I was a child my family celebrated Christmas Eve with a traditional Italian feast, complete with thirteen different nonmeat dishes, representing the twelve apostles and Christ, a tradition taught to us by our Italian grandmother, our nonna, who had immigrated to the United States from southern Italy. From the boys' earliest years, we had re-created this feast each Christmas Eve, so the boys and I decided to prepare a similar dinner for our extended family and friends.

On December 23, the day before the big event, the three of us shopped together for all the necessary ingredients. We each had specialties to prepare: Jeremy always made crab soup and *spaghetti con vongole* (pasta with clams), while Jeff was in charge of baking two kinds of fish and roasted potatoes seasoned with olive oil, rosemary, parsley, and a touch of oregano. I completed the menu of linguini with ricotta, roasted vegetables drizzled with olive oil, marinated *calamari* (squid), *baccala'* (dried cod), fried smelt, marinated shrimp, cheeses, and fruits. We decorated the house with kid-made specialties Jeff and Jeremy had constructed during their elementary school years and professional wreaths and bows. When we opened our doors to our guests, they would know that we three were one united family.

On the morning of December 24, I stood at the stove as Jeremy sat at the kitchen table eating breakfast. His tall, muscular form was hunched over his bowl of cereal as he ate quietly, my younger child, now seventeen years old. By contrast, I was a whirlwind, already div- ing into the many preparations. As I recounted the litany of things that needed to be done, I started verbally jabbing at Jeremy with or- ders about what he needed to do and when. He ignored me and ig- nored me, until finally he had had enough.

"Leave me alone. I'm tired. I'll get started soon enough, but let me alone now. I wanna eat breakfast in peace." He didn't look up as he continued to eat.

I was relentless, urging him to get moving, telling him to get up and get started, like a drill sergeant, like my dad.

Finally, Jeremy looked at me, exasperated. "Shut the fuck up."

I was shocked. He had never used this word with me. He had never talked to me with such disrespect. I flew into a rage and began yelling. Jer held his head, sighing, as Mother Hell erupted around him.

Jeff, hearing all the commotion, ran down the stairs and into the kitchen. He stopped at the threshold and leaned against the door- jamb dressed in the rumpled sweat suit in which he slept, rubbing his head. He was clearly bewildered by what was happening be- tween Jeremy and me.

I ranted about what Jeremy had just said and repeated the phrase.

"Don't talk to Mom like that. What's wrong with you?" Jeff coupled the words with a slap to Jeremy's head.

Even as I write I can see what happened next. Jeremy's huge body rose from the chair and he grabbed Jeff by the neck of his sweatshirt. At that moment, Jeff swung at Jeremy, but Jeremy's arms were too long for Jeff to make contact. A sudden look of fear came into Jeff's eyes, almost a look of terror. He was realizing that his little brother was not so little, that he was in fact bigger than Jeff, and that Jeff was powerless.

Jeremy did not miss the fleeting look of anguish in Jeff's eyes as he flung him into the wall, smashing the Christmas wreath. I had never seen my boys fight. Sure, they played, and even gave each other a punch every once in a while, but this scene was incompre- hensible to me. While Jeremy's huge hands shook Jeff's body as if he were a puppet, I was shocked and stood frozen in place in front of the stove, paralyzed in my own skin.

The two wrestled as Jeff's body bounced off the wall, with Jeremy in control. As Jeff fought desperately to make contact with Jeremy, Jeremy threw Jeff into the family room, past the Christmas tree, and Jeff crashed onto the coffee table. By this time I had regained my senses and started screaming, "Stop! Stop! You'll knock down the tree. It's Christmas." Jeremy picked Jeff up and held him at arm's length. "Please stop! You're brothers!" I wedged myself across Jeremy's arms to separate the boys with my body, and my physical presence hampered the path of attack. Jeremy dropped Jeff to the floor.

As Jeff fell loosely from his hands, Jeremy looked at me with eyes filled with confusion and hurt. He shook his head as if to clear it, and he tried to regain his composure as he scanned the room, seeing the damage in his wake. He could no longer bottle up his grief, all the anger of past hurts and betrayals. He had finally erupted like a volcano, spewing lava and toxic gases. Words couldn't express his pain, and only his fists had been able to give his emotions a voice. He lumbered out of the room, exhausted and depleted.

Jeremy had sworn at me and beaten up his brother, and I didn't know what else to do but to make Jeremy leave. Of course I understand that this was not a wise response from me, but for me, at that time, this had been my standard formula to fix things: first a consequence and then a conversation. I was wrong, and it would be years later before I would learn better skills to fix my personal problems, like having a conversation first and then deciding together what to do. Jeremy stumbled out of the house, shunned on Christmas Eve.

Jeff and I talked about the sequence of events that led to the fight. We saw it like this: Jeffrey had reacted as Jeremy's father, which was the responsibility that he had felt most of his life. Jeremy, in an effort to refuse Jeff's paternal dominance, used his fists to express the words he could not say. For me, I had tried for years to be both mother and father to my boys, but it was impossible. I was a woman, a mother, and try as I might, I could not be a man. There was too much tension in the house during this Christmas season, exacerbated by my relentless desire that we be joyful together. I wanted Christmas to be perfect; I wanted my sons to feel the strength of a unified family of three. But my will could not obliterate all the grief that both boys experienced with the breakup of the marriage, the drugs, the deception, the confounded loyalties, and the silence within the family.

As I recall this day, I am still surprised that Jeremy only shoved Jeff. But Jeremy later told me, "I never wanted to hit my brother. I loved him. I wanted to provide Jeff the same protection he provided me."

The rest of the day was sober and sad, and Jeff and I settled down to cook. We had guests coming; we had clams and shrimp to clean, vegetables to marinate, soup to start. We now had only four hands to complete work that needed six. What else could we do?

That afternoon Jeremy sat in his car across the street from our house and called on his cell phone to tell me to read a letter that he had written and taped to the front door. In the letter he apologized for swearing at me, for fighting with Jeff in our home on Christmas Eve, and for not being there to help with the party preparations. He knew we needed him, he knew we wanted him, and he needed and wanted to help, to be there for the family. About six weeks earlier Jeremy had told me, "You're my mother. I'm so confused. Can't you see it? You should be able to look in my eyes and know how I feel." How I wished I could.

In his letter he explained that he was filled with hurt and confusion, that all the breaks within the family were just too hard, and he said that he wanted to be the one to build us back together again. He wasn't little anymore, he wrote; he was big, and he could help; he could be strong for us. His heart was filled with love for his family; he just didn't know what to do to fix anything. "Please let me come home, and I promise I'll do what's right."

Jer came home, the three of us worked together to prepare the feast, and that night we opened our doors to fifty friends. The party was successful, and we worked together. We were a team again, at least for one night. However, it didn't last.

Later that night, after the guests left, I wanted the three of us to attend Christmas Eve Mass together, but both boys wanted to stay with their buddies at the house. Of course, all the kids promised to clean up and to put away the leftovers. I don't know what I was thinking, but I went off to church and left an entire bar full of liquor and beer. When I returned, the inevitable greeted me. They were drunk. Many left as soon as they heard the garage door open. One boy sat in a living room chair, holding his head, crying about his mother's newly discovered cancer. A girl apologized to me: "I'm so sorry. I tried to take care of things, but I couldn't do anything. Everything was just out of control."

Out of control. I knew exactly how she felt.

The boys went to bed, but I was determined to have the Christmas I'd planned, and I stayed up until 4:00 A.M., cleaning, wrapping presents, and making the family room ready for Santa. Grimly, I made sure Christmas went forward as scheduled, trying to forget the day's events. I would create new memories that might somehow eliminate past failures.

As I reflect on this holiday of 1997, it seems that we were caught up in a never-ending drama: Act I was the Christmas fight, Act II was the Christmas cleanup, while Act III was about to begin. At eight on Christmas morning, the boys and I rumbled down the steps to check if Santa had arrived, rounded the angle into the hallway, and rushed into the kitchen in anticipation of turning the corner into the family room. Stunned, we stopped in silence in front of the wall that had held the Christmas wreath that was crushed just the day before. In front of us, on the deck outside the kitchen's sliding glass doors, was a mountain of brightly colored presents, in various shapes, all wrapped in foils of red, green, and gold and draped with matching ribbons. While we were asleep, Tim had somehow climbed onto the deck and delivered, Santa-like, all of his presents.

As we stared through the window, Jeff, noticeably shaken, was the first to speak. "Why did he leave these here? The deck has no stairs; how did he get onto the deck? Why didn't he just wait until he saw us later today, when we go to his house?"

This Christmas drama was not yet over. Jeff's arrest several days later was the epilogue that ended the holiday season. Jeff and his friend were pulled over for haphazard driving, and the police found ketamine in the driver's backpack and syringes stuffed under the seat. Since Jeff had no drugs on him, he wasn't charged, and he called a buddy to pick him up at the station. When Jeff arrived home he told me what had happened, taking no responsibility, and explaining to me with great indignation that he didn't know what was in the other kid's backpack. Of course, I believed him; I wanted desperately to believe. I had little emotional strength left to do anything else.

In early January 1998, Jeff returned to Boston to complete the second half of his sophomore year, promising to pursue counseling through the student health center.

I was no longer able to avoid the truth, and I started thinking about Jeff's problem as an addiction. This was a fragile transition for me, and it felt like a roller-coaster ride; I was uncomfortable and afraid. I started to pay attention to the split screen of my relationship with Jeff: He had been doing drugs all along, I found out later. Once again, the truth eluded me.

January 24, 1998, 4:24 A.M.
I am not doing well. In fact, my heart feels torn into pieces. It's 4:24 A.M., and sleep is not my friend tonight. My mind races with all my problems and I ache for someone to hold me and make them all go away. Pretty unrealistic, huh? I need to find my own peace.

I talked to Jeff Thursday and Friday nights, and each night he

could hardly speak and he slurred his words. On Thursday, he
told me that he was drunk. He said that he had been drinking
malt liquor beer and that he was just messed up. OK, I let that
go. On Friday, I talked with him at 4:00 in the afternoon and he
was a disaster again! He told me that he was drunk. I questioned
him, and he said, "OK, it's Valium. I get panic attacks, and they're
painful, so my buddy gives me pills." He then cried on the phone
and told me that everything was so exhausting. He made little
sense, wept, and was out of it. He told me he has a substance
abuse problem. At least he admits it; this is a first.

Dear Lord, I am so confused, and I feel all alone. What do
I do?

This is the first time I documented in my journal that Jeff admitted he had a drug problem. My writing continued that I thought
he was addicted to ketamine, and I didn't think he could quit. In
fact, during our conversation he had told me that he knew he had to
quit taking pills and drinking, and he said that he hated the way he
used, but he felt stuck. I told him he needed to get counseling before Friday or I would withdraw him from school and bring him
home. I had already done research on a residential drug treatment
program in Annapolis called Pathways, and I decided that I would
take him there.

As I read my journal today I recognize that this was a huge
breakthrough; however, my words go no further, because during
this same conversation he told me that earlier that week he had col-
lapsed in his apartment with almost paralyzing abdominal pain.
His roommate's girlfriend had taken him to Massachusetts General
Hospital, where the ER doctor ran a sonogram and found disten-
sion in his right kidney, apparently due to an obstruction at the top
of the ureter, one of two tubes that drain the kidney. My brother
had the same problem, so I thought it must have been congenital.
Years later Jeff referred to these pangs as K cramps and described
them as much like the sharp and crippling strain an athlete gets in

his calves. He wondered if this condition might have been caused by his rampant use of ketamine, totaling sometimes more than two bottles a day. Ketamine is not well filtered by the body, he explained, and there might have been some sedimentation left in his kidneys. We still don't know the real cause.

I asked Jeff why ketamine became his drug of choice. As he explained, I struggled to understand. To me, it sounded like a nightmare.

K stood out against everything else at the time, and it altered feelings in the most dramatic ways. Like soaking my mind in watercolor paint, K animated everything around me. Landscapes bled together and car rides at seventy miles an hour felt like we were moving at thirty. Whole afternoons seemed to pass in forty-five minutes and I'd hear friends talk without ever opening their mouths. I remember watching energy from Jason's arms move in waves across the living room and thinking I'd been physically transported to places miles away. Bedroom carpet became blue ocean water and I'd be scared to put my feet down. Everything I saw I believed, and unlike hallucinations on acid, things on K are softer and more surreal.

Occasionally, though, I'd do too much, and the high would get scary. Ketamine is an anesthetic for small animals, and when someone overdoes it, it can stop movement and conscious thinking, a lot like being paralyzed. When that would happen, my vision would become smeared and watery, sort of drippy, and I couldn't make out my surroundings. A collage of memories from all stages of life would clutter my mind, and I'd become horribly disoriented. I'd come out of a high totally wiped out and sometimes in tears. The drug was intense, especially the way we were doing it.

On March 3, 1998, Jeff had surgery, and Tim, Jeremy, and I traveled to Boston to be with him. Tim and Jeremy returned to Maryland within two days, when it was apparent that Jeff was fine. I stayed in

Boston and, the following week, Jeff and I flew to Maryland so that he could recover more comfortably at home. Tim picked us up at the airport and drove us to Calvert County. Jeff hobbled up the stairs and into his bedroom, and I helped him put his clothes away, gave him his medicines, and adjusted the blinds in the room to darken it. I stopped at his window, the one that overlooked the tree fort, and I remembered playing hide-and-go-seek there and pushing both boys on the tire swing. As I turned off his light, I noticed the Superman light switch that was still on the wall, and I remembered little Jeff, when everything seemed so easy.

That night, around 12:30, I awoke with a foreboding sense that something was wrong. I listened acutely and heard nothing, but went downstairs on a hunch and found Jeff with one of his old friends from our county. How did this kid even know Jeff was home, I wondered? "What are you doing here?" I demanded. He just stared at me with blank, clouded eyes, silent, and I was filled with anger. Jeff sat on the couch, and he was a disaster, hardly able to speak, slack jawed. He looked up at me with wide, expressionless eyes and said thickly, with a tongue that could barely move, "I was in pain, so I took six Percocets. I hurt, Momma, but I don't hurt now." (He told me later that he had also shot ketamine that night.) He continued, "The pain is gone. I'm OK now. Don't cry, I don't hurt anymore."

I turned slowly away from the room, from his look, from his blurred, nearly incomprehensible speech. I walked to my bedroom and wept, feeling betrayed again, knowing that only a kid who deliberately wanted to get messed up would take enough Percocet to leave him immobile and hardly able to speak. I had no idea what to do. I ached. Jeff appeared at the door of my bedroom, watching me sob as he staggered unsteadily toward me, mumbling that he was sorry. *Sorry,* over and over again. We were all sorry. Jeff stayed home until he healed from surgery. By the middle of March, he had returned to Boston on his own.

I knew I needed to quit enabling Jeff. When he returned to

Boston after his surgery I had, once again, paid his outstanding bills, taken care of all his expenses, including the apartment, food, and credit cards, and given him spending money. Our family doctor had often told me, "Give Jeff love, compassion, and support, but no money." But I didn't want to add to his anxieties or concerns, and thereby increase the likelihood of his continued use of drugs. By now, however, he had learned extraordinary skills of manipulation. He knew how to ask me for things, and he knew it was hard for me to deny him. I understood that I needed to set boundaries and to get tough, but just thinking about it exhausted me. I was tired—tired of divorcing, tired of working so hard at school, tired of worrying about Jeff and his drugs, his drinking, and his health.

That spring, Jeff and I talked often on the phone, and he assured me that he was in counseling and had been drug free since taking the pills at home. He talked about his continuing anxiety attacks, but he clearly recognized his responsibility to live a sober life, and said, "I'm the only one who can do this, Momma. I must stay drug free."

I couldn't believe him. Even though it was only spring, I had already started to worry that he might want to come home for the summer. His track record in Maryland was terrible. I was fearful that he could not stay straight in Maryland, or, in fact, that he could not stay straight anywhere.

On May 4, Jeff called. He did not want to remain in Boston and work for the summer. He was making plans to come home. I asked him what he would do at home, what kind of job he might find, and if he would stick to a curfew. Finally, I told him that I didn't think his coming home was a good idea, because I didn't trust him to not use drugs.

He was stunned. "I don't know what I'll do during the summer, but I'll work; I'll do something. I just want to come home. You're my mother. How can you tell me not to come home?"

My son, my firstborn. What had happened to us?

May 4, 1998, 10:06 P.M.
I don't have the energy to deal with this. I'm exhausted. Where
do I end and where does he begin? How much do I give? How
much of a safe haven do I allow, do I provide? I'm confused. I
need to think.
Part of me, the Mom part, says, "Be there for him. Trust him.
Believe him. Open the door and allow him to come home." The
other part, the logical part, says, "He's lying and he'll just come
home and get high. He'll have too much time on his hands and
trouble will follow. It always has." Two extremes! Where do I fall?
My guess is I should do something like outline parameters,
boundaries. For instance, if he comes home, he must enroll him-
self in a rehab center. If he comes home, he must work. Do I let
him live at home? Do I?

The next day I attended a conference on leadership at the Four
Seasons Hotel in Washington, D.C., but after a short time, I couldn't
concentrate. I went out to the lobby and spent the day calling one
drug rehabilitation center after another. As I inquired about facilities, fine-tuning my questions, I discovered a long list of possibilities, and I felt totally overwhelmed by the choices. I called Hazelden,
Caron, Pathways, and many more. Each one outlined their requirements for acceptance and explained what Jeff needed to do, what I
needed to do, and what insurance needed to do. My head was in a
whirl. In desperation I called a social worker friend, and she checked
with some nurses at our local hospital, who recommended Father
Martin's Ashley, a residential drug rehabilitation center about two
hours from our home. My next and final call was to Father Martin's
Ashley. Finally, I knew what to do.

The years of Jeff's slurred words, arrests, and near arrests, of
missed curfews, of glazed eyes; and of me closing my eyes to his use
of Valium, ketamine, cocaine, crystal meth, and Percocet; and all
the years of ignoring the comments of friends, of trying to pry in-

formation out of Jeremy, all assaulted me simultaneously. I saw the wreckage that was my son's life. I took a stand.

"You can come home, Jeff, if you go to rehab at a place called Father Martin's Ashley for twenty-eight days. If you go, you can come home and stay. If you do not, don't come home."

A long silence. Nothing. Then: "I'll come home. I'll go. I need to go."

Chapter 3

Starting Down the Rehab Road

On May 11, Jeff and I drove to Father Martin's Ashley, silent, as if driving to a beheading. Jeff was nineteen and had agreed to enter residential treatment, but he was still in a place of tentative acceptance. I understood. We both felt scared; we were traveling into uncharted territories. Jeff packed a small bag with enough clothes for a week, explaining that if he decided to stay for the twenty-eight days, I could bring other items from home. Of course, I assured him.

Father Martin's Ashley was nestled in a cul-de-sac at the end of a long tree-lined driveway, on acres of lush, green, well-maintained grounds in Havre de Grace, Maryland. We parked next to a large, white-brick, colonial-style building and trudged up the concrete steps without saying a word to each other. As we entered the brightly lit reception area, we were greeted warmly by a woman who explained to Jeff that he needed to be interviewed by an intake counselor before he could be admitted. I felt comforted by her respectful and gentle approach with Jeff; in this world of addiction, kindness is not always the norm. A young man about thirty years old, thin, tall, serious, with just a hint of a smile, soon appeared, introduced himself, and shook our hands. He focused his attention on Jeff and, as he led us into an adjoining room, where we settled into large upholstered chairs, he explained that he was a recovering addict with over ten years clean. He and Jeff talked directly to each other, and I sat quietly, grateful to be an observer of the process. The counselor asked Jeff lots of questions about his drug use, and with each answer, he'd nod without a hint of judgment. Jeff acknowledged, "I've abused most every drug I could find." The young man listened calmly, as if he had heard it all before. Jeff continued, "For years it was just a party, but things have changed. My using seems different from other people's."

I have since learned that the patterns with addiction are pretty similar. Addiction specialists are not surprised by the abuse of alcohol and multiple drugs, the escalation of lies, deceit, and manipulation. The tragic part is that the majority of families seem to make a solitary walk through this hell because we feel shame and guilt.

The interview went well, but in order for Jeff to be admitted he had to acknowledge that he wanted and needed help, and to make a commitment to stay for a minimum of twenty-eight days. Which he did.

Jeff had done what he needed to do, and this felt like a gigantic step, for all of us. I thought about when he was just a child and stood in wonder watching replays of Neil Armstrong's first step on the moon. But he wasn't little anymore; he was nineteen, and he had to make this journey for himself, by himself.

When I arrived home I found a card on the kitchen table.

Mom,

Know that I never mean to hurt you. These last couple months have been hard—for both of us. Thank you for not giving up on me. You believe in me at times more than I believe in myself. You give me strength. You're my mother, and I love you. Happy Mother's Day.

Jeffrey

Father Martin's Ashley provides care for addicts, but their philosophy also includes a commitment to supporting and educating those of us who love addicts. Their statistics indicated the growing enormity of the problem with addiction since, they projected, for every one addict at least four other people are affected. Tim, Jeremy, and I were among those numbers. They offered a series of educational sessions, covering issues from the causes of addiction to the obstacles to recovery. I sent Tim the literature so he would know the dates of open visitation and education periods. Parents were strongly encouraged to attend an intense three-day program, during which we would work together and individually with Jeff. Tim did not attend due to business constraints, but I blocked off the time, stayed at a local bed-and-breakfast, and was determined to learn more about this disease that was strangling our family.

The schedule began with a required one-hour overview session, during which we saw a film of a lecture given by Father Martin, called *Chalk Talk*. He began delivering these chalkboard presentations in 1972 at an Alcoholics Anonymous meeting, and I listened intently to his no-nonsense approach, heard clearly his compassion, and remember especially one phrase: "The express elevator to sobriety is broken. Take the steps." After the film, a counselor prepped us as to what to expect from both the facility and our visit. We were dismissed through large, glass double doors and onto a concrete patio that led to the grassy common area. I felt anxious to see Jeff again, concerned about how he was adjusting to being in a residential rehab center and nervous about how he was reacting to his treatment. My nerve endings felt raw. As I walked slowly across the lawn, a vast expanse of green with a panoramic view of the Chesapeake Bay, my eyes caught in the distance an image, a shape. First, I made out a body, moving easily with a free stride, arms swinging naturally as the form emerged from behind a massive tree. Next, the sun reflected my son's smile, radiating a sense of peace as if saying, *I'm OK, Momma. I'm OK.* When I reached him, I hugged him closely. I felt contentment and relief.

For me, the tree provided a metaphor for my prayer for Jeff's future.

May 18, 1998, 9:50 A.M. Father Martin's Ashley
Lord, let him grow as the tree does. Let his roots grow deep with Your love, to hold him grounded no matter what tries to dislodge him. Let him grow tall, to the sky, and proud. Let him hold his head high and provide support for others. Let his children, wife, and family climb into his soul, play on his limbs, knowing that he will always try to keep them safe and secure, because he is grounded, centered, and strong. Let him experience the seasons of life, always knowing that he is loved, that he is fine. Let his winters help him to appreciate the sunshine of his springs and summers.

Jeff took me on a tour of the campus and introduced me to the people he knew as we made our way through the chapel, the cafeteria, and the garden. He was comfortable, his head held high, and I could see that he was physically stronger, and had a secure tone in his voice. He told me that he was grateful he had come. "It's all starting to make sense. I understand so much better." He sounded proud as he explained that even though he was the youngest member of his group, they had chosen him to be one of the leaders. Jeff explained it this way:

Father Martin's was a tender place, but at nineteen it was all so new. Early seeds were definitely planted and my perception of drugs started to shift. It's hard to escape your first time in treatment with a carefree regard for drugs intact. I began hearing words like "addiction" and "disease" in the same sentences as "friends" and "parties." Counselors talked about cravings and they had clinical terms for the anxieties associated with my personal world of drugs. I was shocked that they knew so much, and I was shocked that other people felt the same way that I did. There were no secrets; no feelings were uniquely mine. I still owned the details, but at Father Martin's there was a community of other people, across all ages, who used drugs as I did, and faced issues similar to mine. On some level, everyone was dealing with the same type of broken relationships, legal issues, and personal shame. I remember being comforted by the commonalities, thinking that time in treatment would fix the addiction.

The three-day family training program was scheduled from early morning until late each evening. Our group totaled fourteen, all parents and spouses. We worked sometimes in large groups, other times in small groups, and we also met with our loved ones both in groups and individually with a counselor. The days were long and exhausting, both physically and emotionally, but I could start to feel the gap narrowing between Jeff and me as our conversations became more and more honest. Each night, when I returned to the B&B, I documented in my journal what I had learned. For instance, the counselors at Father Martin's believe that addiction is a disease. They used a medical model when talking about addiction, and called it a malady that addicts must learn to live with, like arthritis or diabetes. Such diseases never go away, and Jeff would need to attend to his disease all his life. The one certainty, they explained, was that whenever Jeff used drugs he felt a kind of euphoria that triggered more drug use. Jeff would need to manage his patterns of behavior and his choices in daily life. They explained that Jeff would need to change people, places, and things.

I also learned about the twelve steps of Alcoholics Anonymous, a program developed in 1939 and documented in the Alcoholics Anonymous bible, called the *Big Book*. The twelve steps provide a framework for recovery and health; they are the North Star to continued sobriety. With the twelve steps, addicts are given the tools to share their experience, strength, and hope with each other, so they can work together to solve their common problems and help each other. Al-Anon meetings were developed for the singular purpose of helping the family and friends of addicts. During my first Al-Anon meeting I heard stories harder and more difficult than ours, and I marveled at the strength of the people in the room, these other mothers, fathers, wives, and husbands. We were all desperate to learn how to help our loved ones, to know what to do, to know how to provide support without enabling. There was a young mother in our group, about thirty-five years old but looking much older than her years, her face tired, her countenance sad. She proudly showed us a picture of her family—her husband, herself, and their three little girls, all with long, curling, blond hair and bright blue eyes, ranging in ages from two to six years old. Her husband, a successful Philadelphia attorney, was an alcoholic, and he was in Jeff's group. Jeff had introduced me to him just the day before, and he seemed like an affable guy. His wife explained that she loved him dearly, but that she could no longer expose her girls to the extremes of his alcoholic behavior. She could not go forward with the marriage, and she had brought divorce papers, which she planned to give him at the end of her visit. Hearing this, we were all sorry. Addiction is a family disease; no one is spared.

In the group sessions with Jeff I was repeatedly impressed by his remarkable capacity to see concepts from different viewpoints. He listened carefully when others shared their stories, and he talked about the shame and guilt that he felt. He also began to talk about the effect of addiction on our family, and he used words like betrayal, loneliness, resentment, and confusion. Jeff's anxiety, I learned, came from his drug use; his sleep problems came from drug use; his weight loss came from drug use. We also met with his counselor, who pointed out Jeff's many strengths, his leadership abilities, and the respect he had earned from the members of his group. He was young, and this was in his favor, she explained. He was intelligent, and while this was positive, it was also potentially negative, because there were times when Jeff expressed the feeling that he could manage his own addiction, that he was smart enough to handle his own problems. "Jeff," she warned, "be careful of pride. You need to learn humility; you need to learn to accept help and to rely on others who know your walk, who know the powers of addiction. Sometimes you are too smart for your own good." She ended our meeting by confirming her great hope for Jeff, but also by reminding us both that Jeff's recovery was in his hands.

I only touched the tip of learning about addiction during those few days at Father Martin's Ashley, but I began to learn the basics, the scaffolding I would need if problems continued. However, I didn't think the problems would continue; everything seemed so right. Jeff later wrote,

> The family sessions helped me to see you, my mother, as a person. Treatment lifted the backdrop of everyday life and allowed us to look at the drug use alone. You were afraid, and I could feel the weight of that pain. You couldn't fix my addiction patterns and your fear was evident. I began to understand that parents carry the full weight of their children's hardships.
>
> Also at Father Martin's, I was told that recovery required vigilance and commitment, that in order to stay sober I'd have to regularly attend AA meetings and work with a sponsor. I didn't realize that sobriety was an ongoing thing and I wasn't sure that I was ready to do the work. Although my drug use was causing problems, it wasn't devastating. Not yet.

The next weekend, Jeremy and I visited Jeff, and we attended, as required, the introductory one-hour educational session. Jeremy was nervous about visiting his brother in an institutional setting, but all hesitation evaporated the moment the two saw each other on the lawn, by the tree. Jeremy broke into a run and hugged his brother. At that moment their roles seemed reversed: Jeff appeared timid while Jeremy, sensing his brother's apprehension, quickly wrapped his arm around Jeff's shoulder and gave him a reassuring smile. Jeff greeted me with a quick kiss, and they took off together. I sat under the tree, wrote in my journal, and didn't see them again until it was time for Jeremy and me to leave.

Jeff was still in treatment when the end of May brought Jeremy's graduation from military high school. We had a wonderful weekend, as my mom, Tim, my brothers and their wives, and many of Jer's friends made it almost complete. The incompleteness came from the absence of my dad and Jeff. My dad was tired, aging, and he didn't feel he could make the journey north from Florida. Jeff had to choose to put his rehabilitation first, and the graduation, his counselors told him, was something to which he would have to say no. At the time I asked Jeremy how he felt about Jeff not being there, and he never replied. Years later I asked again, and he told me, "I was so psyched that day, with all my family and friends around me. Sure, I wanted Jeff to be there; I was achieving and conquering a major part of my life."

Jeremy planned to start university in the fall. Out of the many colleges to which he had been accepted, he chose BU, because "I wanted to be with my brother, so I went to Boston. It's that simple."

On June 9, 1998, the three of us were together again, living at home. Jeff had returned from Father Martin's after completing his twenty-eight days, and a sense of confidence mixed with realistic caution emanated from him. He knew that his sobriety was not a slam dunk. Jeff and I had developed better communication skills while he was in treatment, and we negotiated boundaries around his time at home: a curfew each night; a work schedule each day; strict rules about no alcohol and drugs; and attendance at AA meetings.

The summer was calm, yet I always felt on edge, fearing that Jeff would resume a life of drugs. Yet all was going well. Jeff had a full-time job as an intern in a commercial real estate company and, as always, he was a responsible worker. My only concern was that he was not attending AA meetings regularly. He told me that although he wasn't drinking, he believed that he could drink, because he was a drug addict and not an alcoholic. His problem, he explained to me, was drugs, especially ketamine. Alcohol was a problem for some, but in Jeff's mind it was not the primary issue. I was concerned about his dismissive attitude about alcohol, and he and I talked about this, but I never called Tim to discuss this with him. He had not attended the educational sessions at Father Martin's and didn't know about the twelve steps, the need for Jeff to attend AA meetings, or the problems with relapse. Sadly, neither did Tim talk with Jeff that summer about his rehab experience or his recovery.

In the *Chalk Talk* film, Father Martin frequently explained how addicts relapse and careen back into their world of drugs and alcohol. He offered the example of the alcoholic who stops at the bar on the way home from work to have a drink. All goes well, so the next night he has two drinks. He's still feeling fine, as though he can control his drinking, and so he stops at the bar again. In short order the dam breaks, and he is back into active alcoholism. All mind-altering chemicals are a slippery slope for the addict, no exceptions.

In September 1998, at the start of the new school year, Tim drove Jeremy to Boston just as he had taken Jeff two years earlier. When Jeremy climbed into the passenger seat, he looked so big and so ready. I kissed him, waved good-bye, and stood in the driveway to watch my last child leave home, drive off to college, and take with him a piece of my heart. Three days later Jeff packed his own car, a used red Acura that he had bought with the money he had saved from working during the summer, to return also to Boston.

The summer had been a healing time for the three of us. We had talked openly and honestly, approached all subjects with candor, and we loved each other through it all. We were learning. Late, I admit, but we were learning.

That night I found a note on my bed. Jeff must have placed it there before he left.

This summer has been a blessing. I'm glad I came home. I love you more than you know.

Hope had been reborn, in both of us.

With both of my sons off to college, I was left in the house with myself. It was then, at this unfamiliar juncture in time, that I decided to focus on my own progress.

September 5, 1998, 5:00 P.M.
I have defined myself as a mom, and now my kids are gone. I'll always be a mom, but my role has changed. I'm now relegated to praying for them from a distance. That's it—I'm a long-distance mom. Maybe that's what bothers me so much. I like the feeling when the boys are at home, as if I'm in charge. Really, I'm in charge of nothing; close or far I can't control what they do.

So, I sit in our family house inhabited by me. It's all in my mind, you know. I could sit here content and happy that my boys are both in college, proud even. Yet, I sit here fighting myself. Now I need to reorient myself. I think the problem is that all my wants, desires, and plans always revolved around my sons. I'm not very seasoned at thinking about myself alone, by myself. I need to take control of my life, move forward, "hup, two, three, four," as my dad the drill sergeant would chant.

I remember well a character in Michael Dorris's *A Yellow Raft in Blue Water*, who said, "I never grew up, but I got old. I'm a woman who'd lived for fifty-seven years and wore resentment like a medicine charm for forty." That's how I felt. I was forty-seven years old, but there was still so much I didn't understand about the events in my life, and I harbored great resentment about the problems with my marriage, Jeff's drug addiction, my inability to help Jeremy, and other family turmoil past and present. Emotional traumas don't just appear from nowhere; they grow from the inside out. The damage is internal, hiding, growing under the skin, like a bruise. I was full of signs, of bruises. Some I could see; others were yet to appear. The problem was seeing the whole, and I knew I needed help connecting the internal dots.

I began my journey inward guided by an intuitive woman therapist who asked questions, listened, and probed deeply. When I called her to make my first appointment, I told her that my life was in chaos and I needed help to understand what had happened and what was happening. I explained that my son was a drug addict, and that although I was a highly functioning professional woman, I was unable to save Jeff or to be fully present for Jeremy, the two most important people in my life. I thought that the therapy would help me manage my conflicting feelings. I knew that the stronger I became as a woman, the stronger I would be as a mom, and this fueled my intention to delve deeply into my own motivations, my goals, and my past.

As I filled my journals with my self-discoveries, my life as a mom continued.

Jeff and Jeremy were together again, so on October 9, I traveled to Boston to spend the weekend with them. I wanted to see Jeff's apartment and check out Jeremy's dorm room, to stock their refrigerators, and to offer them a dose of Mom's care. Jeff and Sophie were still together, and I was eager to see her again. The boys and I enjoyed two full days with each other as we shopped, talked, and laughed. We were a team.

Sunday night we ended our adventure with a wonderful Italian meal in Boston's North End. We parked Jeff's car and ran through the rain without an umbrella, laughing like children, arriving at the restaurant wet but happy. As we climbed the stairs the familiar sounds of Italian and the comforting smells of garlic and olive oil enveloped me.

I fell back to when I was a child, when I would run away from home, run to my mom's mom, run to my nonna's house. While climbing the thirteen gray concrete steps painted by my uncles every other year I would smell these same smells, and I knew I was safe. Nonna was my bastion of security, an Italian immigrant who couldn't read or write either Italian or English. My older brother once told me, "Nonna was the smartest woman I knew who was illiterate in two languages." Memories of Nonna touched me that night in Boston.

The owner of the restaurant knew Jeff, and he greeted us with hugs and a kiss on each cheek. We were seated at a small circular table in front of a window in the corner of the room, quiet and serene. As we watched the lights of the neighborhood glisten in the rain, we talked, told stories about their youth, each boy remembering something different, a twist to the tale that embellished the memory and made each story even more remarkable. We talked about Jeff's bike trails and skateboard jumps; a golf outing when Jeremy got the cart stuck in the woods; a childhood theater production of *Peter Pan* that we put on in our front yard; and the time Jeremy and his friend tried to smoke out a rabbit burrowed in the field next to our home and an acre of brush caught on fire, bringing the local fire department. Their eyes danced, and the bonds among us sounded a familiar chord, a kind of family harmony. The food was rich in textures and flavors; *my boys are Italian*, I thought, *all in spirit, half in blood.* Jeremy's wit was impressive, fluid, keen, subtle, and as always he watched with an intensity that encompassed every nuance. Jeff, the older, always felt responsible for taking care of everything, yet he was comforted by my presence and supported by Jeremy's. I was not sure that Boston was good for Jeremy, but I was sure that he reminded Jeff of family, values, and centeredness. I knew that Jeremy understood better than I did his brother's frailties and indiscretions.

As we walked back to the car through the evening mist, we en-twined arms and sang the songs that my dad used to sing to me when I was a little girl. We sang old Italian songs, and then we raised our voices to "When You Wore a Tulip," "Till We Meet Again," "Play-mate," and a slew of others. When I was young I would sing melody, and my dad would sing harmony. I'm sure we sounded terrible, the three of us, off-key even, but what wonderful times, what wonderful memories, and there on Hanover Street in Boston we sang.

October 12, 1998, 7:00 p.m. Return trip on the plane
What a wonderful time I had with my sons. Jeff and I went to an
AA meeting, and I was delighted and proud that he allowed me
to accompany him. His recovery is so important to me (maybe
even more important to me than to him?), and I know he has
relapsed several times. He's not honest enough to tell me. I wish
he were. I just sense that he has tripped along the way, just a
feeling, that mother feeling. But I'm confident that he will make
it.

Three weeks later, Jeff came home for a visit, and the days were crystal blue, "glad to be alive" days. Sunsets were magnificent, pink and purple skies, a sliver of moon. We golfed, walked, and laughed. I cooked my nonna's spaghetti, with her rich, red, tomato sauce; Jeff's favorite chicken and peppers; and Italian *minestra*. I needed to build a nest of security, and food was my way of offering a feeling of home and comfort. However, I couldn't help but see that Jeff was melancholy, slower, slightly thinner, and a little more distant than usual. His energy was diminished; he didn't laugh spontaneously; and his vocabulary wasn't quick. I sensed that ketamine was back on the scene, along with lots of alcohol. When I asked him, he assured me that he was OK. "Trust me, Mom. I'm fine. I learned a lot at re-hab; I won't go back to drugs. I'm just tired."

I didn't know what to do. Setting boundaries at home was hard enough; setting boundaries from a distance seemed impossible. Jeff

told me just enough to appear to be truthful, yet hid enough to protect himself. This back-and-forth tug between the joy of mother-
ing my son and the despair of disbelieving my son kept me always
on edge. I struggled between basking in our mother-son relationship and being a detective looking for clues. I had learned in therapy and at Father Martin's that I needed to learn to let go. Jeff knew
about his addiction, and he had learned at rehab what he needed to
do. It was his time to be strong for himself.

Two days following Jeff's return to Boston, I was awakened early
in the morning by a bad dream, of which I could remember only
snippets: Jeff was using PCP and trying to explain that it was OK;
Tim was sleeping on the couch and couldn't be awakened, while a
woman, and then a woman and a man, tried to break in the front
door. Tim slept. I screamed his name until finally I stopped. I'm not
even sure how it ended, although I seem to recall running and grab-
bing my cell phone and calling 911. I feared that my dreams were
continuing to give me insight into my subconscious, reflecting my
fears of Jeff's possible relapse and my feelings of isolation and abandonment. The holidays were coming, my sons would be home, and
although I had missed them deeply, I found I had conflicting feelings about Jeff's return. I was afraid of drugs and drinking.

Despite my dreams, the holidays passed with both serenity and
tranquillity. All was well. As we ended 1998 I felt content and at
peace with my sons and my life. Our holiday had been successful,
and then it was January 1, 1999, a day I remember as I might remember a slow-motion black-and-white movie, in movements and
shadows that are both stark and distinct, yet at the same time mud-
dled and garbled. I can almost smell the day.

I had invited thirty neighbors to our home for a New Year's Day
brunch for a woman whose husband had recently died. Everyone
was glad to come, happy to bring a little relief to a friend.

By 10:30 A.M., I'd already been in the kitchen for four hours.
Roasts were in the oven, appetizers prepared, and the dining room
table was scattered with all the serving pieces needed to pull the

party together. As I pushed the chairs against the walls in preparation for a house filled with friends, the phone rang.

Probably just someone calling about the party, asking if there was anything I needed, I thought, walking slowly from the dining room to the kitchen and answering nonchalantly.

It was Jeff's girlfriend, Sophie, and she spoke to me in hushed tones: "Libby, is Jeff there?"

"Yes, he's asleep," I responded calmly. "He came back from New York City last night. We're getting ready for a party today, and I'll soon have to wake him to help. Do you want him to call you?"

"How is he?" she continued. Her voice was trembling; her words rushed together like one continuous whisper.

I was glad I could reassure her. "He's fine, really, just tired. We didn't talk much. He was pretty quiet. I think he came home from New York to get away from all the drugs and drinking, all the craziness." I offered again: "Sophie, I'm busy here in the kitchen, but do you want me to have him call you when he wakes up?"

She hesitated and finally stated, "He's not fine. He's getting high again. It's ketamine. He's shooting it into his arms and legs. You've got to do something. I'm so afraid."

Her words smacked my cheek where the phone was resting. Stung and confused, I questioned her: "How do you know?" Struggling to understand what she was telling me, I added quickly, "He looks fine, he sounds OK." I paused, searching for the right words to counter what she had said. Finally, I pleaded once more, "How do you know?"

"I saw the bruises on his body. I know a lot of things, but I can't tell you everything. And please don't tell him I called you. He'll be so angry with me, but I love him, and I'm afraid."

I thought about all the progress he had made at the treatment center and how I had believed that he was serious about his recovery. I thought about being in Boston together, and how we sang my dad's old songs, and how we laughed in the rain. I thought about all the promise that this firstborn son of mine held. I felt betrayed, as if the floor had dropped out from under me.

Sophie had called me in an attempt to help Jeff; this was the only thing she knew to do. I had to comfort her. I tried to sound strong as I promised, "I won't tell him you called. My guess is he didn't even hear the phone ring." My voice trailed off as I ended the conversation. "Don't worry. I'll do something."

I stood in the kitchen clutching the receiver, not knowing whether I should sit or stand, throw the phone or hold it, believe or not believe what she had told me. I remember the smell of the roasts in the oven; I remember looking out the window at the same trees my sons used to climb when they were little. All the memories of past bad times and broken promises crashed down on me. Nothing had changed, and everything had changed.

What do I do this time?

When Jeff finally realized that I had first shaken him awake and was now yelling his name from the bottom of the stairs, he stumbled in a haze down the steps, dressed in sweatpants and a T-shirt, and dropped sleepily into a dining room chair. He was not happy. He wouldn't even look at me. He bent his elbows, propped them on his knees, and buried his head in his hands. I sat in another chair, each of us positioned in a corner of the room. I told Jeff about the phone call (I didn't tell him until years later that it was Sophie who had called), and he tilted his head and looked at me as if I were not even there. We stared at each other across the trappings of a party, the white linen tablecloth, the silver serving trays, the crystal glassware.

At first he denied everything. He had done nothing. I was crazy. The caller was crazy. Everyone was crazy, until finally he rubbed his head, leaned back into the chair, and snarled with deep hostility, "Yeah, I'm using K again. Now you know. For chrissake, leave me alone."

"How are you using K? How?" I pushed.

"It's none of your goddamn business how I'm using. I'm using— that's all you need to know."

None of your goddamn business. None of my business. When he said this my mind felt like a hurricane had picked up debris and

hurled it against my senses. I almost heard the roar of the winds
and the cries of the injured, but I knew that I was the one who had
been flung, I was the broken thing, too splintered to rescue my son
from the storm. My son, he *was* my business.

In the end Jeff admitted that he was shooting K into his arms
and legs. I wrapped the food, stuffed it into the freezer, and can-
celed the party. Everyone knew about Jeff. They always had.

Jeff retreated back to his room, waiting, I think, to see what I
would do. I didn't know what to do. I needed help, but it was New
Year's Day, and I didn't know where to find support or advice. I
called the crisis center at Father Martin's, and they told me that a
counselor would contact me soon. I called a woman friend of mine;
I needed to talk. She would come to the house immediately, she told
me, and she would bring a friend named Erika with her who had
lost her son to drugs. She was sure that Erika could help me. By the
time they arrived I was distraught and confused. Erika offered to
talk with Jeff, so I called Jeff to my bedroom, where she, Jeff, and I
could talk privately. Jeff didn't know Erika, and I had met her only
briefly through my friend.

Little did I know that the conversation between Erika and Jeff
would chart the course for the dramatic outcome of this day. While
I sat on a chair in my bedroom, weeping, Erika stood toe-to-toe
with Jeff. Her image was fierce as she stood tall against him. Jeff
didn't cringe at her approach, and he became increasingly aggres-
sive. I watched the scene playing out in front of me as if I had no
control. I heard Erika accuse Jeff, "You're doing drugs. Aren't you?"
He responded crossly, "Yeah, who are you? What are you talking
with me for?" He looked questioningly at me. "Mom?" Erika took
another shot. "What did your mother say would happen to you if
you continued to get high?" He fired back, "She told me she'd take
my tuition away. That she'd pull me out of college." Erika leaped in,
"Well, that's what is going to happen. You're out of college." With
this Jeff backed down, shocked, and he turned to me. "Mom, that's
not true, is it? You wouldn't really take me out of college." I looked

up at my son from my seated position, and I heard words drift out of my mouth as if I was talking to myself: "If I were stronger, Jeff, I'd take your tuition." The words floated back at me, into me, and I heard my weak tone, my bewildered words, and I reoriented myself, paused, and said strongly, "Well, yes, that's what will happen. Erika is right. You're out of college."

Erika nodded to me as if to say *a job well done*. Jeff stared at me, speechless. He glared at Erika. "Fuck this," he hissed. "You're all crazy." He stormed out of the room, down the steps, and out the front door. I didn't know where he was going. I could do no more. Enough damage had been done. My friends left, tears all around, and I sat in the house, alone. Jeremy was in his room, but we didn't speak to each other.

Jeff returned to our home less than an hour later, quieter, ready to talk. The decision to withdraw Jeff from college was made and I could not, would not, reverse the judgment. It was right; I had told him that his college education was contingent on his sobriety. Emotions hit him, hit me, and I regretted all the past actions and hurts. I felt bewildered at his continuing drug use, confused as to what had gone wrong, and frustrated at the failure of all the attempts to do the right thing. Tears, mine and then Jeff's, and the circle opened outward, because I didn't want to be the one who called my mom and dad. At my insistence Jeff telephoned them and told them that he had lost his college tuition, and that he was again using drugs. I called Tim and a few concerned friends. We all railed against a demon of addiction that we couldn't stop. All, that is, except Jeremy. Jeremy watched silently, stayed close to Jeff through it all, and never left his side. Jeremy told me years later, "I was pissed. I was angry at everybody and all the intrusions into our family by your friends who thought they were helping us. I felt rage that we were taking Jeff out of school, cutting him loose, not helping him, just making him leave. I felt bad for you; you were so confused. But I was more sympathetic for Jeff than anything. I wanted to protect him, but I couldn't."

In the end Jeff did leave the house, although he lingered for a few days, trying to decide what he would do next. During that time we talked, all three of us—Jeff, Jeremy, and I. Somehow, after the storm, we seemed to be able to communicate. Jeff later told me:

> After rehab the previous summer and back in Boston, drugs reentered the picture. I started drinking, which opened doors to coke and pills, then K, then everything else. If you're not working against addiction, it returns. It's inevitable. The time in treatment was helpful, but it was still too early for me to take sobriety seriously. It was undeniable that consequences were becoming more severe, but they were still tolerable, and I was convinced that I could ultimately manage my using. I refused to accept that drugs were outside of my control.

I gave Jeff options. He could go back into a rehab center, live with his grandparents in Florida, or go to Pittsburgh to live with my brothers. I didn't even know if any of these family members would accept the responsibility of my son, but I felt helpless, used up, powerless. Tim was done. I didn't know what to do, and I hoped desperately that maybe someone else could heal my son, give him what he needed. In the end, however, Jeff decided to return to Boston. There he had his apartment, his friends, and I guess all his connections. He began packing his car again. But this saga was not yet over.

Two days later, on the night before he was to leave, he came home smelling of alcohol. I had fallen asleep on the bed while reading, lights on, as I waited for his return. Sometime shortly after midnight, I awoke to him standing next to my bed as he bent over to kiss my cheek. A good-night kiss from son to mother, a normal gesture. The smell of the alcohol registered on me even before I opened my eyes. As I brought him into clear focus, I raised my voice accusingly. "Were you drinking?"

"Yeah," he replied coolly. "A buddy and I stopped at Abner's and we had a few beers. I'm out of school anyhow, so what difference does it make?"

Why, I wonder yet today, did he have to drink that night? And why did he kiss me good night? I still don't know.

That was the last straw. I had had enough; I could take no more. As I rose to confront him, to search his eyes, he had already begun walking away from me as though nothing had happened, as though he were invincible, as though I could do nothing. Maybe he thought there was nothing else for me to do. "Pack your bags and get out tonight," I told my son. "You can't stay here."

He did exactly that, and calmly. Maybe this is what he had wanted all along? The night was dark, and it was now well past midnight. Jeff packed his things and marched down the stairs, me trailing behind. When he reached the front door he paused with his right hand on the doorknob, his back facing me, his duffel bag clutched in his left hand, and his backpack flung over a shoulder.

I had no tears left. This time I needed, wanted, to say something that might be right, something that might make a difference. The words formed in my heart and rose to the surface, and I spoke clearly: "I look forward to the day when I can welcome my son home again."

I moved toward him to kiss him good-bye, expecting him to turn and face me, but he opened the door and never looked back, slamming it shut behind him.

Chapter 4

The Mothers in Al-Anon

January 13, 1999, 12:30 A.M.

Can't sleep. Jeff is back in Boston. Where will this addiction end?
How it will end could be the scariest of all scenarios. My world is
rocked to the center. I have no control over what happens now.
He uses drugs, pops pills, drinks too much. Dear God, what pain
is he trying to kill, and will he kill himself first? I must wait and
pray. I don't wait well. I can do nothing now. How does a mother
do nothing?

After Jeff left I asked Jeremy what had happened in Boston during the preceding months. He told me nothing; he was Jeff's protector. Eight years later, however, in October 2007, he made the decision to talk with me, and he related story after story, remembering the time as clearly as if it were yesterday.

When I got to Boston, doors opened immediately to me because of Jeff. I got into any party, got the prettiest girls, a whole world that other freshmen didn't have access to was there, waiting for me. Jeff was well connected, and his reputation translated to me. He had looks and personality, plus he was a major player in the drug scene. At that time, drugs were a total status symbol.

But with Jeff, it was bigger than drugs. For instance, once I took out a girl, and we were sitting on the stoop of her apartment, drinking. Three upperclassmen walked past and they kept staring at her. I jumped up and said, "What are you looking at?" The guys turned and started coming at me. All of a sudden, one of them stopped and said, "Wait a minute. Aren't you Jeff Bratton's little brother?" I fired back, "How do you know my brother?" He turned to the others and said, "This is Jeff's brother. Leave him alone." Another time, a friend of mine and I had too much to drink, and we were standing in the middle of Brighton Avenue holding up traffic, for no reason—we were just playing, stupid really. The police pulled up and were furious. I thought we were going to jail. At that same moment, from nowhere, Jeff drove up in his car, walked over to the cops, and talked with them. The next thing I knew he was putting us into his car. He took me home to his apartment.

When I first got to Boston he tried to play the good guy, the big brother. At first, everything seemed pretty normal. He went to classes, and he seemed OK, balanced. But, over time, Jeff's dependency on drugs became more and more obvious. Like his nodding off during conversations. I used to think he was just tired. But I listened and watched. I started to hear about trips to New York City, and I paid attention to his out-of-town visitors.

I saw it all: yellow rows of K in shrink-wrap, bags of powder and pills, and sheets of acid. I started to become more concerned as his drug dependency became more evident. He'd get wasted, black out, and people would call me. I'd go and get him from parties or wherever he was, take him home, and care for him.

In time I started getting physical with people to keep them away from Jeff—I'd sit outside on the steps of his apartment with two of our football player friends, and we'd keep people out just by our presence. I don't know what happened when we weren't there, but I can tell you, when we were there, none of Jeff's drug friends entered that building. Another time, when a close friend of Jeff's and one of the biggest dealers on our side of Boston came to see him, I pleaded with him, "Please don't deliver anything to my brother. He's in bad shape." The guy told me to stay out of things and that Jeff could make his own decisions. No one wanted to hurt Jeff, but he was a centerpiece of that drug circle. At this point I realized that drugs were bigger than Jeff, bigger than me, bigger than brotherhood. They were a business.

Because Jeff loves me, he tried to keep me at a distance, but I'm so me—it's hard to keep me at a distance. I'd show up. I'd go to his apartment, and Jeff and his buddies would be blown out on K and pills. He couldn't walk or talk, and he'd make no sense. I hated to see him like this. Sometimes I was so angry and full of rage; other times I'd laugh to hide my feelings, sad that this was my older brother, my role model. I wanted to say, "Look at you. You were everything I wanted to be." I was crushed. Drugs were robbing me of my brother.

The rambling narration wound down, and Jeremy's eyes were far away, as if caught somewhere in his memories. I both ached for my son and was grateful to him. I was sorry for his pain; I was grateful that he finally decided to talk to me; and I hoped that in the talking there would be healing. I was sure there were more stories, stories that he kept to himself, stories that he wouldn't tell me. After a silence in which each of us wandered, lost in our own thoughts, I asked, "Why, Jer? You carried so much alone. Why didn't you tell me?"

Jeremy looked away. "He's my brother." He paused and said it again, as if to himself: "He's my brother."

Jeremy had tried, I had tried, Sophie had tried, Father Martin's Ashley had tried. We all had tried, but we couldn't fight the drugs, the addiction, and I finally understood that addiction was not our enemy to fight. It was Jeff's.

In February, around Valentine's Day, Jeff called home for the first time since that January night. His voice was soft, contrite; it was clear, the words not garbled.

"Last year I sent you a dozen red roses, Momma."

"Yes, Jeff, you did."

"I don't have enough money to send you roses this year, so I thought I'd send you twelve Valentine cards."

"That would be nice," I replied quietly. Tears streamed down my face. I held the receiver tightly, hoping somehow to touch my son through the air, hanging on every word, tucking each syllable into my heart.

"I don't have money for stamps. Will you send me money for stamps?"

"No, Jeff, I won't."

"I didn't think so."

Years later I asked Jeff why he went back to Boston.

Although tuition was pulled and I wouldn't be taking courses, major pieces of my life remained in Boston. The explosion at Christmastime was sudden, but I still had a girlfriend, close friends, and a social scene that I wanted to be a part of. School and classes were only a part of my time in town. I'd been at school for more than two years and knew lots of local kids who were around to hang out with. Filling time was never a problem.

I got by selling bottles of K hooked up through a friend from New York, but I was a notoriously bad drug dealer. I'd do more than I'd sell, share with friends, and spend money indiscriminately. If I had to pay outright for the amount of drugs I did, I'd never have survived. Drugs weren't about the money, at least for me. They were always a "get high and break even" kind of thing.

Without the academic rhythm, though, I started feeling aimless. I never lost track of my reason for being in Boston, at least not cognitively. A degree was my goal and when I stopped and really processed my situation, it was clear that drugs were doing bad things to my life.

It was during this time, when despair filled me, that I reached out to Al-Anon. I had been introduced to Al-Anon meetings during Jeff's stay at Father Martin's, and I had seen the sharing that occurred among those of us who love addicts. I was now at the end of my emotional rope with Jeff, and I needed help from those who knew firsthand the trauma of addiction. I had heard about Alice, a nurse at the local hospital who was married to a recovering alcoholic and committed to helping others. I called her. When she answered the phone, I began, "You don't know me, but I heard that you help . . ." and then, gulping down the tears that wouldn't stop, I explained to her that I wanted, needed, to find an Al-Anon meeting. My words tumbled out in chunks, but the key words were there: my son, drug addiction, chaos, powerlessness. She took the lead without hesitation. She would meet me in front of a nearby convenience store at 6:40 that night. We would go to a 7:00 P.M. meeting together.

As I drove to meet Alice, I felt lonely and anxious. When I climbed into her car, however, her smile welcomed me, as if saying, *It's OK. I've felt the same things you're feeling. We all do.* She had short-cropped, blond hair; meticulously clean fingernails, clipped short and brushed with clear enamel nail polish; and a competent, in-charge look. Her voice was gentle, musical, as she explained that she had found a meeting in another county, since she thought I might feel uncomfortable seeing people who might know me from school. I trusted her. We traveled to a church, parked alongside several other cars, and walked down the metal steps into the basement, where we entered a cold and dimly lighted room. There was a small circle of metal folding chairs where twelve people were already seated; eleven of them were women, and all of them, I would learn later, had alcoholic husbands. Alice seated herself, but before I sat next to her I searched the faces to make certain that I didn't recognize anyone. This, I knew, was my own ego, my pride; I knew that. Al-Anon is founded on anonymity, but I was conflicted. I hated being in need, yet I knew I needed help.

When the meeting opened, everyone welcomed me as a newcomer; all eyes were on me, and with this attention, I regretted being there. The facilitator focused the group by reading from an Al-Anon book called *Courage to Change*, emphasizing one particular sentence: "We are best able to help others when we ourselves have learned the way to achieve serenity." Then each person in the circle spoke, going around clockwise, talking about how she struggled to find her peace and serenity, so that she might be stronger for herself, and, consequently, better able to help others (usually the alcoholic husband, but also the family in general). I sat doubled over in a kind of fetal position, with my arms crossed in front of my chest and pressed into my belly, and my head rested on my knees, and I silently wept.

The others continued with the meeting, introduced themselves, spoke, and opened their lives and their stories to us, but I knew I couldn't share the story of my addicted son, my twenty-year-old gone bad. I couldn't tell my story in front of these people I didn't know, and who seemed to care more about their own peace and serenity than in helping me learn how to help my son. When it came time for me to say something, I lifted my head, looked around at all the waiting faces, and whimpered something about not wanting to speak, a reaction that I later learned is not unusual for a newcomer. They all understood. The meeting ended with all of us standing, holding hands, and saying a group prayer. "Keep coming back," they told me.

Keep coming back—were they crazy? I had no intention of ever coming back.

Alice, however, called me the next day. She had found another meeting in another county, and we would try again. When I got into her car this second night, she handed me a wrapped gift, the Al-Anon book *Courage to Change*, and she encouraged me to read and meditate on the daily passages. I found myself in another church basement, another folding chair, with my head on my lap again. This meeting focused on the principle of taking one day at a time, keeping our focus on today, and neither regretting the past nor fearing the future. I didn't want to hear about taking one day at a time; I didn't want to hear about how I needed to take care of myself. I was a mother; I needed to know what to do to save Jeff and to help Jeremy. I wanted advice, clear and simple. The group consisted of only women, and I'd look up every once in a while to study their eyes, where I began to see understanding, even compassion. Their voices floated over me, and I didn't register much of what they said, but I listened acutely to the cadence of their tones, and I heard lots of grief, just like mine. I didn't hear individual words, but I did hear chords of hope and faith and love. When it came my turn to speak, I said nothing, just as before. We ended the meeting with a group prayer and another round of "Keep coming back."

The third meeting that Alice found for me was in yet another county, distant from where I lived and from where my school was located. Another church basement and more folding chairs, but I sat upright this time, next to Alice, and this was the first meeting where there were parents, three mothers of addicted children who also knew the pain of a lost child and the powerlessness of not being able to rescue their son or daughter from the demons of addiction. One woman talked about her daughter, who was living in a homeless shelter and whom she hadn't seen in seven months; another had a son who was an alcoholic, his girlfriend was pregnant, they had moved back to the family home, and neither one would work; another mother's son had been missing for the last two weeks and she suspected that he had relapsed on cocaine. These three women talked about trying to stay strong, trying to find a sense of peace for today, trying not to lose themselves in their children's illness. I felt these women would understand my hurts; I felt safe here. I had found my home meeting.

And that's the way with addiction: We help each other by reaching out a hand to another. Thus began my lifeline in Al-Anon. And I kept coming back.

> February 23, 1999, 6:45 A.M.
>
> I went to an Al-Anon meeting last night, and I found a peace that has eluded me. I'm truly amazed that my soul quieted there, in the basement of a church. What made the difference? I heard such pain from others, and I listened intently to how they are struggling to survive. I saw in their eyes a determination to get healthy, their intense love for their alcoholic or addict, and true compassion for each other. Yes, something happened last night. Many of them have worse pain than I, and all seem to struggle with similar issues—worry, fear, detachment. I can find strength in their strength. Maybe I've been searching for someone to give me strength. Maybe I can find strength and comfort in Al-Anon, and ultimately in myself.

I didn't realize how soon what I was learning at Al-Anon would be sorely tested. It began with a phone call.

On February 26 at 3:30 A.M., I was awakened by a phone call from Jeremy. He was in tears, almost screaming, "Don't give Jeff any more money. Don't. Do you hear me?"

I struggled to gain some level of alertness. "I haven't given him a penny since he left in January. What's wrong?" I pleaded, "Talk to me."

Jeremy choked on his tears and fought through his rage to tell the story. He and Sophie had been at Jeff's apartment and all was fine. "Then," he said, "some kid came to the apartment to see Jeff."

Jeremy had threatened the boy. "If you're coming with drugs, you're dead." The boy sneered at Jeremy. "I came to take a piss."

The boy and Jeff went into the bathroom. After about five minutes, Jeremy continued, the boy opened the door and stumbled out, laughing at him. Jeff didn't walk out of the bathroom, so Jeremy rushed in and saw Jeff struggling to stand up, mumbling to himself, falling over. Jeremy looked on top of the medicine cabinet and found two syringes. He was outraged, sickened, and his anger erupted. "I grabbed that fucking kid and I threw him through the glass door in the front of the building. I threw him, yelled at Jeff, and then ran out of the apartment. Jeff's a mess. He gets high and can't even move his body. He's gonna die." Jeremy was filled with regret, disgust, and fear. "I don't know what to do." And then he pleaded, "Mom, you gotta do something."

Jeremy had broken his silence. I felt afraid and confused, and I was also grateful that he had finally asked me, trusted me, to help him carry his burdens. I knew that I needed to stay calm that night on the phone with him; I needed to sound sure and in charge, so that he could rest. I told Jeremy to go to bed. I told him not to worry. I told him that I would handle the situation with Jeff. But I felt helpless: Jeff had already been to a treatment center, and I had already made him leave the house. *What would I do now?*

It was 5:30 A.M. and I was sitting alone in the blue chair in the living room; I had been wide awake since Jeremy's phone call. I couldn't move, couldn't write, couldn't do anything but read my Al-Anon books, searching for an answer as to what to do next, devouring page after page of addiction literature, hoping to find the solution to our problem. No revelation came to me that early morning, but the literature gave me a touchstone of information and, as I read other people's stories, their experiences kept me from losing my sanity, and kept me somewhat grounded.

Finally, at 7:30 A.M., four hours after Jeremy's phone call, I couldn't stand the noise and confusion in my head not knowing what was happening with Jeff. I called him, thinking that since he had a job as a temp at the Harvard Business School and needed to be at work, he should be awake. (They liked him so much they were considering offering him a permanent position. I didn't understand it: They liked him so much and knew him so little.)

Jeff answered on the second ring. He sounded fine. Incredible, I thought, after what I knew had occurred. I asked him what he had done the night before, and he told me that he and Sophie had gone to the movies, even told me the name of the movie, and assured me that all was well. I was shocked. I wasn't sure what to say next. I couldn't tell him that I knew what had happened; I couldn't tell him that Jeremy had called and recounted the story of the drug use. From prior experience I had learned not to divulge my source of information—if you tell the name of your informant, you never hear again.

I struggled with how to move forward, and then I said, "Jeff, I've told you that the board has given me a sabbatical, and that I'm going to Italy. I would love for you to come for a week or two, but you have to be clean. How's your sobriety?"

"I'm doing really well. I'm working a program, going to meetings most nights, hanging out with sober kids. I'd love to come to Italy."

Unbelievable. I was speechless. I wondered at how OK he managed to sound and at how instantaneously he created lies.

After a long pause, my mind searching for the correct response, I just blurted it out without any explanation. "Jeff, I don't believe you. I think you're like dirty dish water, always gray, never clean. I think you lie about your drug use and your friends."

"Why do you say that?" He laughed calmly. "I'm fine. I don't know what you're talking about." Then he paused, a kind of careful silence. "Has someone been talking to you, telling you shit about me?"

Even in his addiction he could almost smell that my call was in response to some event. I had to get off the phone quickly.

"You lie, Jeff. You lie to me and to yourself. You need to get yourself into another treatment center. And until you get help you can't come home, you can't come to Italy. Until you get honest, forget the phone number here, forget the address. You need help, and you know it."

A silence. What would he say?

"Fuck you."

I got dressed. I had to go to work. I was the head of school, and what else could I do? Work was the place where I felt capable and intact. I usually arrived around 7:30 A.M., well before the students' first class of the day, and today I was late. By 9:00 A.M., I was driving to school, eyes red and swollen, but I knew I needed to drag myself forward. I was in the car about five minutes when my cell phone rang. I thought it was probably the school calling to ask me if I was on my way, and to make sure everything was fine. I answered. It was Jeff. I couldn't believe it. Hadn't I just told him to forget the phone number? Why was he calling?

He began, "Just listen to me." His words rushed together; he was intent on delivering his message. "After I got off the phone with you, I called Father Martin's and asked them for the name of a good halfway house, a place where I could go to get clean—where people volunteer to go. They gave me the number of a place in south Florida. I called there. I talked with a guy at the Boca House and told him that I could come immediately, that I had to come. He told me there were no empty beds available. So, I called Father Martin's again and asked them to call on my behalf. They did. When I called back to Florida, they accepted me. I need to be in Florida in twelve days. Can I come home now? Can I come home before I leave?"

He had made the call. He had made the decision. Maybe this was the time that would make the difference. Maybe this was the time when my son would turn his life around. I opened my arms to him. "Yes, Jeff. Come home."

February 27, 1999, 8:30 A.M.
Jeff enrolled himself into a three-month halfway house. I'm
thrilled; his actions bring me some peace, since he made the call
and the choice. I'm cautious; I'm not in control of when his tur-
moil will end, if it will end. Jeff is making his walk. My heart has
a steady drip about Jeff. His name is mentioned, and I ache.

Dear Libby, I know you're afraid deep inside, but give yourself
a break. Jeff has taken a positive stance. Celebrate your family's
strength instead of wallowing in self-pity and misery.

Dear Lord, I've written to everyone else, why not You? The
saving grace is that we're finally facing Jeff's drug addiction, filled
with lies, fears, and broken hearts. I need help. Everything feels so
wrong. I know it's not, but I'm so tired. You are working mightily
in our lives. Protect us and hold us, the three of us, in Your
hands. I need You to help me stand alone. For Your glory and our
good.

Jeff and Jeremy arrived home from Boston together. I had already
made Jeff's plane reservations, and I was hopeful that the Boca House
would make the difference in his life. On March 10, just twelve days
after Jeremy's phone call, Jeff was scheduled to fly to Florida.

I never knew, really, why Jeff made the decision to go back into rehab, and it was years later when I asked him. I wish I had asked him
earlier.

Being in Boston around a predominantly college-oriented crowd
was starting to make me feel disconnected from the community.
Friends were lining up internships, doing cool things with academic majors, producing music, starting businesses, and building real
relationships with people around them. On the other hand, I was
constantly fighting with the important people in my life, wasn't in
school, and was running with a crew of kids who were oftentimes
in far more trouble than I was. I couldn't help but recognize the cir-

cumstances, and I eventually decided that above all else I needed
to settle down and finish school. The only chance I had of getting
tuition reinstated was to go back into rehab.

I went to work the morning of Jeff's departure to give him time
to pack and to give me an opportunity to organize my school com-
mitments before leaving at noon. Even though I arrived at school at
6:00 A.M., I got caught in last-minute problems as I tried to leave.
Rushing home, I felt comfortable, because I anticipated Jeff being
ready to walk out of the house at 12:30, as we had agreed. Instead,
when I opened the door from the garage, I heard the shower running.
I bolted up the steps, two at a time, as I shouted, "We're leaving. . . .
Now." I tried to sound calm, but I was hysterical inside.

"I don't think I'm taking the plane," he responded absently. "I
think I'll drive to Florida; I'll need a car anyhow."

Fifteen minutes later a disgruntled Jeff sat slumped in the passenger side of my car with his carry-on bag and backpack.

"Do you promise that Jeremy will drive my car to Florida if I
need it?"

"Yes." I could say no more.

We rode in silence. I was praying. Jeff was listening to music on
his Walkman; he was quiet, headphones muffling the sound. We arrived late at the Baltimore airport with no time for me to walk with
him to the gate. I screeched the car to a halt at the departure curb,
jammed the car's gear into park, and left it running as I darted to the
passenger side, opened the door, and stood impatiently, encouraging
Jeff to hurry his exit. No such luck. He was in slow motion. In an instant my mind saw the plane leaving and my son left out of recovery.

Gently, I yanked him out of the car as he donned his backpack
and picked up his carry-on. Like walking through mud, we trudged
toward the entrance. The glass doors slid open automatically, and we
stepped inside. There we were, standing in that quiet place where I
felt as though I could not breathe. To the left people smiled and
kissed good-bye as they prepared to leave for their journeys. To the

right, others rushed to check luggage, made final calls, stood in line, even laughed as they readied themselves for their flights. For my son and me this was a journey that he must make alone. He was sick with the disease of drug addiction, and I could do nothing but let him go.

In the vacuumlike space between the glass panels, I focused on the face of my six-feet-one-inch-tall son, just twenty years old, but I could only imagine the lives he had lived, the sights he had seen. His face, with elegantly chiseled bones, deep and gentle brown eyes, long lashes—his complexion was mottled with red blotches, I saw; must be nerves, I thought. I cradled his face in my hands, as I had when he was just a little boy.

"Mom, I'm scared."

"Me, too, Jeff. Me, too."

With that I kissed both his cheeks and made the sign of the cross three times on his forehead, just as my nonna and mother used to do to me. Jeff closed his eyes for an instant, as if he knew this was a rite of passage, the sign from mother to child. I wasn't sure whether Jeff even believed in God anymore, but I believed that he knew that the sign was my way of saying "I love you and I'm praying for you, and I send you with my blessing. My mother angel is with you—always." He then opened eyes filled with tears and began to move away from me.

No, I cried inwardly, *not yet. I can't let go just yet.*

Jeff moved toward the glass as if to walk into it. The door sensed his arrival, his time, and he slipped through.

Without a word my son walked away from me, toward the gate. I stood helpless, watching his thin body, straight back, strong shoulders, and the heavy backpack slung over his right shoulder as he slid out of my protective net once again.

I stood frozen in place. I prayed for his flight, his safety, his recovery, his strength. I prayed for his healthy return home.

Jeff moved away, moving—I hoped—forward.

Chapter 5

Doing the Next Right Thing

March 11, 1999, 9:00 A.M.

Jeff called from Florida, from the halfway house, and he sounded happy. "I feel safe, Mom. It's a crazy feeling. The guys here seem genuinely committed to sobriety." And so my twenty-year-old son joins 150 other men to work on his own health. He told me that at his first AA meeting, an older man named Jack sat next to him, turned and faced him, made a fist with his right hand, and held it a little above his belly and grumbled, "Don't tell me, but I know you have a hole right here, about this size, that sucks everything right down the back of your throat. I know you have it because we all have it—we all come here with it." Jeff was surprised that this guy knew about the anxiety, a knotted nothingness that Jeff says is right below his breastplate and pulls his breath down into it.

My journal continued, reporting that Jeff said another man told him, "Religion is for people who don't want to go to hell. Spirituality is for people who have been there." I knew that AA had a spiritual base but not a commitment to a certain religion, because the second step states, "We came to believe that a Power greater than ourselves could restore us to sanity," and I wondered if Jeff would embrace a higher power. Jeff told me yet another phrase he had heard: "Work on your inside first and the outside will come."

My son had chosen to enter a halfway house, which is a mandatory residential center at night and an open campus during the day so they can work: half time on the property and half time off the property, while it provides drug monitoring, structure, and support for recovering addicts and alcoholics. He had chosen to begin his own healing, and I was grateful. Mothers and our sons—how do we know what to do to help them? When do we allow our children the opportunity to feel the weight and consequences of their own mistakes? What do we do with our fear when we think their choices will lead to dangerous outcomes, when we know that the possibility is high that they are headed toward disaster? I didn't have answers to any of these questions, and I didn't know what to do about Jeff's addiction, but I did know that it was time for me to learn how to be a better mother to my sons. I thought about the words that another man had told Jeff—"Work on your inside first and the outside will come"—and with this in mind I planned a two-month sabbatical, a time for me to think, reflect, and write, and to research my ancestral roots in the south of Italy.

When I was a child, in fact from as early as I could remember, my nonna, my mother's mother, an immigrant to America during the early 1900s, had provided me with a sense of security. I'd spend most weekends with her, away from my parents and brothers, and I grew up confident of her unshakable devotion. She was the one who taught me how to twirl spaghetti without splashing sauce all over myself; the one who taught me how to make bread, the kind you make with only flour, water, salt, and yeast, measuring nothing, a handful of this and a pinch of that. After our noonday meal we'd sit on her porch swing, rocking gently, and she would tell me about her home in the small village of Rotondella, in the poorest province of Basilicata. After dinner we'd sit together in her living room, she in her chair in front of the window, me on the carpeted floor next to her knee, resting my hand on her leg, feeling a sense of comfort with the additional touch, the added closeness. She loved *The Lawrence Welk Show* (which she pronounced "Velk"), and as she would listen to his big-band music she'd sway her head to the beat, her short gray hair held in place by a hairnet, and her coal-colored, black-brown eyes would sparkle. She loved to see the beautiful young people dancing, and she'd *oyee* when the show ended with a spray of bubbles raining like confetti. During each commercial break I'd badger her to tell me stories of the old country, of the Italy she left. She was reluctant to reminisce about these times, because they were sad stories for her: hard years of hard labor, and the hard choice of leaving her mother behind as she traveled to a country she did not know. But she would soon grow tired of my nagging, and she'd relent. "When I came to America . . . ," she'd begin. Her words were like music, each word ending with the uplift of a vowel, and I'd hear the rhythm of *ven-a, eye-a, came-a.*

Her voice would drift away from me. "I went very north to Naples to take the boat, during the first war, the big war. I left my mother in 1915, November, I left my family and I came alone to America. I was young and afraid. I had big fear." I'd plead with her to tell me, over and over again, the stories of her youth, of when she and her mother and sister, along with the other *contadini* (peasant farmers) from their village and their donkeys trekked down the mountainside to work in the wheat fields at the foothills around Rotondella, where the boss, *il padrone*, paid her either a loaf of bread or a penny for a full day's labor. Her eyes seemed to look into the distance when she talked about washing clothes in the water fountain at the bottom of the steep hill, where she worked alongside her mother and the other women of the village. They would fill large water barrels (*varril*, in Rotondellesi dialect) that were made of wood, oval-shaped, rounded, and topped with a wood stopper; roll a cloth called a *corona* and place it on the top of their heads, to help balance the weight; and then they'd hoist the *varril* of water upward and trudge back up the steep mountainside to their homes. She told me about our family's humble beginnings in Italy, and of the many other people from her town and the surrounding villages who joined the exodus from poverty and a seemingly hopeless future to come to America.

Nonna's stories seemed to root me in a time and place in our history; however, she was more than a storyteller—she was my bastion of safety. When I got into trouble with my mother I'd jump onto my bike and speed away to Nonna's home, and she would open her arms to me. I would run and bury my head in her breasts, and she would listen patiently to my muffled complaints. Her perfume was tomatoes and garlic and her smile radiated homecoming. Italy became my mother parent, and the need to travel back to touch my nonna was embedded deeply in me. She called to me; Italy called to me.

March 11, 1999, 9:00 A.M.
Guilt, control, and fear are all alive and well and living in me. I want to leave for Italy, but I'm afraid to leave my sons, and I feel guilty that I'm taking this time for myself. I must acknowledge these feelings and let them go. Jeremy told me, "If you know you made the right decision, even if it hurts you gotta let go. If you know it's right, that's all that matters."

Jeremy. What a juxtaposition of little and big, innocent and wise. I tried to talk with him about Jeff's choice to go to the halfway house, but he said clearly, "Momma, I love you and Jeff, but this is the first time in my life that I don't have to deal with Jeff's drug addiction. For three months, I'm free. I feel like a huge burden has been lifted from me. Let me enjoy my three months without talking about drugs."

"You're exhausted, aren't you, Jer?"

"Yes, Mom."

As I readied for my trip abroad, I struggled with the idea of leaving the country, of being so far away from my sons. Even though Jeff and Jeremy supported this adventure, I wondered what would happen if Jeff had problems in Florida or, worse, if he decided to leave the halfway house. Less likely but still possible, Jeremy might need me in Boston. Leaving my school only compounded my feelings of guilt. Even when my preparations were nearly complete, I felt especially uneasy about Jeff; however, in late March, before I left, the answer came.

Momma,

We've been through tons together—a lot of painful memories and a lot of beautiful ones. For years we've watched each other struggle and grow. In order to grow it seems you need to experience tension and strife. Three months ago I was so mad at you, I was convinced that you were being wicked and spiteful and had no right to stop tuition. I couldn't understand what I was doing wrong. The reality is that you were allowing me to take an honest look at my life. Thank you for loving me enough to let me go.

Always,

J.M.B.

With a feeling of release I accepted my doubts and fears, and I boarded the plane to Italy. As fate would have it, I left on April 5, my nonna's birthday; she would have been 110 years old. I flew into Florence, where for the first time I met a distant cousin and his family. After their warm greeting into the country of my heritage, I took the train to the small hill town of Cortona, not far from Florence. Here I rented an apartment and began Italian language classes to prepare for my trip south, to the birthplace of my nonna, Carmela Perciante. All the time that I was basking in many new experiences of culture, food, and language, I stayed in regular contact with both sons.

I knew from phone calls to Jeff and his counselors at the halfway house that all was well, and that he was making progress. One of the requirements of the house was that he had to work during the day. Before I left for Italy he had started work as a valet parker at a nearby resort, and he loved the physical exercise and the camaraderie of the other kids. He was trying to change, and he told me, "I put all the tip money into the bucket, not into my pocket, because it's the right thing to do. I'm trying to live honestly. I even pick up trash from the ground and throw it away. Believe me, things are changing."

After several weeks as a runner for cars, Jeff was hired at a clothing shop in a nearby mall. Since he had no car he caught the bus outside the halfway house to report to work on time. He was learning new skills and creating a new life for himself, one based on honest work and the principles of AA. He attended meetings regularly and chose a great sponsor, a young man a few years older than him who had three years clean and was committed to living both in sobriety and with dignity. They spent lots of time together, and he supported Jeff's work through the twelve steps. Jeff's sponsor taught him that he had to acknowledge his many mistakes, make amends, and move forward. "Do the Next Right Thing" became Jeff's motto, words that helped him to redirect his life. He was learning that the past didn't have to dictate the future, that he didn't have to repeat his use and abuse of drugs, and that he could *do the next right thing.*

All the signs pointed to recovery for Jeff, yet I felt caught in the space between gratitude for his safety and concern for his possible relapse. This was not good—for me, for Jeff, for Jeremy, for our futures. I had to see this, and so I made the decision to address my fears and begin my own renewal while I had the time in Italy, away from the demands of work. I was determined to come to grips with my life as the mother of an addict; I was determined to work hard to be better for myself and my sons. I knew that AA held truth about understanding the disease of addiction, and so I began to work through the steps myself. This process challenged me, as I examined myself and our family life with rigorous honesty. Like finally seeing a figure emerge through the fog, guided by the steps and helped by my own doggedness, I began to understand myself better and to see more clearly my journey as a woman and mother.

After several weeks of quiet reflection in Cortona, and after lots of journal writing and daily language lessons, I felt ready to make the trip to my nonna's birthplace. My Florentine cousin's girlfriend, Ombretta, who was fluent in English, was appalled that I intended to travel south alone. "You can't even speak Italian yet," she said, "and you don't have any understanding about the south of Italy. You will certainly never understand their dialect, and you cannot go alone as a single woman. Impossible." She offered to accompany me, and since I had liked her immediately and trusted that she was right, I happily agreed.

We stayed in Rontondella for four intense days. I immediately found family, children of Carmela's oldest brother, and as soon as we met we embraced each other with long hugs and kisses, with a familiarity that transcends the prior knowing. Near Rotondella I walked the dusty fields where Nonna had labored, and I visited the graveside of our family, a rough wooden shed covering a deep hole where the bones of all the poor were heaped together. I ate the familiar foods of the region, the ones that Nonna used to cook, and I meandered through the winding stone streets of the tiny, impoverished village of Rotondella, imagining the young Carmela, who had traveled alone, north to Naples, to take a boat passage to Ellis Island and join her husband, Vincenzo LaGuardia, in Pittsburgh, Pennsylvania, to start a better life. I could feel my nonna's strength being transfused into my bloodstream and embedded in my soul. I had rekindled the memory of the woman who for me held the key to understanding my own strength and destiny. As if looking into double mirrors reflecting my life, I saw my present and my past at the same time. I knew I was a woman birthed of strong women.

I felt changed by my adventures in Italy, by learning more about my heritage and myself, but life doesn't change, and when I returned to Maryland on May 27 I was still the mother of two sons, one an addict, and head of school. I returned to my Al-Anon meetings; they had become an anchor of balance and hope for me. I mentally recited their slogans: "Let go and let God"; "Courage is fear that has said its prayers"; "Progress not perfection"; and "Easy does it." Al-Anon was my first point of support and help, and I knew they would not leave me in times of trouble.

In June, Jeff had a weekend pass from the halfway house to come home for a short two-day visit. I hoped that after my time of growth in Italy I would better understand my son and the disease he suffered from. I knew that my spirit and my understanding had grown deeper through my own work through the steps, individual counseling, and the Al-Anon meetings. I felt more prepared to love my son through his addiction.

Jeff returned home with health, vigor, and joy. He seemed more centered, more sure of himself. He was embracing the steps, although relinquishing his will to a higher power, to God, proved to be difficult for him during this period, and for years to come. Although raised Catholic, he did not have a strong faith. He said he wanted to trust, he wanted to give his problems to God, but the concept felt too contrived, too unbelievable. During that visit he told me about an AA meeting:

An old man with twenty years of sobriety, "old-timers" they're called in the program, sat in the first row of a meeting. His hair was gray, his body was frail, and I could hear his deep breathing from where I was sitting several rows behind him. Time had tilted him some and he sat crooked in his chair, leaning on a cane in his right hand. Halfway through the meeting he raised his arm to share and we all listened closely as he pounded his cane on the floor and said sternly, "God's will *will* be done." That was it.

These words touched Jeff, grappling as he was with the concept of God's will and not his own. "God's will *will* be done" became a cornerstone phrase for him, for the two of us, and for years that followed, when we wrote to each other, we would often sign our letters and notes GWWBD. I prayed that Jeff would learn to rely on his higher power, his God, to help him live a sober and fully recovered life. I also wondered what God's will was for my son, for our family. I wondered about the intersection of God's will and Jeff's will.

Only twenty days after Jeff's visit home, on June 27, he called to tell me that he had been kicked out of the halfway house. He had lied about his mandatory attendance at AA meetings, one of the requirements of the house. Jeff explained that when he returned to the property and signed in, he wrote that he had attended a meeting, but he had not. When questioned, he told the truth; when he told the truth, he was dismissed. After two weeks, however, he was allowed to reapply and possibly reenter. Jeff struggled with the decision, but he did it.

In my mind I could see this as a victory for my son. The important part was that he chose to start again, I knew. What I did not know was that this sequence of dishonesty, truth telling, and making amends was one that would be repeated for years.

July and August continued without eruption, and my journal entries are calm and filled with thoughts of pride about my sons: "They are still vulnerable, but they are charismatic, strong, smart, playful, kind, and wonderful. They know how to love." Jeff had returned to the halfway house, was working at the clothing store, and was scheduled to complete the program in November. Jeremy had decided to stay in Boston and work for the summer, and to continue his studies in the fall.

On November 20, 1999, Jeff left the halfway house and Florida, having been there almost nine months. This nine-month time period, the actual length of it, signified to me a second birth, one that Jeff had accomplished himself. Jeff decided to return to Boston University in January 2000, to complete the last three semesters necessary for his bachelor's degree, and expected to graduate in December 2000. In January 1999, he had taken a leave of absence from the university, and since he was a student in good standing, his return was seamless. However, his counselors in Florida did not support the idea of him going back to Boston. They were concerned that he would be immersed in the "same persons, places, and things," and might be tempted to return to his old patterns of behavior, his old friends, and his old connections. Jeff remained adamant about returning to BU, citing the fact that if he transferred to another school, he would lose credits he had earned toward his major. He didn't want to delay his graduation date further, and so he pushed to go back to where the course work toward his major remained intact. Over all objections he remained steadfast and determined.

In December 1999, after having successfully completed his time in Florida, he traveled to Boston and found an apartment to rent where he would live alone, within walking distance of campus, above a coffee shop on the corner of Brighton and Harvard avenues. He located the list of local AA meetings and time schedules, registered for his academic classes, met with his adviser, and completed all the necessary requirements for his January return. Sophie was still in Boston; she had remained loyal and loving through all his trials in Florida and the halfway house, but she and most of Jeff's friends would graduate in May 2000.

An additional complication for me about Jeff being in Boston was that Jeremy was now a sophomore, and he felt conflicted about Jeff's return. He was plagued with doubts about how much responsibility he would feel for Jeff's sobriety. What if Jeff started hanging out with his old drug connections? What was Jer to do?

December 1, 1999, 12:20 A.M. A letter to Jeremy in my journal

We just got off the phone, and you said, "Mom, I'll take care of my own business." You are correct and, ultimately, we need to take care of ourselves, because we have no control over anyone else, and we need to protect ourselves. With Jeff's return to Boston, I hope and pray that you protect and take care of yourself. You and I are both afraid, and Jeff is afraid, but we can't live our lives in fear. He can't give up his entire life because of drugs. He must face his fears and win. Maybe he will—it's his walk. It's his walk with his God. Let's find our peace in the Serenity Prayer:

Dear Lord,
Grant me the serenity to accept the things I cannot change,
The courage to change the things I can,
And the wisdom to know the difference.

Tonight, our Team is alive and sober. If that changes for Jeff, I will have the courage to change the things I can.

The entire family wanted to guarantee Jeff's success, and for this reason my dad, knowing that Jeff needed to attend AA meetings, gave him a used four-wheel-drive SUV, a good vehicle, said my father, to negotiate the Boston winters. For Christmas I gave him a keychain with his new car key attached. On one side of the silver charm I had engraved J.M.B. On the other side, G.W.W.B.D. 3/10/99, the date of his entry into the halfway house. When Jeff saw the letters he immediately knew their significance and said quietly to himself, "God's will will be done." He nodded and smiled that kind of knowing smile, as if all the memories of the past nine months flashed through his mind in that split moment.

We, mother and son, had both grown through this last year. I had learned a lot about myself, but as time would tell the full story, I still had many hard lessons to learn about addiction. I should have paid more attention to Jeff's smile—I should have wondered if he knew what would happen in Boston.

Chapter 6

The Functional Addict

Confident in his abilities as a student, Jeff returned to Boston. Naively, I thought he was also confident in his abilities to live a sober life. Although I was well aware that my prayers and hopes could not guarantee his recovery, I decided not to worry about what might happen in the future; therefore, I chose to live in the present. Jeff was good today, and although the earlier years had been filled with unrelenting tension and anxiety, I was determined to enjoy being a mother. I understood that Jeff's patterns of behavior of drinking and using drugs would be difficult to break, but I was resolute—I would trust him and his recovery. In the end, however, I was short-sighted: I had underestimated both the power of drugs and my son's functionality when using them.

The year 2000 started as a hopeful year in Jeff's life. It was, on the other hand, a difficult beginning for Jeremy: The combination of

BU's tough academic program and Boston's social scene proved to be challenging.

> January 1, 2000, 1:06 A.M. The new millennium!
> Jeremy left BU. He's upset; he's irate. Legitimate feelings. But where will he go? What will he do? Boston wasn't a good place for Jeremy from the beginning—too big, too many distractions, he took on too much responsibility for Jeff and all the chaos of drugs and addiction. I need to trust that Jer will be fine. He'll walk his walk; he's the only one who can do it. He has inner strength.

I wasn't sleeping well, often waking in the middle of the night to write in my journal. I was filled with anxiety, searching for some direction about how best to help my sons and, by writing, I tried to understand my emotions. I had anticipated Jeremy staying in Boston to complete his education and Jeffrey transferring to a different university to wrap up his degree. This was not the case. Jeremy would return to Maryland, while Jeff would go back to Boston.

I didn't know what had happened, really, and as usual Jeremy refused to talk. Years later he offered me this explanation: "I knew it was coming; it was inevitable, creeping up. I went to Boston to be with Jeff, but I didn't blame Jeff directly for what happened. I consciously chose a social lifestyle. I never got addicted to drugs, although I did experiment. I never felt like I needed them. In the end, I left Boston—and it killed me."

During these days of transition, Jeremy was a bundle of emotions: One minute, he'd dance and laugh; and the next minute his temper would flare, and he'd rage with frustration, humiliation, and disappointment. One night, as he was dressing to go out with friends, he looked at himself in the mirror in my room, pant legs rolled up, then down, and he turned back and forth. "How do I look, Mom?" he asked. I batted back the question, "How do you feel, Jer?" He examined his reflection. "I wish I were going back to Boston. I wish the situation were different, but it's not. So, I'll make something happen here." He was nineteen, and I wanted to protect him, but I, his mother, could do nothing, only stand back and allow him his time.

By the end of the month Jeremy had proved true to his words: He had enrolled himself in a local community college and set his sights on fulfilling the requirements of a two-year associate degree, after which he could transfer to another four-year college. He rented an apartment in Annapolis with one of his buddies, moved in, and settled into his new routine.

With both boys back in college, our lives took on an academic pace. Jeff once again proved his scholastic competence. He attended classes regularly, completed assignments seriously and on time, and achieved high marks on his tests and written work. He was clear: "I've got a job to do. It's time for me to finish school." His goal was to achieve, and I felt hopeful for him. Jeremy was enjoying his new course of studies and had begun coaching a boys' high school lacrosse team. I immersed myself in the demands of my school.

While Jeff was in Boston, he and I spoke regularly on the phone. I had promised myself that I would not continue to behave as if I were a detective on the trail, always questioning him about attendance at AA meetings and trying to determine the social habits of his friends. Unfortunately, I wasn't successful in this promise, and on February 12, I wrote, "Jeff sounds good, but who knows? When I asked him if he was going regularly to Alcoholics Anonymous meetings, he told me no." My journal continues that Jeff wasn't upset with my vigilance, and he tried to justify his absence at meetings by citing his busy school schedule. He fumbled through reasons preventing his presence at meetings, and tried to downplay the role AA had once played in his life. He reminded me that his problem was drugs, and especially ketamine; therefore, he rationalized, alcohol was not his problem. I had heard him say this before, and Father Martin was clear that this was perilous thinking. Drugs were drugs, and all drugs were dangerous to addicts and alcoholics. Jeff and I talked about this; he understood my concerns. He assured me that he would start to attend more meetings and get a sponsor.

In order for me to help myself with the process of letting Jeff go, and to find some sense of serenity in my life, I became a regular at Al-Anon meetings. I knew that the other people in the room were struggling with the same issues as me. During one particular meeting we talked about how those of us who love alcoholics and addicts want to believe what we are told and not what we see. Words are easy to believe, and many of us had heard statements from our loved ones like "Believe me—I'll get it right this time" and "I'm done with alcohol and I'll never take another drink" and "You can trust me. This time is different." I needed to remind myself that Jeff was both smart and manipulative, and that he would tell me whatever he thought I needed to hear in order to keep safe his own drug use. Truth was in his actions, and I had often been deluded by his words. I understood that I needed to watch what he did, but he was in Boston, and how could I know what was really happening? The distance made it almost impossible: I knew this; Jeff knew this.

In February, I received a Valentine's Day card from Jeff, and I was reminded of Valentine's Day 1999, just one year earlier, when he said he had been unable to buy stamps for cards, or to send flowers, and couldn't even talk cogently on the phone. This year, however, was different. He was becoming Jeff again.

Mom,

So much has changed. Thank God we're where we are today. Last year my life was very different, but I'm learning that everything falls into place in God's time, but trying to work within it feels almost impossible. Thanks for all you do!

A & F (Always and Forever),

J

My boys were growing into young men, and I clung to each good memory, each written word, and each accomplishment. I wanted desperately to believe that this was and would continue to be a good year.

In April, I traveled to Boston for a long weekend to visit Jeff. He and I had a great time together, and I could see no evidence of anxiety or problems: His physical appearance and health looked good; his apartment was handsomely decorated; he and Sophie were together; and, although we didn't spend any time with her during those few days, I noticed her robe hanging in the bathroom and her flip-flops arranged neatly on the floor. He even took gentle care of a neighbor's cat that roamed the halls of the apartment building, feeding and sheltering it when, from time to time, it meowed at the door of his unit.

I wanted to believe that Jeff was sober, to rejoice and be glad, yet even though all the facts seemed to support his continued recovery, I found it hard to trust that all was well. While I was staying in his apartment I had several opportunities, when he was in the shower or went out in the mornings to buy fresh brewed coffee and muffins, to look through his papers or riffle through his drawers for any indication of drug use. I could have, but I didn't. Even when he was living at home, I never searched through his room or closet. Maybe I was foolish, but this was my way. As head of school, we had an honor code, and the children had no locks on their lockers, and even when the buildings were empty I never violated my students' trust by searching through their belongings. I knew that I needed to trust my son, and I also knew that I couldn't control his choices. This internal conflict felt like a noose around my neck, and I knew that I was the only one who could remove the rope and stand squarely in the present. I feared that I was becoming my own worst enemy.

During this time, a friend felt my fear and saw my angst, and he sent a quotation from Pascal's *Pensees* that I kept on my refrigerator for years:

> We do not rest satisfied with the present . . . for the present is generally painful to us. We conceal it from our sight, because it troubles us; and, if it be delightful to us, we regret to see it pass away. We scarcely ever think of the present; and if we think of it, it is only to take light from it to arrange the future. So we never live, but hope to live; and, as we are always preparing to be happy, it is inevitable we should never be so.

I had not learned to live in the present. At times I wallowed in the past, in moments of guilt about what had been, how I had not created strong enough boundaries for the boys, how I had not taken care of Jeremy's needs, and how I had allowed myself to deny Jeff's addiction. At other times I cast terrified glances into the future, wondering what would happen if Jeff returned to drugs, if Jeremy didn't stay committed to his academics, or if I didn't have the resources or health to help them. Even when things were good, I saw that I barely paused and noticed. I needed to learn how to live today, to live in the present.

In late May, both boys came home to celebrate Jeremy's birthday and Mother's Day. While we were together I told the boys about my decision to sell the family home, because now that they were in college the house was too large for me to take care of. They were in agreement, and for several days we packed boxes and joined forces to sort through the mounds of twenty-one years' accumulation in the basement. After three days of sorting and hauling our possessions, Jeffrey and Jeremy left to attend BU's commencement ceremonies. As they pulled out of the driveway, laughing, talking, and bobbing their heads to the beat of the music, I felt glad for their closeness, proud of their achievements, and hopeful for Jeff's sobriety and Jeremy's academic success.

This BU graduation was significant for Jeff, since it signaled the time when not only Sophie but also his friends would leave Boston to pursue their next career moves. Jeff would have graduated with them had he not taken the nine months' leave to go to the halfway house, and he was now face-to-face with a major consequence of that decision. I feared that this might trigger his return to the comfort of his old life of drugs and drinking. Years later, Jeff told me:

> Lots of changes during that period. I was back in Boston, but people were moving on. At home people were moving on, too. Everyone seemed to be doing something new and exciting, taking next steps and advancing their lives. But all I saw was myself not going forward with them. I was still three semesters away from a degree and had to remain in school. I measured my progress against everyone else's, and at that age, motion is tied to things like graduation, jobs, new cities, and different people. In essence, I saw myself being left behind.

The realization of this fear appears in my journal when on June 2, 2000, I wrote only one line: "Jeff is in bars and drinking." I don't remember how I found out about this, and I don't mention my source; maybe he called me and slurred his words or maybe I called him and heard bar-type noises in the background. Whatever the reason for this statement in my journal, I continued by writing that I wanted to jump into action and lay down my mother's law, saying, "If you don't go to AA meetings, I'm not paying for college," or "If you go to bars, don't come home," or even "I believe you are drinking, so I'm telling you that your education's on hold and you're going to have to stop school and get a job." Of course, I was fearful that the cycle of drugs and drinking would begin again. I had heard countless stories from people in AA and Al-Anon that relapses happen like this, with a few drinks, with a couple of hits. I feared that Jeff was on a slippery slope. I felt as if I were standing at the bottom of a canyon hearing the pebbles and stones start to scatter down the mountain, smack into the bigger boulders, and ricochet around me. I wanted to scream at Jeff, destroy the drugs, and interrogate his friends. I wanted to do something, but I didn't know what to do. My dreams gave me no rest.

June 12, 2000, 6:30 A.M.

Last night I dreamed that some young man walked into the house (somehow he got through the door) and turned off the security system. I was on the phone, and I told the caller, "Hold on, I think someone just broke in. If it's true, you call the police." I went downstairs and the man was standing in the foyer. I told him I would call the police, so he said he'd leave. He left, but he forgot his pen and he wanted it back. I opened the door a bit and handed the pen to him through the slit in the door, but he put his foot in the doorjamb and forced his way inside the house. He wanted jewelry, so I gave him a bunch of fake jewelry and ran upstairs and hid the good jewelry.

Then I dreamed I was lost in a large city, maybe New York. I couldn't find my way home, but I knew where I needed to go, since I saw a cathedral dome in the distance. I ran through the streets looking for a way out, but couldn't find one. Two kids, a boy and a girl, tried to help me, but they couldn't travel past a certain point. I finally ran into a bagel shop and called Jeff. I told him to take a taxi to the shop and then the taxi could take us home. He said he couldn't come, that he had made plans with some girl and a kid named Jimmy. I remember telling him that was fine, and that I would find my way alone. I awoke afraid.

Dreams continued to be messages from my subconscious about feelings of aloneness and abandonment, of the violation of my sense of security, and of my desperate desire to feel safe. Dreaming of the

intrusion into the house, the theft, being lost in the city, and Jeff's re-
fusal to help me came from my feelings of fear and helplessness that
I pushed down into my own quiet abyss. However, these feelings surfaced during the depths of the night. My life felt exhausting. Pascal's
words came back to me: "And as we are always preparing to be happy,
it is inevitable we should never be so."

Whether Jeff was drinking or not, I was not certain. What I was
certain about was that our lives were changing. On June 16, 2000,
after twenty-one years, we moved out of our family home. Home
was now an apartment that I rented in the same county where our
house had been, and the boys shared a bedroom where they could
stay comfortably and in close proximity to their friends and familiar territory. Even though Jeffrey and Jeremy were both busy with
college requirements, they came home often. My response to the
changes was to dig into my work at school, attend Al-Anon meetings, continue my own individual therapy, and try to understand all
that had happened. If I couldn't control what was happening in
Jeff's life, I would try to control my life: I could work harder to en-
sure the academic success and growth of the school. I quit asking
Jeff questions, especially those concerning his sobriety and his attendance at AA meetings. We talked often about his classes, course requirements, his excitement about being back in Boston, and even job
possibilities after graduation. He shared nothing about his recovery
work, and I didn't ask.

During the summer and fall of 2000, Jeff flourished. He not only
took a full course load of classes, but he applied for and was awarded
two internships, one with a boutique leather studio on Newberry
Street and the other with a large international public relations firm
headquartered in Cambridge. He did well in both jobs, and especially
enjoyed the opportunity to help create communication strategies. His
performance with the PR agency earned him an interview for a

full-time position in the firm's New York office, with a possible January start date, right after his December graduation. All the while he earned extra money by working at a clothing store in Boston. He was on a roll, and on September 10, I could write: "I am surrounded by peace."

I continued to convince myself that Jeff was living a sober life. It seemed to me that this must be true, since he was not only achieving a strong grade point average, but also was enjoying successful work experiences. If he were drinking or doing drugs, I reasoned, the facts would be different.

It is true that Jeff did well in Boston. There were some events, however, that occurred during the fall that might have sounded the alarm bell in me. These are documented in my journal, but my entries are written without reflection, without concern. For example, in September, Jeff returned home because he and Sophie had ended their relationship again, and this time the rupture seemed final. I wrote on September 17, "I see how he feels—hurt and empty. This break is affecting him deeply." I was sad for my son, but Sophie had moved to New York, which made the break seem somewhat predictable. Jeff also wrecked his car that fall. He said a truck had sideswiped him, and since the police report supported Jeff's explanation, I accepted it as an accident. Also, there are several journal entries commenting on my conversations with Jeff about his feelings of anxiety and angst about completing assignments, applying for jobs, and managing money. But my written words stop there. I wanted to feel confident that Jeff had been sober for one and a half years, and I was making an effort to let go. I was forcing myself to trust him.

On the scale of wins and losses, he had much in his favor: His course work earned him high grades and his internships brought him further work opportunities, indicating a strong work ethic. I was quick to overlook what I considered smaller events because the bigger issues seemed all in order. He was scheduled to graduate on

December 16; he had been hired by the PR agency for which he had interned; and he and a close friend would share an apartment in New York on the corner of Broome and Mulberry streets in Little Italy. In my mind, he was realizing his dreams.

In November, I received a birthday letter from him that I wanted desperately to believe was sincere:

> Momma,
>
> Lots of smiles when I look back on the past year. As a team, we've overcome obstacles, survived tough periods, and celebrated victories. And as individuals, we've grown and learned from each other. Your example is a strong one and your message to us is always hopeful. You know how it feels to hurt and you know how it feels to keep fighting.
>
> With love and respect,
> J.M.B.

Things seemed to be in good order with Jeff. If my internal alarm bell sounded, I didn't listen to it. Or perhaps I chose not to hear.

We ended the year in joy. Jeff was on his way to New York and a job. Jeremy was nearing the completion of his degree and was happy coaching. And me? I was the mom, and my sons were in a good place. Of course, I was happy.

> January 1, 2001, 8:50 P.M.
> As I look forward and back, we are blessed. There was a time when I was afraid to dream—even hope was difficult. Now, I believe in a life of health and spiritual strength. I know it's there; I'm beginning to see it, and I can dream again.

This journal entry is true; this is how I felt—that I could dream again.

However, if I had known that in the previous February Jeff had begun drinking, and if I had known that in March he again began to use cocaine, ketamine, and Xanax, and especially if I had known that in November he was introduced to heroin, I would have understood the undercurrents of fear that haunted me.

But then, I would not have been able to celebrate his very real accomplishments—in the present.

Chapter 7

Trusting Lies

Sunday, January 7, 2001, 9:30 A.M.

Jeff and Jeremy are still asleep. It always feels right to have my sons at home. I'm trusting that this will be a perfect year! Like the earrings the boys gave me for Christmas—knotted three times, welded together, the three of us, bringing each other strength in unity. Jeff is good today, and soon he leaves for New York to start a new life. He'll either grow stronger or he'll get immersed in the negative side. Oh my son, I pray you find the strength that steels you.

A few weeks later, on January 19, Jeremy and I took the train to New York to visit Jeff. He met us at Penn Station, and we traveled by subway downtown to his apartment on Mulberry Street, above an Italian restaurant. His building had no elevator, and he lived on the fifth and top floor, so we carted our luggage up the stairwell. Even though we started our climb with enthusiasm, we slowed midway, legs achy and lungs lurching between breaths and laughter. His apartment had two bedrooms, one narrow bathroom, a tiny kitchen, and a compact living area, but it was perfect, it was home to Jeff and his roommate. Jeff's bedroom was at the top of a circular metal staircase, in a loft space, and it had access to a private rooftop, where the three of us stood and spun 360 degrees to see the whole of New York City glittering around us. Jeff, our tour guide, pointed out highlights, including the World Trade Center, the Empire State Building, and the Chrysler Building. We felt as if we were near the center of the universe, spying on everything below us. The city glowed brightly for Jeff on this evening, and I felt content there, standing with my two sons, knowing that Jeremy would return to college and Jeff was moving forward into the life he had temporarily lost track of.

One week later, however, I was awakened in the middle of the night by a phone call. I should have known that nothing was that easy with Jeff.

January 27, 2001, 7:20 A.M. On an airplane shuttle to New York

The phone rang at 3:45 A.M. It was Jeff. "Momma, how are you? Were you asleep?"

I was awakened, just like in the past, immediately alert. "Jeff, what's wrong?"

"I'm in Beth Israel Hospital. I was hit in the face with a bottle last night. We were celebrating my roommate's birthday, and I was in a fight. We were at a bar on Spring Street, and I was talking with a girl. Some guy, must have been her boyfriend, was nearby, frustrated, and he approached us. She rolled her eyes. Next thing, a beer bottle, or a cocktail glass, maybe, came screaming at my face. My eyes are OK, the doctor said, but one of the tear ducts is lacerated and my face needs surgery. I'll be OK."

My mind is a whirlwind: how, why? I assured Jeff that I would arrive on the next shuttle. Then I called Jeremy, who said, "Don't *worry. We'll get through this. We always do."* I called Tim next and told him what had happened, and that I was on my way to the city.

I ask myself why? Why did this happen? What lessons do we need to continue to learn? Why isn't it over for Jeff? What else is necessary?

I'm exhausted. My dad's words echo: "You'll do what you need to do." And I will, with the Lord's help.

After I landed at LaGuardia Airport I jumped into a taxi, explained the situation to the driver, and urged him to take the quickest route to Beth Israel Hospital in Union Square. I'm not sure I made much sense, words tumbling out in fractured phrases. I am sure, however, that my face and voice told the story of a son who needed his mother. Or maybe it was the mother who needed the son.

As we began our rocketlike trip down highways and over bridges, I received a call from a doctor at the hospital, who told me that Jeff had been transferred to Manhattan Eye, Ear, and Throat Hospital on East Sixty-fourth Street, where he would receive specialized attention and surgery. Although I was grateful for the call, realizing that Jeff must have given the doctor my cell phone number, my heart felt ripped, as if to say, *Here you are in New York, and you don't even know where your son is.* With a shaky voice, I gave the driver the new destination. The streets and sights of New York became a blur.

I was single-minded in my need to reach my son, but my thoughts were scattered. Jeff had just moved into his apartment and he was scheduled to begin work in two days. Here he was again between, not here or there, not firmly in New York and not started in his job. My son and his life never seemed settled.

The driver stopped directly in front of the hospital, and at that moment I was somewhere between frozen in time and racing through actions. I was like an eight-millimeter film, offtrack, stopping and then bumping along, the dialogue cut here, cut there. I felt caught in my own movements, in slow motion, yet my brain ticked off things to do. I knew it was happening in real time, but I didn't register things clearly. In a blur, I paid the driver and grabbed my carry-on bag.

I pushed through the emergency room doors and found myself standing among a small group of people huddled uncomfortably together around a receiving desk, where a security guard was stationed. People stared at me as I entered, coat hanging off my back, suitcase clattering behind me. The room fell silent. I claimed the moment of shock and demanded of the man standing behind the large central counter, "My son is here?"

He responded as if he read my face, my mind: "You're the mom of the kid who just got here by ambulance—the kid with the face wound?"

I must have nodded. I don't think I said a word. I don't remember.

He gave me directions to the optometry surgical ward, but I heard nothing. I did, however, watch the movements of his hands as he pantomimed my route.

I was off like a shot. Left, right, white walls, directional markers, lots of people, and I heard my boots pounding with each step as the wheels of my suitcase whirred behind me. I felt cold, distant. My singular goal: to find one boy with a bloody face.

In the eye surgical waiting room Jeff sat slumped in a chair. He never moved when I entered, only lifted his head a tad to look at me through his one unwounded eye. I stood in front of him, frenzied, alert to every sound, a mother who would protect her son at all costs.

"Don't cry, Momma," was all he said. "Please don't cry."

One of Jeff's friends had stayed with him, and as I stood gaping, stunned and rigid, the boy stood up and left, wordlessly. I never even acknowledged his presence as he nodded at Jeff and respectfully, silently, left us alone. I think he must have been relieved by my presence, and also frightened, maybe thinking about his mother and how she would have felt, that palpable bond between mothers and sons.

My son's face was as raw as ground meat, smashed and wounded. His left eye was gashed and swollen, indistinguishable from his forehead. His lips had swollen to double their size; they were sliced, rivulets of blood had hardened into tracks that ran down his face and onto his chin and neck. His nose had taken the brunt of the assault, and it was broken, misaligned, like fissures in rock. He was all shades of red: the red on his white sneakers like a battlefield flag; the red soaked into his jeans now turned brown; the red on his fingers that must have tried to wipe away the hurt; the red-splattered shirt unbuttoned and stained; but mostly the red blood-encrusted face. His face disfigured, all because of a beer bottle and a girl.

A nurse came from behind me and asked me to sit. Sit? Was she crazy?

The surgeon met with Jeff and me to explain the procedure. I remember looking closely at the size of his hands, thinking that he would need small hands and delicate fingers for eye surgery. He smiled benevolently when I asked how many of these operations he had completed. "About two or three a week. They're actually pretty common. This is New York City." He continued, "Jeff's lucky, because the nose caught the force of the bottle." The anesthesiologist interviewed Jeff privately before surgery, and Jeff explained his history of drug addiction. In short order the nurse hauled Jeff off on the stretcher.

Tim arrived while Jeff was in surgery, and we greeted each other kindly. I was glad he had come to support Jeff and to help with registering Jeff's health insurance information with the hospital's business office. During this waiting period I also talked with Jeremy by telephone; he remained staunchly Jeff's protector, declaring, "If I had been there, with Jeff, this wouldn't have happened." He paused, heavy with thought, and continued, "I would have watched out for him. God made me big and strong to take care of my family."

Time passed slowly as I waited in the hospital lounge, listening to the nurses' whispered comments about patients, to phones ringing, to the beeps of the hospital machines as they ticked off measured medicines, until after about three hours, Jeff was returned to the room, seventy-eight stitches in his face. The doctor assured Tim and me that the surgery had gone well, and within two more hours Jeff was discharged, and the three of us left the hospital together.

Tim flew back to D.C. and I stayed with Jeff during the night. We each slept fitfully: me ever ready as I dozed, watched, and waited, while Jeff moaned quietly from time to time, probably his mind reliving the incident in a jumbled mess of glass, laughter, and pain.

The next day, after Jeff dressed, he couldn't be contained in his apartment. Before we left we took pictures of his face so that we would have photo evidence, in case the guy who hit Jeff was ever found, or if necessary for medical insurance purposes. Immediately following the incident the police had arrived, and the barman and witnesses were questioned. We really didn't expect anything to come of it, but maybe there would be some resolution, someone nabbed, the perpetrator brought to justice. That was what I wanted. Actually, nothing or no one was ever found. Jeff was left with an open-ended investigation.

We walked around the city for several hours, buying all the necessary supplies for him to care for his wounds: peroxide, gauze, paper tape, antibacterial ointment, paper cups, and straws, since his lip stitches were deep. Most important, his eye was functioning, although years later we found that his eye never healed well, and when cold winds blow, it tears constantly. Some glass remains in and around that socket, but the doctors say it's harmless, and it might, someday, work itself to the surface. If so, they'll remove it.

That evening, just one day after Jeff's operation, I returned to Maryland. During the following days he and I talked often about the details of what happened that night. The gist of the story remained the same. Jeff explained that he was talking with a girl when a boy appeared, anxious and overprotective, and within a few moments he was standing next to Jeff, almost on top of him, and tension was high. Jeff reacted abruptly, pushing the boy backward, into the bar. The boy stumbled, reached behind him, and in the next moment Jeff was covered in glass and blood.

Our discussions included his reaction to the girl's boyfriend and his need to develop a kind of observing ego, so that he could better monitor his behavior. Through it all I never asked him the important question, the question that nagged at me: Had he been drinking or doing drugs the night he was hit in the face? Why didn't I ask? Maybe I didn't want to know. I had suspected that he had been drinking for a while, and I remembered the single journal entry that I had written seven months earlier, in which I questioned his continued sobriety. Even though my mother's ear heard an internal, unconscious whisper encouraging me to open my eyes and my mouth and to ask the question, I smothered the voice. With his face stitched and healing needed, I didn't want to go back again to all the inquisitions, to all the mistrust. I felt that I needed to continue to trust that he was still sober, and that this senseless act of impulsivity was an unfortunate misadventure. Hadn't the surgeon told me that this type of assault was common in New York?

So I didn't ask. Instead, I reprimanded myself: "Lib, you need to trust. It's your problem, not his. Your problem is trust."

Life continued after the "bottle in the face" trauma. During these months, Al-Anon meetings continued to offer me support and structure. When I first started to attend, I had felt a special bond with the women in my group who had children who were addicts, thinking that they could best understand my family struggle. In time I learned to respect the larger connection of all the people in those rooms, for we were all bound together by the effects of addiction.

After one February meeting, in which the topic was happiness, I wrote in my journal, "I never thought that I would be happy again. Two years ago today, I was sure all was lost and that my life had ended with my son's drug addiction. I used to pray every morning that Jeff would just stay alive. Look at Jeff today. He is good!!" Pascal's admonition of a life spent never living, but having lived or hoping to live haunted me throughout these days, and I reminded myself, almost as a mantra, to stay in the present and to be grateful for the here and now.

While I was struggling to trust him, his life was changing.

We had settled into the apartment on Mulberry Street and I was about to start working for the first time in a professional and full-time capacity. I was excited to be in the city and part of a scene that was new and inspiring, around friends that I had grown tight with during the years in Boston. At the time, it seemed like everyone I knew was living in New York, friends from every chapter of my life had moved here.

In those final months in Boston, however, I'd developed some bad habits that traveled with me to New York. When I was alone and finishing school, I started using drugs that were less social and a little darker. It was a very private time in my life, and I grew more intimately aware of my relationship with substances. Getting high was less about the party and more about feeling connected.

The months flew by. In April, Jeremy and I visited Jeff in New York, and we spent time with Sophie, too; she and Jeff were back together. In May, the boys came home for Mother's Day, after which they traveled back to the city to spend a few days together. In June, my school year ended with the usual fervor of graduation. Jeremy had been accepted into several four-year colleges, placing him back on track toward his bachelor's degree. Most of my journal entries rambled away with thoughts about my growing-up years, mother and father issues, and the need to allow my sons to grow into men without trying to control things. I understood that the desire to control was at my core, learned well in my family of origin. I needed to let go and trust.

Jeff's reports from New York were upbeat, and he was enthusiastic about the good comments and reviews of his supervisors, earning him a salary increase with a promotion. Jeremy was busy preparing to move into an apartment near St. Mary's College, where he had chosen to continue his education. During this time, on August 12, Jeff came home, and I wrote, "Today, Jeff is strong and capable, and I cherish our time together."

The end of August and early September brought increasing activity, as I geared up for the beginning of the new school year, and Jeremy began college life, registering for classes and getting his bearings around a new campus, and he even thought about trying out for the basketball team. In late August, before my school started, I visited Jeff. I wanted to make sure all was well, to see face-to-face, up close, that Jeff and New York were still a good match.

During my visit we talked about his past, and he acknowledged that lying was a way of life in addiction. His time at the halfway house was a pursuit of truth, and he said, "Often when we are angry, we say our truth, but then it's said with ugliness and nothing is accomplished. If we could say the truth without anger, healing might be possible." I left New York confident that Jeff was on solid footing, and I continued to trust that he was sober, and, further, that in his sobriety he was growing in wisdom and honesty. I was tired of all of the grief of past years.

Upon my return to Maryland, I had a dream. I dreamed I was in a car with a young boy—faceless, not Jeff or Jeremy, but maybe. I was trying to locate the correct road to audition for the soprano section of the opera. To my right was the alto section, so I turned left. I drove up a hill toward the SOPRANO sign. As I reached the top of the hill I found myself out of the car and walking down an outside corridor of a motel-type place. I sensed someone behind me, but I didn't turn around to look. I felt afraid and I just wanted to get to the room. The next moment I was inside the room, and I could see the bedroom area, where Jeremy was asleep on the bed and Jeff was asleep on the floor. I turned around, and the man who had been following me was in the bathroom. I didn't know how he got there or why he was there, and I looked once again into the boys' bedroom. The light from the bathroom was shining in Jeff's face, and I watched as in his sleep he covered his eyes with his blanket. I went into the bathroom, closed the door so the light wouldn't bother the boys, and told the man he had to leave. He laughed at me, so I raised my fists and I screamed at him to leave. He pushed me and laughed again, and I put my fists in his face and said, "Get the hell out!" He was stunned and said, "You're serious." "Yeah," I hissed. "Get out. Now!" I awoke afraid, and my heart seemed to be beating out of my chest.

I was never sure what my dreams meant, but I knew that I needed to honor them. This dream seemed to signify that I was standing strong for myself and my sons, that I was fighting to keep them safe, and that I could and would take care of them both.

Then came September 11, 2001, a day forever chiseled into our nation's history: the terrorist attack on the World Trade Center and the Pentagon. While this atrocity ripped through our nation on a macro level, our school became a microcosm, and fear and confusion ran rampant. Through the long hours and chaos, I attempted to lead our community with strength and resolve, and I kept communication open among board members, faculty, staff members, and parents, and I conferred with outside experts as well. By this time we had 430 students, and our school was located within forty-five minutes of Washington, D.C., and the Pentagon. Many of our parents worked for the federal government in the District and Virginia. That day I held assemblies with the students, so that they would be informed about what was happening, and I answered their questions with honesty. A police officer was stationed at our school, and at every school in the county; parents were frantic to come and pick up their children; and the teachers expected me to offer guidance, calm, and clarity. I felt I met expectations during that frantic day, and cared for our community, while all the time my mind spiraled with concerns about Jeff in New York City. I tried to locate him while simultaneously dealing with all the events popping around me, but the cell phone towers in New York were overloaded, and neither his cell nor office number answered. After an hour, while I was addressing the middle- and upper-school students, standing on a chair so I could see each child's face within the group, and while the television in the media center replayed the strike over and over again, Jeff called. He was safe. He had been on his roof and seen the towers collapse. He was in a state of shock. The whole world was.

In the days that followed, Jeff's neighborhood was barricaded at Delancey Street, which was considered off-limits because of its proximity to Ground Zero. Jeff had to show identification proving that he lived below Delancey before he was allowed to pass through the blockades. During the week his eyes reddened and became irritated, probably due to the debris and dust in the air as he walked around his neighborhood. His office was closed, and he decided to return to Maryland for a few days. He arrived by train, clearly shaken by what he had seen. He explained that nobody in the city had escaped the devastation of that day; everyone was pierced by the experience. He and his friends saw the towers smoldering; firefighters trudging back and forth from Ground Zero covered with soot, exhausted; and people on the street crying, suddenly hysterical. How does a person assimilate such horror?

Three days later Jeff returned to New York, and we continued our phone conversations, primarily about issues other than the attack. During one discussion Jeff told me that the long-term director of the halfway house in Florida had relapsed, and was back on the streets. Jeff explained how it troubled him that someone he so admired for getting and staying sober for over fifteen years would relapse, fall back into cocaine. This news also worried me, because relapse is always a concern with addiction, yet I wrote in my journal on September 24, "Jeff has made it through the toughest times. Jeff is our victory tale."

Life seemed to settle down, and on October 21 I received an e-mail from Jeff: "I opened my blinds this morning and sunshine poured in the windows. . . . I thought of you and Jer." His words touched me as always, and I was able to write in my journal, "Jeff and Jeremy are good. Enjoy, Lib. Your kids are safe; why don't you dance?" The next week, on October 28, Jeff called to ask me how to cook green beans. The next day I wrote him an e-mail:

> When you called about cooking green beans, a memory, at razor speed, slashed through my mind. When I was little, maybe eight or nine, Nonna would cook green beans just for me. First, she would boil them until they were less tough, but not tender. Then she would steep them in tomato sauce, the rich, robust, meatless sauce that she made only for vegetables. When I would arrive at her home, usually on my bike, which I always imagined was my horse that I rode like the wind, I would climb her thirteen concrete steps and round the corner, peeking in through her screen door into her kitchen. She stood always in the same spot, in front of the stove, stirring the sauce and moving her lips in inaudible prayer. When she would see me, she wouldn't move, for what would the green beans do without her, but she would smile and open her arms. I'd run into her soft breasts which would envelop me, and I'd smell garlic and tomatoes, and I'd hear her mumble into the top of my ponytail, *"Mangia, mangia, Nonnanade."* I always felt safe; I knew I was home.
>
> The neat part about this is that no one else really liked green beans, only me. When Uncle Tony and Uncle Jimmy would stop by Nonna's on their way home from work and they'd smell the

green beans, they'd know I was somewhere close by. So, when I think of cooking green beans, I think of a singular love— tomato-rich green beans, just for me.

This was the kind of love I wanted to offer my sons. The rich, red, tomato-sauce kind that would immerse them in comfort and security. I wanted to embrace my sons with the scents and touches that healed.

The next month brought my birthday, and my boys planned a surprise. Jeremy coordinated events in D.C. while Jeffrey completed his part from New York. Jeremy invited me to dinner and arrived on time, carrying a dozen peach-colored roses. He then hustled me out of the house, on our way to an Italian restaurant in DuPont Circle, telling me we had to be there at 6:30 sharp. When we walked into the restaurant, Jeff was sitting at the table. I looked at Jeff, looked away, and then looked again, a quick double take—not believing that he was really there.

Dinner was wonderful, and the night was perfect. Jeff and Jeremy both slept at home that night. Early Friday morning I took Jeff to the airport for the 6:30 shuttle, because that morning he had to be at work, back in Manhattan, and he was off.

For Christmas vacation the boys and I visited the Florida Keys, ending in Sarasota to spend five days, including Christmas Day, with my dad, who refused to come north during the winter months, even for the holidays. During these days I made a conscious attempt to cherish each day, to hold it, and to feel each moment of grace and love.

On the third day of the trip, Jeff and I knocked heads.

We were all together watching TV in the living area of a condo that I had rented. Jeff got up and went outside, without saying a word. As he left he seemed distant, felt far away. After about thirty minutes I grew uneasy, because that night his attitude seemed different to me. I went outside and looked for him but couldn't find him, and immediately all the old concerns about drug use returned to me. Jeremy tried to allay my fears. "He's out using the phone, just talking. It's a beautiful night, let him alone." But I was inconsolable.

When Jeff finally returned, I told him, "I'm very upset. I need to talk with you." I hit him with this out of left field, and he must have seen the tension in my face, since he responded calmly. "Sure, let's talk," he said. "Walk with me to the shore; it's beautiful out." As we walked I told him, "After you left the house, you were gone for a long time. When I looked for you, I couldn't find you. I need to ask you: Are you doing drugs again?" He was stunned and appeared hurt: stunned that my mind would jump to drugs and hurt that I would assume that to be true. He said he understood how I would think these things, but he was also frustrated that I had such little confidence in him. His eyes looked harder than usual, and although he said nothing more, his eyes seemed to say, *I hear you. I understand where you are, and I've been there, too, but I'm not there anymore, and I can't give this inquiry much more time. I've done all I can do to be all I can be. I'm twenty-three, and I'm here in Florida with you. I'm done with this inquisition; I'm done with your fears and worries. I empathize, but I can't do anything more.* He never said these things, but by his expression and his silence, I thought I understood at that moment that he wanted to get on with his life. We continued our walk under the light of the moon, and finally returned home. Jeremy was awake and waiting for us. Nothing more was said.

I admonished myself, my internal dialogue repeating, "You need to let go, Lib. Sure you're afraid, afraid to go back to the chaos, afraid that Jeff might be drinking and doing drugs again, but your fears are yours." My fears taunted me—again and again—but I thought that trust was my problem.

As the year 2001 came to a close, I thought about its changes: We started the year with the blood red of Jeff's lacerated face and we ended the year with the comforting, tomato red of the memory of Nonna's love. I prayed that Jeff would grow stronger within the concrete of New York. I wanted to believe that Jeff was sober, and I submerged the feelings of unease that rumbled in my belly, and that flowed out into my veins. I decided that all I needed to do was to trust my son.

Chapter 8

The Double Life of
My Chameleon Son

For the two years following Jeff's return to Boston, I had been unwilling to understand the split screen of my son's life: the life he was living versus the life he allowed me to see. Instead of accusing Jeff of any wrongdoing, I blamed myself for doubting him. I thought I watched closely (I was always vigilant), but I realized later that Jeff carefully orchestrated what I was permitted to know. He was well practiced at keeping me in the dark—and he wanted it this way. As long as he kept safe his lie, he could keep safe his addiction. When I finally learned the truth, much damage, maybe too much damage, had been done.

We started the New Year, January 1, 2002, together in Maryland, as a family of three, enjoying a dinner at home while we talked about music and friends and relationships, but we spent most of the time laughing, as Jeremy recounted his lacrosse coaching experiences. The next day we returned to our duties: Jeff to New York for work; Jeremy to St. Mary's for college classes and coaching and to Leah, a young blond athlete who had stolen his heart; and I to a school that demanded my constant attention. My journal entries noted problems with budgets, faculty, and students; my plans for summer travel to Italy; and reflections about my own personal growth. I didn't hear much from the boys for about six weeks, but I was not concerned.

Jeff's first trip home was the weekend after Valentine's Day, when he stayed just two days. My journal notes only one phrase: "All seems well with Jeff." In March, he returned again for another short visit; however, my journal then gives voice to my internal alarm system.

> March 10, 2002, 10:30 A.M.
> Jeff is home—he celebrates THREE years drug free today—he left for the halfway house on March 10, 1999, so that's three years. I pray he's really drug free. In truth, I don't think so, and I know it's not so if we consider alcohol a drug. He does drink, and my guess is he drinks more than he should.
> Enough. He's growing into a fine man.

My entry ends here; however, I'm struck by my own unrelenting persistence in ignoring what I knew was true. Those last seven words, the juxtaposition of those two statements, represent pure and simple delusion. With one word—"enough"—I admit that I don't want to deal with what I suspect is true, and it was obvious that I didn't want to dig deeper. Maybe I was afraid that if I admitted the problem, I would have to do something—and I didn't know what to do. Maybe I convinced myself that he would only drink and not use drugs, because, after all, he was an addict, not an alcoholic. I couldn't face the truth.

. . .

After Jeff's early March visit I didn't see him again for nearly two months. Again, my journals do not indicate any anxiety about his absence, but I did note that Jeff and I talked less frequently on the phone, which was unusual, because my sons and I were typically in regular communication with each other. In April, Jeff talked about requesting a leave of absence from his job, during which time he wanted to travel abroad for the summer. As usual, he wove his story well, explaining that he had saved money and this would be a great experience for him. I summarized my thoughts on April 20: "I think it would be a great experience for him—traveling abroad."

My pattern of denial continued even though things with Jeff didn't seem right: I had seen very little of him since the beginning of the year; he called less frequently; his two visits home in four months had been oddly brief, only a day or two; Sophie had broken up with him again, but he didn't seem distraught; and now he was planning a hiatus from work. All spring I continued to shut my mind to what I felt in my bones. This seemed to work for me during the daytime hours; however, during the night my dreams weren't as forgiving. For several months, I had a recurring dream.

I was walking in Manhattan, carrying two big shopping bags, juggling them awkwardly while trying to keep track of my purse, which I had hung over my shoulder and tucked under my arm. I was having difficulty carrying the bags, but I was determined to get to the theater district to buy tickets for a Broadway show. I took a cab, but accidentally got out several blocks too soon. As I walked up Seventh Avenue toward my destination, I called Jeff on my cell phone to tell him that I was struggling with these bags. A little girl was walking next to me, and she was also burdened with bags. I recognized her immediately: She looked like I had when I was young.

The next moment, I was no longer near the theater district, but in a dark, desolate area, deep in the bowels of the city. I was convinced there was a walkway that connected this area to the theater district, and I was desperate to find it. I passed through a bar, climbed a flight of stairs, and walked down a hallway, tripping and stepping over the feet of several drunken men, who were sitting on the floor. I also noticed other men drinking in various adjacent rooms. At the end of the corridor I found myself facing a locked closet door, and I felt frustrated and afraid as I retraced my steps. A man saw me coming back and told me that the passageway for which I had been searching had been closed a few years earlier. As I left the bar, other adults and their children were clambering up a ladder to get to the top floor to find the same aisle, and the parents were carrying playbills from the theater. I explained to them that the path was closed, but they ignored me and continued on their way.

Next I found myself in a hotel unpacking the shopping bags, and I discovered that I had lost my purse. I was upset, because my wallet was in the handbag, with all my credit cards and personal information. I opened all of the bags searching for a sales receipt, hoping to find the phone number of the store in which I might have left the purse. Using my cell phone, I called a store and explained the situation to the clerk. She answered, "You don't seem very upset." I responded calmly, "I've had a bad day. I'll either find it or I won't." At this point I woke up, exhausted and spent.

My dreams were discomforting, and they were warning me of the chaos that was coming and building in intensity. During sleep I was burdened with two shopping bags and trying to call Jeff, while also searching for some corridor that would lead me back to where I wanted to be. In the end I lost my valuables, my identification, my money, my credit cards, all the things that helped me to survive each day. Even in my dream, I continued to hold tightly to the shopping bags, feeling overwhelmed, knowing that I couldn't do any more. Through it all, however, I never lost my cell phone. I was determined to stay in touch with Jeff.

And for a moment, I was accompanied by a little girl who looked just like me.

Jeremy's birthday was in May, and this celebration brought Jeff's problems front and center. An "incident" is the word I write in my journal, a "fight" is the word Jeremy used. Although I was not there, and my journal gives no specific description, I puzzled the pieces together afterward by listening to both boys.

Jeremy wanted to celebrate his birthday in Manhattan with Jeff, so Tim offered this as his gift to Jeremy. Jeff organized everything in New York: Tim and Jeremy would sleep at Jeff's apartment; Leah, Jeremy's girlfriend, would stay in a hotel on West Fifty-ninth Street; tickets were bought for the theater; and dinner reservations were made.

Upon their arrival, Jeff assumed his role as tour guide. They walked around the East Village, had lunch in a café, made their way uptown, and strolled parts of Central Park. That evening, after the three men dressed, they picked up Leah at the hotel, enjoyed the show, and then went to dinner near Madison Square Park. The restaurant was busy, and they had to wait for their table, so they went to the bar, where their drinks multiplied. After more than an hour, at 11:30 P.M. they were finally seated, and Jeff was drunk and falling asleep, nodding off, time and time again. Intently, Jeremy watched Jeff, and each time Jeffrey closed his eyes, Jeremy would shake him to awaken him. With Jeremy's every nudge, Jeff became more and more surly.

After dinner the men accompanied Leah back to her hotel, and then returned to Jeff's apartment, but as they were walking up the stairs, Jeff realized that he didn't have the keys. They were in his jacket, which he had given to Leah to wear because she had been cold. They had no choice but to return to the hotel to retrieve the jacket and the keys, but Jeff, in his agitated state, started to criticize Leah for keeping his jacket and not dressing warmly enough for a night in the city. Jeremy said nothing, but his anger at Jeff, which had started in the restaurant, was growing with each insulting remark about his girlfriend.

After they had retrieved the keys and returned to Jeff's apartment, Tim went into the bathroom to take a shower, and the boys were left alone. Jeremy's anger could no longer be contained, and Jeff's mouth was out of control. A verbal battle began. Jeff's words were vitriolic, as he verbally struck out at Jeremy: "You're putting your time into a girl who's not worth it."

The tension between the two boys exploded, and Jeremy grabbed Jeff by the collar, towering over Jeff in height and overpowering him in weight. Jeff was helpless, so he rained insults: "You should've never come here. You're nothing without me. I wish you'd go your own way." These vicious words cut Jeremy, and his reaction was quick and forceful, as his muscles constricted and his hands grasped Jeff's shirt even more tightly. He lifted Jeffrey off the floor and hissed at him, "You're nothing but a fucking drug addict." With this Jeff spat in Jeremy's face.

Jeremy had no words left to play in this verbal volley. He released his right hand from Jeff's collar, clenched his fingers tightly into a fist and rammed it into Jeff's face, smashing and bloodying his nose. He then threw Jeff into the wall with such force that Jeff's head cracked a hole in it.

At this point Tim heard the noise, ran into the bedroom screaming at the boys to stop, but it was too late. Jeremy's rage was out of control, and as he looked at the damage, the destruction, and his brother's face, he grabbed his bag, ran down the stairs, and caught a cab to Leah's hotel. He later told me with both sadness and remorse, "I never hit Jeff in the face before, Momma, never. His words shattered me. I didn't know what to do. That night, I cried myself to sleep."

The next day Jeff and Tim called Jeremy and Leah to meet for lunch. Four dispirited people ate together, and three returned to Maryland.

For myself, I wasn't there, and I can only recount the story, telling the pieces as they've been told to me. I wanted to call Tim and ask him about what had happened; I wanted to scream at Jeff for drinking; and I wanted to thank Leah for stroking Jeremy's head while he tried to find solace in sleep. But I didn't do any of these things. I ignored the fight, called it an "incident," and moved forward.

After that night, Jeremy refused to see his brother. He was finished. This was confusing to me, since, although I understood the facts of what happened, I never really understood the gravity of what had happened, something so significant that it would cause Jeremy to turn his back so completely on the brother he had adored. Years later I asked Jeremy, and he told me that this night was his turning point. It was bigger than the fight, he said: It was the drugs, but it was also the words. He explained that this was the first time since Jeff's departure from the halfway house over two years earlier that he feared that Jeff was using drugs again. Jeff's nodding off triggered Jeremy's anger and fears and pent-up resentment, since Jeremy was convinced that Jeff's behavior was from taking something, a drug of some sort. Jeremy could no longer deal with the addiction, betrayals, and lies. But Jeremy's feeling did not end here, with Jeff's addiction.

Jeff was everything to me, but I didn't know him anymore. That night I went blind with rage. I don't even remember hitting him. He touched the deepest place in me. He was the only person who could truly hurt me. His words and actions hit me in a way that our relationship was never the same. I cut him off completely. I hated him after that, and I didn't care if he was in my life or not. I decided that only when he was Jeff, my brother, not the addicted Jeff, would I care again. Maybe he was as hurt at my birthday as I was, I don't know. From that night on, I talked to no one. I buried it. Then I gave up on everybody. I felt alone. I became a tower because I felt I had no one. I had always wanted Jeff's approval, but I didn't have Jeff anymore, not after that night.

As I listened to my son, my heart ached for him. Who looked out for Jeremy? I had been involved in school and immersed in Jeff's addiction. Tim's life was his business. Jeremy was left to find his own way, and for all those years he had had Jeff, his father figure. Now things were different, and as always, Jeremy shoved his feelings into his belly for no one to see.

After Jeremy and I were quiet, lost in our own thoughts, I asked him why he never told me about his fear that Jeff was using drugs that night, or about the grief that Jeff's words caused him. He didn't know, and he just shook his head and shrugged his broad shoulders. Maybe he understood that I was powerless to stop what was coming for Jeff, for us. Maybe he wanted to protect me. Maybe he felt helpless when faced with his brother's addiction and the chaos that accompanied it.

Years later, Jeff wrote about the fight.

That weekend really split us. To this day, I'm not sure all the damage done during that trip has been repaired. I was always able to love Jeremy through the drugs, almost in spite of them. They never stopped me from being his big brother. But with the fight, uglier things came to the surface. I was drunk and high and aggravated, and I said things that I downright didn't mean. Out of nowhere I attacked him with words that caused pain. Our relationship suffered real trauma that night.

This fight in New York marked Jeremy's emotional line in the sand. He wanted and needed his family, but he could give Jeffrey no more. He was done.

Jeff came home for Mother's Day, but Jeremy refused to see him. In fact, Jeremy didn't see Jeff again until the holidays in December. And even then, Jeremy held back, and was distant from his brother. Jeremy never quit loving his brother, but he had built a wall to protect himself against the hurt.

June 1, 2002, 7:45 A.M.
*My sons continue to feud. I'm sad through and through. I'm sad
that my sons aren't good together. I'm sad that our family is
wrought with a sort of bad blood, an undercurrent that seems to
run through it. I want to break the bonds and make them free,
but they are the only ones who can liberate themselves. Jeff and
his drinking—I know there's only so much I can do, but I cannot
support his using alcohol as a substitute for his past use of ketamine and other drugs. Jeff is struggling—we'll see how he lands.
I think he'll be fine, but he's very vulnerable. I'm done writing—
my mind is off.*

I should have realized that the slippery slope on which Jeff had
been walking had given way, and the boulders were already smashing us. My therapist once asked me, "How many red flags do you
need?"

The journal containing my written thoughts and reflections for
the next six months, from June 2, 2002 to January 6, 2003 is missing. I never thought I would write Jeff's story, so I handled it ca-
sually. It traveled with me on vacation to Italy for the month of
July, which I spent on the Tuscan seaside near Florence. My Italian cousins and their friends visited on the weekends, and true to
the culture, we cooked big dinners and dined for hours while talking into the night. People prepared traditional meals, especially
fresh fish and homemade pastas, and I wrote the recipes in the
back of my journal. I wanted a written record much like a cook-
book, and when I returned home to Maryland I would sometimes
leave it in the kitchen, sometimes in the drawer or on the book-
shelf. In my random handling of this journal, I have lost it or mis-
placed it, and I have no access to my words that document this
stretch of time.

However, I remember well the feelings and truths that started to
seep through Jeff's conversations, usually when he wasn't conscious
of who was listening or at times when he was too tired to filter his

words. I remember discovering pieces of information, details, usually a bit at a time. The consequences of his addiction had started to pile up.

At the end of June, Jeff left New York and visited friends in London and Greece, and then he joined me in Italy for two weeks. When he arrived he looked rested and tanned, his smile radiating with health and vigor. Our time together was ideal: We rode bikes every morning when the air was crisp and cool, then I would write for several hours while Jeff ran through trails in the nearby woods, music pumping into his ears as he became stronger and stronger. On the way back from his runs he would stop at the local fish market to buy something fresh, typically fillets of tuna, and we would cook together and linger through lunch on the *terrazza*. Afternoons were spent at the beach, where we would walk, talk, and rest, although Jeff, quickly bored sitting in the sun, would usually bike into nearby towns, returning later with observations and stories to tell. Sometimes he would bring back a richly flavored dessert from a *pasticceria* for after dinner or a late-night snack. Nights were calm and beautiful, and we would ride our bikes to the nearby outdoor amphitheater to hear concerts by local musicians or orchestras that stopped in our village on their summer tours. From watching his behavior, I felt sure that he was clean and sober.

The only worrying thing was that he told me that he had quit his job. He offered the information easily, explaining that he hadn't been happy with his position, and that he had already lined up something else to do, a delivery service that would pay him enough to live while he applied to graduate schools. He wanted an advanced degree, maybe in law or maybe a master's in business administration. Much of our time was spent discussing his future education and what he wanted to do with his life. Our conversations were open and upbeat; he sounded content with this decision and comfortable with his next steps. I remember feeling uneasy about what he would do, and how he would support himself, but his life was his. Not mine.

Our fourteen days together were beautiful, almost perfect. I remember well his smile and his gentle personality and manner with our cousins and friends when he would greet them with a kiss to both cheeks and a welcoming *buona sera*. I remember his laughter, the way he would bend his head back and look into the sky, and his joy would resonate, deep with pleasure. I remember his muscular and toned body as he ran through the woods, taking long strides to the rhythm of his feet. I remember his bartering with the woman at the fish market for a good price for tuna, while he spoke only English and she only Italian, but somehow their communication was held in the eyes and the softness of the voice. I've kept these memories safe in a precious mental recording, much like a music box that sits silent until the lid is lifted, the music plays, the ballerina dances.

Our time was almost perfect—the "almost" is because there were moments and statements that caught my attention, like the catch of a breath, there and then gone. For instance, an eclectic mix of people came for dinner, including professionals, artists of all kinds, and young people who seemed to live life on the edge. Jeff gravitated toward the most bizarre people, the ones who seemed to drift directionless through life. Then, at the end of July, instead of following his itinerary and flying back to the States, he insisted that he would travel to Amsterdam for several days, even though he had little money left, certainly not enough for lodging. This caught me out of the blue, but he was adamant, saying that he would tape his remaining three hundred dollars to his leg inside his pants and sleep in the park for three days before returning to New York. I thought this was crazy, and in the end he didn't reroute his flight schedule because he didn't have enough money to pay for both the airline change fees and limited expenses in Amsterdam. The most unsettling jolt hit me after Jeff left Italy. Ombretta, my Italian friend, the woman who had traveled with me to Rontondella, told me that Jeff had confided in her that over eight months earlier, in November 2001, a boy had died of a heroin overdose in his apartment. Jeff assured her that he had not been using drugs, but his two friends were using at his place, and one of the boys had died. He and the other friend, he explained, called the police, were detained, questioned, and later released on bond. He was shaken after the death and the extended legal battle that followed it, and that is why he decided to quit his job and leave New York. He shared nothing more with her, and she didn't probe. I was deeply concerned—he had never mentioned a word of this to me, and obviously it was important to him and caused him pain, so much so that he told Ombretta. Maybe he didn't want to tell me because he knew I'd question him and be suspicious. Maybe he just didn't want me involved. I knew Jeff's mastery of words, his extraordinary functionality while using drugs, and the intuitive sense of survival that had kept him alive. As I packed to leave Italy, the word "heroin" was alive in my mind, followed by two more words: "death" and "Jeff."

In August, I returned to Maryland to dig into the final preparations for the new school year. I never asked Jeff about the death in his apartment; time had passed, other problems were present, and Jeff was back in New York. During the following five months, from August to December, Jeff moved into an apartment with friends on the Lower East Side. He told me that he was working for a bicycle delivery service and was making enough money to pay his bills. He seemed at loose ends, living life on a whim, almost on the run: He visited home sporadically, sometimes staying with me while other times staying with friends in D.C., and when he was home he seemed edgy, not sure of what to do with himself nor clear about his direction. Although he talked easily with friends and family, and his verbal skills were still strong, his work ethic had diminished, and he seemed satisfied with the bicycle job. At times, I would notice that his eyes were glassy and distant, and he would often close them for a moment while his head would bob to the side, as if he were falling asleep. When I questioned him, he would explain, "Everything's fine, Momma. Don't worry. I'm just really tired. I'm allowed to be tired, aren't I?"

Jeff later told me what was really happening.

Those were scattered months. I returned from Europe and rode a bike for a delivery service that sold high-quality pot. I got the job through a friend who also rode for the service. Every morning, about five days a week, I'd meet a boy named Christian at a coffee shop in Astor Place. He'd give me a prepaid cell phone and a small box of plastic cubes sealed with stickers. Each cube contained a few grams of pot and cost $50. Throughout the day Christian would call me with addresses and phone numbers for deliveries, and I'd ride around the city and meet customers, typically in parks and apartments, and sell to them. It was a simple and efficient system. At the end of the day I'd reconnect with Christian, and he'd collect the cash. It sounds easy, but the job was miserable. Fall weather is unpredictable and Manhattan feels really big on a bicycle, but I worked when I wanted to and it gave me everyday cash.

When I wasn't doing the bike thing, I was high. Even when I was doing the bike thing, I was high. At this point, I was using heroin every day, and my lifestyle revolved around it. My friends that weren't carrying habits themselves were pretty unimpressed with the routine, and some even tried to intervene. I was on my way down and everybody knew it.

At that time the fact that my son, who had a college degree and had recently left a job with an international agency, was riding a bike for a delivery service made no sense to me; however, I chose to accept that this was just an interim position, and that Jeff was in a kind of holding pattern. He said he was paying his bills, he didn't ask me for money, and we each lived our own lives. There is a saying in Al-Anon: "Let go and let God," and this is what I was trying to do. I needed to get out of the way, and Jeff needed to live his life.

The three of us spent Christmas visiting my mom and dad in Florida. Jeff stayed close as he golfed with Granddad and took walks after dinner with Grandma, but they both noticed Jeff's lack of focus and his laissez-faire attitude, his slowness. My dad repeatedly told me, "He has no fire in his belly, Lib. You've gotta do something. I don't have a good feeling about him. There's no intensity, no commitment." Although this was true, and we all felt the same way, no one confronted Jeff. We tried to enjoy Christmas, and kept quiet about our concerns.

After the holidays Jeff decided to leave New York and move back to Maryland, to live with me, to work somewhere close to home, and to apply to graduate schools. I welcomed him home because I thought I could keep track of him, monitor his actions, and understand better what was happening with him. When Jeff was in Boston and New York, his life was a mystery, and it had been difficult for me to know how he spent his time.

I ended the year straddling an emotional hump between knowing and not knowing about what was happening in my son's life, and this caused me both discomfort and profound pain. Although I knew about the fight between Jeremy and Jeffrey, Jeremy had not told me that he felt sure that drugs were back. I had seen Jeff in Italy, and he was good—I saw his health with my own eyes.

I didn't know then, at the end of the year 2002, that Jeff had led a double life for almost two and a half years. He was a master of illusion—careful to show me his life as competent and solid—but his behavior and lifestyle choices were catching up with him. I wanted to accuse Jeff of using drugs, to call him out as an addict, but I was terrified to blame him unjustly and lose any kind of communication with him. I wanted desperately to believe that all was well, but I knew in my soul that all was wrong, and I didn't know what to do. My confusion and internal quarreling were like ropes, heavy, so much so that they seemed to cut into my skin, rubbing me raw, and obscuring my true feelings and best judgments.

I truly never knew that my son was lost or so deep in trouble. I suspected that he had created big problems in his life, but I never imagined the depths to which he had fallen. Moreover, I didn't want to turn my back on him. I wanted to be a good mother, and all that that means. I was, however, no longer able to deny that with each passing day my son was becoming someone I no longer recognized.

Chapter 9

What Happened in New York

As 2003 began I wrote in my journal about the early years of my sons' lives and I wondered what my sons would be like, wondered if I could have changed the course of Jeff's addiction if I had those years to do over again. I couldn't even say I knew Jeff now, not my Jeff. This was made clear to me by a series of events: a phone call; a monetary dispute; and the truth about a boy's death. I was catapulted into despair, confusion, and helplessness.

Jeff's lease on his Mulberry Street apartment had ended more than six months earlier, and his half of the initial security deposit of twenty-six hundred dollars, which I had paid, was to be returned to me pending no damages. I had been expecting the reimbursement, but in January Jeff explained that the landlord had kept the money because Jeff's roommate had failed to pay rent during the last few months, and my deposit had been confiscated in lieu of one missing payment. I was angry at being charged with Jeff's roommate's rent, and I demanded that Jeff instruct his friend to re-pay me.

Jeff did as he was told, but nothing was clear and simple with Jeff, as nothing is clear and simple with addiction. His roommate would return the money, but only on one condition: that Jeff tell me the truth about why he had moved out of the apartment and had refused to pay rent.

With so many people involved, including the landlord, his room-mate, and me, Jeff conceded, and agreed to tell me his version of the truth. Late one night, when all was quiet and I was reading in my bedroom, Jeff knocked on the opened door and sunk wearily into the chair opposite me, his eyes unfocused and his shoulders bent into his chest. His movements alerted me to an impending problem: My brain clicked into gear as my heart simultaneously sank into my belly.

A heroin overdose, he said. He explained that after returning to New York on November 30 from my birthday celebration in D.C. (I wish I had kept him home), he was with two friends, Justin and Paul, and they wanted to get high. He said he offered his apartment as a safe place to use.

Jeff told me about it in a lifeless voice that seemed to come from far away, his words almost hollow, just shells, as if it were too much for him to remember. As he talked, I could almost see the boys strolling down Mulberry Street in Little Italy, enveloped in the sounds and rhythms of the city. Maybe they shoved each other on the 6 train, joking and jostling the way boys do. Maybe they were greeted by the waiters cleaning up after the restaurants' busy night as they walked to his apartment. Maybe they laughed as they bounded up the well-worn marble steps, five flights, no elevator, to Jeff's top-floor apartment. Maybe they were silent; I couldn't know. When Jeff unlocked the door, the three would have spilled into the small entry that was also the living room, where Jeff's roommate kept his music equipment, records, and turntables. I wondered if one of them stopped in the bathroom, to the right, small, almost impossible to

turn around in, before they began their dance with death. I don't
know if they used downstairs or if they passed by the tiny kitchen,
next to the bathroom, so small that the refrigerator door banged
against the wall when just halfway open. They climbed the black
wrought-iron circular staircase next to the kitchen, up to Jeff's bedroom, the steps clanking as their shoes banged heavily. I didn't know
what they looked like, Paul or Justin, their size, the color of their
hair. Jeff I could see in my mind's eye in his apartment, a little over
six feet and one inch tall, twenty-two years old, slender, with liquid
movements, soft, and a laugh (did he laugh that night?) that rippled
like waves, deep and resonant. My guess is he was in the lead, since
it was his apartment. His bedroom, in the loft, was handsomely decorated in shades of navy and maroon, had plants on the windowsills,
an oversized mounted poster above his bed of Miles Davis, assorted
artwork from friends, and snapshots of our family, him with Jeremy,
laughing the way they used to. Maybe the boys trailed first onto the
roof that was accessible through Jeff's bedroom and sat in the lawn
chairs that Jeff and his roommate had arranged outside. Maybe they
smoked a cigarette before they went back inside to heat the heroin in
the spoon, tie off their arms and clench their fists, ready the syringe,
find a suitable vein, pull the plunger back to snatch a patch of blood
to make sure they had the right place, and then drive the elixir into
their forearms. I've never seen this happen, but I've heard about it,
and about the extraordinary high that follows, your head dropped
down in a flood of warmth and relief, your eyes prickly as they begin
to cloud over, time slowing down and blocking out the world.

Both Paul and Justin used, Jeff told me, and all seemed well until
about two hours later, when he glanced around his bedroom at his
friends and noticed that Justin, who sat on the futon, looked bad: His
head was slumped down onto his chest and a small mass of red bubbles dribbled from the corner of his mouth. Jeff shook him, splashed
a cup of water in his face, yelled at him to wake up, but Justin's body
couldn't move—he had overdosed. Paul and Jeff decided to try to

move the body from Jeff's fifth-floor apartment to the street, where they wanted to put Justin in a cab and send him to St. Vincent's hospital, but they were unable to move him more than two flights of stairs. In maneuvering Justin's two-hundred-pound body down to the first landing, his shirt and shoes came off and his head banged against the steps, and they had no choice but to call for help. Maybe Jeff called, maybe Paul called. The police arrived and the apartment was searched while paramedics paddled Justin's heart, trying in vain to start it again. Jeff and Paul were taken into custody, where Jeff was charged with possession of drugs and tampering with evidence. He was placed under investigation for negligent homicide.

Jeff's voice now filled with emotion, and I could hear the strains of his distress as he told me that during the following five months he was an emotional disaster. He hired an attorney who helped him, and in the end, after torment and uncertainty, pleaded guilty to attempted tampering with evidence. He was placed on probation for three years and given one year in jail with the sentence suspended.

I remember looking at Jeff and struggling to recognize my own son, as if I were looking at the shadow of someone who had once been my child. I had listened acutely to all he had said and I was trying to understand all that he had told me, but I felt disoriented, shocked, and confused, grieving for the life of a young boy I didn't know while I stared at the face of the boy I did know.

Jeff sat quietly, waiting for my response. At that time I knew little about heroin or drug overdoses, and I tripped over questions as I tried to get to the truth of what had happened that night. I told him that I could only believe that he, too, must have been shooting heroin, because the boys would not have used in his apartment unless he was also involved. He looked at me calmly, without a blink of an eye, and stated flatly that he was not using heroin. I must have looked doubtful, because he said then, "You're just gonna have to believe me. I hate needles. I'd never stick one into my veins." My words gained me nothing.

Justin's death has stayed with me all these years, appearing in the corners of my mind, always there but never exactly there. I've continued to wonder who he was, what he had been like, and how his parents suffered their loss. The truth is that at the time Jeff told me about Justin, I was afraid, and I didn't want to know any more than I did. The attorney had dealt with the resulting legal problems, and over a year had passed, so at the time I didn't question further. I didn't talk to Jeff's lawyer, and I didn't call the boy's parents. All I wanted was for Jeff's drugs to stop.

After the case concluded, Jeff's lawyer recommended that he leave New York to avoid further complications: This was the real reason Jeff had left the city. For over one year Jeff had held the death away from me. No wonder he didn't come home much during the first six months of that last year; no wonder he quit his job and traveled to Europe.

Jeff's roommate sent the money, but it felt stained with the red of blood, the black of death, the silver of needles, and stained also with my sense that I couldn't believe anything Jeff told me. He hadn't told me until he was forced to, and then he denied using himself. I knew, deep in my bones, that the situation was more complicated than it sounded, if only because with Jeff the truth was typically hidden underneath layers of lies and deceit.

I was baffled and felt desperate as to what to do. How does a mother respond to a combination of death and drugs, all made somehow more degraded by money, all wrapped around with lies? I felt disoriented. Part of me wanted to lurch forward into forceful action, while the other part wanted to fall back into fear and inactivity. I was well aware that the event had happened over one year earlier, and that what was done, was done. But still that night I listened to Jeff, I asked questions, and I accepted (I felt ill inside myself). I didn't know what to do, but I knew I had to do something.

After several days I made demands of my son, telling him that he needed to return to AA meetings and begin to work with a psychologist, a specialist in addiction therapy. He appeased me by agreeing to go. A friend of mine, in an effort to give me some space away from Jeff, offered him a room in his house in Annapolis as well as a car to use. This would allow him greater opportunities to find a job and easier access to his psychologist appointments and AA meetings, and provided us both a physical distance from one another.

Before long Jeff wrecked the borrowed car, explaining that he had taken several pills to help him sleep the night before, and that he shouldn't have been driving—the pills hadn't entirely worn off, and he had nodded briefly at critical moments. He always had answers to problems, never claiming culpability; nothing was ever his fault. I was miserable, disgusted with seeing Jeff's glazed eyes, hearing his slurred speech, and watching his lack of work as he fumbled between cities and offered excuses. Jeff lived between worlds, in a kind of gray area, engulfed in fog. My parents had been right; there was no fire in his belly, there was no fire in his eyes. The fire that had once been in my son, the desire, the passion to be alive, was being suffocated by the drugs that took him into places so distant from me that I couldn't communicate with him.

I wrote only one journal entry in February, and I didn't write again until April 21. Not only did I not write, but I did not talk with my family about Jeff and our problems. What could they do? My parents were in their eighties and living in Florida, and my brothers were in Pittsburgh and they had no experience in dealing with addiction. Neither did I call Tim, even though he was the obvious one to help, because he had written a letter to Jeff stating that he considered Jeffrey a liar, a manipulator, and a deceiver. Explaining that Jeff had lied to him too many times, Tim ended the letter by declaring that he wanted no further contact with Jeff. My life was imploding: Work was relentless; Jeremy needed my support; I refused to involve my family or colleagues; professional advice seemed to lead to dead ends; Tim had closed himself off; and Jeff was lost in his addiction. I was filled with fear and shame and didn't know what to do, so for two months I silenced my words, I silenced my self-expression. I cut the pathway from my heart and head to my hands. I was unable to express or clarify or validate my emotions in my journal, where for years I had had the power to discern reality more clearly, the only place were I felt safe to say my truths. I was handless.

In April, I announced my retirement from the school, effective at the end of the following academic year. I was exhausted. It was time to leave all the work behind.

> April 27, 2003, 4:00 P.M.
> The sun is trying to bake the sadness right out of me. Work your magic, Sun. Bake me thoroughly so that I am happy—like blue and yellow instead of gray and the color of mud.
> I struggle with knowing how to be a good mother to my son. I struggle with knowing how to let him go and to keep him close at the same time. I know I need to let go, but how? I try to extricate myself, to free myself, even if only in my own perception, even to keep myself safe, but I remain staunchly enmeshed. I'm his mother.

May was always one of my most hectic months at school, as we prepared for the end of the year and graduation, and I was inundated, pounded with work. At the end of May Jeff's addiction chased me down, again. A girlfriend of Jeff's called me at my home. They had been getting high together since February, she said, but Jeff was using ferociously, and she feared for his life. His drug of choice this time: heroin.

Hadn't I noticed his nodding off, she asked, his eyes closing as if he were about to fall asleep? She explained, almost incredulously, as if I should have been well aware, that this was the telltale sign of heroin use, the indicator, the red alarm signal. She didn't know who to call, so she called me, his mother.

Monday, Memorial Day, May 26, 2003, 11:55 P.M.

Jeff. I want to scream at him, but screaming has never been the
answer. I want to shake him until he rattles and say, "Why, why,
why? Why are you throwing your life away? Why do you insist on
killing yourself?" I want to say, "Look at all the great kids out
there who love life. Why can't you be one of them?"

I want to shout, "Now, what do you want me to do? You mess
up your life, and it comes home to me because I'm your mother.
What am I to do? Is this my responsibility? When will it quit
being my responsibility to be here for you?"

I don't even know what to do. What in his life is so painful?
Why does he return to drugs? Heroin.

I was forced to see the truth—my son was a junkie. I had to understand that I could never understand it. I had to accept it, but
how can a mother accept that she is losing her son?

I telephoned Jeff and found him with friends in D.C. I told him
to come home, because we had to talk. He must have heard the concern in my voice; he said little and agreed to meet me, but not until
the next day. He found me in the kitchen, and when he rounded the
corner from the hallway and saw me, he met my gaze directly and
paused: He knew that I knew. In that perceptible connection between child and parent, he knew that his lies had multiplied during
the years after he left the halfway house, tumbling over each other,
one catching on the other, and although it took all these years for his
ascent to reach crescendo pitch, he was finally unable to contain it.

He told me that it was all true. His relapse had started years ago,
almost as soon as he returned to Boston from the halfway house,
first with pills and cocaine, then ketamine, and then in November
2000, he was introduced to heroin. Initially, for about a year's time,
he used the drug occasionally, afraid that he would develop a habit,
but by September 2001, he was using it almost exclusively. He explained that heroin provided him peace, a comfortable level of
belonging—much like a love that a person had always been search-

ing for, heroin was like a warm cocoon of affection. It quieted his mind, body, and spirit; everything would shut down, and he was left in a still and predictable space. Nothing was great on heroin, but nothing was particularly bad, either. Everything just was. When he was high things were finally consistent.

Also, heroin was bought and sold on the street, in bad neighborhoods, and on some level this intrigued him: the chase after the drug and the daybreak trips to the rougher sides of cities. As a result, an ongoing series of legal issues had become commonplace with Jeff, who had apparently been arrested numerous times throughout this period. Misdemeanor possession charges now dotted his record. He had been living a life about which I knew nothing, a second life born out of drugs and darkness.

Sitting in my kitchen I listened quietly as he told me that during the months of the bicycle drug-delivery job in New York, he had carried a heroin habit, spending all of his money on the drug. The past few years had been dominated by heroin and everything that came along with it. No wonder he was unable to find a job or maintain a bank account. The car crashes and constant head nodding finally made sense. Overdoses were common, he said, and once, in his friend's apartment, his buddy's girlfriend found him unconscious on the bathroom floor. They had dragged Jeff into a cold shower and pounded his chest until his breathing revived. Even that didn't stop the flow of heroin into his veins.

He had also been using heroin the night Justin died; all three of them had gotten high together. In the months following the death he became uncontrollably anxious and afraid of everything, and his heroin use skyrocketed. He would use all day, every day. All his money went into drugs. He explained that he needed to. He used even at work but few people seemed to notice. When someone did, he had excuses at the ready, blaming stress and restless nights. Somehow people believed him.

He both loved and hated his addiction: He cherished the high from heroin, but abhorred its grasp on him, abhorred the consequences of his use. He told me that he wanted to get clean, needed to detox, and had tried several times on his own, but he couldn't stick with it. This time was different, he said, and he pleaded for my help: "I hate it, Momma, and I've tried twice to kick the habit. I hate getting you involved, but maybe with your help I can get off."

I asked Jeff why heroin had become his drug of choice.

Of all drugs done in excess along the way, heroin resonated with me the most. On it, I was safe and serene and sheltered from feelings, both good and bad. My mind finally stopped, and I was allowed not to care. Like something buried in warm soil, I was unaffected by the world around me. I was all I needed. On heroin I was home.

When Nicole called to tell you about my using, I remember feeling betrayed and unburdened. I was furious that she reached out to you with this, but I was also relieved. For years I'd been holding heroin to myself, but when we spoke it was over. Not the using part, and I knew that, but the secrecy and heaviness. That day heroin became our issue and I knew you were willing to carry it with me.

Even at the time, distraught as I was, I understood that Jeff was finally admitting to himself and to me the grave consequences of his addiction. He needed help and he was trusting that I would help him. I believed him and all that he told me about his drug use. I understood myself well enough to know that I could not turn my back on my son. Of course I would help; I never gave it a second thought.

Monday, Memorial Day, May 26, 2003, 11:55 P.M.
And what to do? Wouldn't I be glad if there was an answer to this one? There's never an answer with addiction. Some good ideas, maybe, but never a singular, obvious solution. I think I was always waiting for this day to reappear. I knew it would come back. I knew he hadn't done his work and the demons would

return. I need to be calm in front of him or I'll lose him. He'll feel as if no one is in control and he'll run deeper into drugs. I need to be strong about this. I need to be honest, and so does he. Lying will only compound the problem. We'll have to find a detox center. If insurance covers this, great. If not, I'll figure it out. Jeff's health comes first.

I had learned from experts and from reading about addiction that first the drugs need to be stopped. As I write this now, it seems obvious, but at the time, when Jeff was sick and drowning in the chaos of his addiction, this notion seemed like a revelation to me. Kevin McCauley, a medical doctor who specializes in drug addiction and recovery, once asked me, "How can you expect a rational response from an irrational person?" He continued, "Addiction is a disease. Your son is under all the layers of lies, betrayals, and deceit, and once you stop the flow of drugs or alcohol, he can come back, but you have to stop the flow first."

Time constraints compound the problem, because when a heroin addict decides he needs help, the help needs to come quickly, or he gets sick and returns to drugs to relieve the pain. This need for immediate care often leads to another and more critical situation, because the beds at many detox and treatment facilities are full of sick people, so a quick response is often difficult. Drug resources abound, but somehow when I needed help, I couldn't find it.

Pathways, a nearby drug rehab center associated with a local hospital, became my target. I called several times, but I couldn't get through the switchboard to talk with an intake person. It was a holiday, and Pathways seemed to be closed down, closed to new admissions, closed off, closed, closed.

Feeling blocked and desperate, I then called our compassionate family doctor at his home, begging him to intercede for us and to call the center. His response was clear, and he assured me that he would telephone the facility immediately. Within an hour the intake person from Pathways returned my calls. She explained clearly, calmly, and in no uncertain terms that they had no beds available for Jeff, and they would not even see him until Wednesday or Thursday. They had only sixteen beds, and they were all full. In addition, insurance needed to be contacted and, furthermore, both Jeff and I would need to be interviewed before he could be accepted into their program. After listening to what I considered her officious rendering of information, I asked her, "What do I do with him while we wait for a bed? If you won't see him until Thursday, that's not for three days, so what do I do now?"

She responded calmly. "When he's detoxing, he'll get hot and cold and his limbs will cramp. Try to make him comfortable. You can give him ibuprofen for the pain, but that's it. It's not as bad as alcohol detox. Just deal with it the best way you can." For her it was just business as usual. What she seemed to be saying to me was *"That's it, lady. He's your son and it's his problem."*

Jeff had two options: go to an emergency room detox center in Baltimore, one of several large, hospital-run facilities, or begin the process on his own and wait until Pathways had a bed. A glaring third alternative loomed: He could always use again, but that I couldn't allow. I'm sure there were many other choices, but my mental and emotional resources were collapsing. I had a tiger by the tail, a heroin addict who would soon be sick and in need of another fix. I didn't have the time or capacity to look for other facilities, to do the research, to be logical and detailed; doing what I had already done took massive energy, and I had little left. Jeff and I talked, and he chose to wait for a bed at Pathways. His interview appointment was set for Thursday morning.

Jeff stayed at my home. Tuesday, he was in pretty good shape, not very sick; he seemed sedate and intent on making it to Pathways. So I went to work—I still had a school to run. Wednesday was tougher. I came home at midday and found him ill, sweating, and in bed. He'd cover himself with a blanket, huddle tightly on his side, and then throw off his covers and spread his body to allow it to cool, all while his arms and legs jerked achingly. I took him for a car ride to divert his attention, trying to distract him with memories of old times as we traveled through the neighborhood where he and Jeremy had grown up, where he was one of a troop of little boys who rode bikes, built forts, and swung on vines high above the ground. We drove past the playground and past the familiar houses as we ticked off the names of all the children who once lived there and romped through these streets. Wednesday night was the worst. I stood in the hallway near his room and faced his closed bedroom door, listening to him thrash in his bed, a moan, a tremble, and off came the covers.

Wednesday, May 28, 2003, 4:00 A.M.
I hear his movements and I trace the outline of his body in my head as he tosses and turns. I used to stand by the door when he was just a baby and listen when he was in his crib, "Is he OK? I heard him cry, now he's stopped, must be back to sleep." Only this time he is twenty-four, almost twenty-five, yet a mother's memory seems to hold no time limits. I hear him punching his limbs, as if the pain will submit to the beatings and subside. In vain, my son. Into another hot bath he goes, then back to bed, I listen from my bed now, and I do the same, toss then turn, and I pray. In some respects, I'm grateful for the pain. "Feel it, Jeff, remember it. Remember, my son." Maybe it will stop him next time. Next time.

Thursday morning I did not go to work. We left for Pathways. He had an overnight bag, which he had been reluctant to pack. "I'm not staying there. I'm almost through this, and I did it myself."

"Pack your bag, Jeff." He did.

We sat in the lobby of the center for hours, watching a parade of people walk through the door. It was a cold place, really, but a sense of caring permeated the air, almost saying, *Yes, this is stark, but we do our best. We are fighting a tough fight, you know, but someone has to try.* They interviewed me first, then Jeff. After the interviews we sat and waited, eyes down, arms crossed, waiting.

Insurance wouldn't cover anything, nothing, because, "he has detoxed himself this far; he can do the rest on his own." They would give Jeff a bed for three days, no longer, but I would have to pay. I knew I couldn't take him home. He was still detoxing and in visible discomfort; he needed professional help, not his mother. I paid for three days; I paid for Thursday from 1:00 P.M. until Sunday at 7:30 A.M. and the three days slipped away like ice on glass. They flew by, and yet I was aware of every minute of every hour. I didn't want Sunday to come—I wanted Pathways to keep Jeff forever, but I couldn't wait to see my son again.

When Jeff and I debriefed with the counselor at Pathways on Sunday morning, she was kind, caring, and hopeful for Jeff. He had already registered in their outpatient program, which included three-hour meetings four times a week, and he agreed to attend Alcoholics Anonymous meetings and to find a sponsor. He was familiar with this routine from his other treatment centers, and he knew how to return to the process. His counselor explained that Jeff needed to put in hard work to remain sober and, if he did, she said, "the hole the size of a fist that sucks his tongue right down and chokes him" would eventually begin to heal.

I thought about Jeff's ability to adapt to whatever situation in which he found himself. He was at Pathways only three days, and she said that he had contributed significantly to the groups and had made a strong impression on the staff. When he was home with family and our adult friends, he was considerate and good humored, even when he was nodding off. I once asked him how the Jeff I knew could survive on the back streets of inner cities up and down the East Coast because, to me, it was inconceivable. He smiled and said, "I've learned to adapt to most anything. Within seconds, I can change colors and become part of the environment."

My son was like a chameleon, I realized; he could change and blend into places without anyone even knowing his position. He knew how to weave in and out of social situations, and even though some of this seemed to me to be utter manipulation of systems, he also had characteristics deeply embedded in him like empathy and tenderness. My son, yes, he was a chameleon, but I felt strongly that he would never lose the inner flame of his humanity. Maybe this was just a mother's wishful thinking, but I held to this belief—and never quit believing. With all this thought, I wondered if he would do the work necessary to place himself in sobriety and come home to his one, true self.

My mind returned to the debriefing, and I heard the woman saying that Jeff knew well the steps of Alcoholics Anonymous and was a born leader. He was talented, she offered, but warned us that these natural skills could also lead him back into severe trouble. People gravitated toward him, listened to him, and liked him. His verbal skills were strong, but he could quickly use these abilities to be cunning and manipulative. His life on the streets was well honed and systematized. My chameleon son later explained some of the duality of this time.

As an active drug addict, you don't have the freedom of a singular lifestyle, much less an honest one. Different stories go to different people and nobody gets the truth. On one hand, I was a heroin addict, hustling to make heroin work every day. On the other, I was a young professional who still had social and personal responsibilities that needed to be protected from the drugs. These worlds didn't mesh well, and I struggled constantly to keep them separated.

When I was living in Maryland I reconnected with some old friends who were also into heroin and understood the demands of daily drug use. Every day we'd drive into the east side of D.C. and buy dope in bad neighborhoods. Local kids would post up on certain blocks and sell heroin and crack. We'd hit popular sets on Old Central, Division Avenue, or the projects on Fiftieth Street called Lincoln Heights. These neighborhoods were violent and

unpredictable, but the drugs were consistent. In D.C., especially
on the streets, if your business is steady, people take care of you.
If you're in the projects every morning with cash, they know that
you're carrying a habit and will be back. And if you never burn
anybody, you're usually safe. In time, though, things got desperate and we found trouble. We'd be broke, pretend to have
money, and drive away when the drugs were in our hands. Or
we'd get overextended with certain dealers and have to watch
out for them when we were in the 'hood. It was mostly hand-to-
hand deals through car windows. We got stuck up a few times
and hassled by police, but when we needed to score, nothing
kept us out of there.

The counselor forcefully delivered the promise of continued use:
If Jeff didn't stay clean, his options were three: jails, institutions, or
death. I branded these words onto my heart, because I knew they were
true. The answer for him as for all addicts was sobriety, and he had to
find the strength in himself, in his God, and in the steps. As I listened
to her, I feared for my son, but I knew I could not change what was to
come. As we left I heard a lilt in Jeff's voice, a kind of optimism I
hadn't heard in a long time, and my heart lightened. A parent's love—
no matter how painful the hurt has been, parents always want to hope.
And believe.

Jeff began the Pathways outpatient program, attended AA meetings, started to meet with a sponsor, and applied for a job through
the county recreation office at the Annapolis skate park. Although I
wasn't happy with this position, remembering his early years with
his skateboarding friends, I felt relieved that at least he was working
and had to report to a job. Also, he began applying for professional
positions with D.C. and Maryland public relations firms. He was
clean again, and his verbal and organizational skills were returning;
he approached finding a job with his old enthusiasm.

Once again I had made plans to spend July in Italy, and Jeremy was going to join me, so I decided I could travel. Six days before leaving the country on June 21, 2003, I wrote:

> Rain. I think it's rained for months now. Everything's soaked.
> Trees are uprooted from the wet soil, the roots losing their grip,
> losing their footing—all metaphors for the inability to hold on.
> Maybe for me it's the same, the inability to hold on to anything,
> especially Jeff. Maybe it's the same for Jeff, the inability to hold
> on to himself.

I was exhausted by school, by drug addiction, and by all the people who I felt needed me. I knew I needed to change myself, and that Jeff would change only when he was ready. My mind understood, but my emotions were another story. Hope was all I had, and Jeff was sober today. I left for Italy on June 27, determined to find peace, and to enjoy Jeremy's visit.

While I was abroad, Jeff and his problems seemed a million miles away. My family didn't live in Maryland, and although Tim did, he wasn't talking to Jeff, so I tried to convince myself to trust that Jeff could be independent and would take control of his life in a good and positive way. During this month I wrote often in my journal about finding the balance between loving Jeff and knowing when to help, and loving Jeff and knowing when to let go. I had forced Jeff into treatment three times, and I wondered when it would be the right time to allow him to struggle with the raw consequences of his behavior. I knew I had missed many clues in the past, ignored or been blind to many red flags, and at times I wallowed in guilt and self-pity about my naïveté, my delusion. Other times I felt anger at Jeff, and recognized that it was time for him to take control of his life. My innermost self felt bruised, beaten up, and enervated.

On July 7, Jeff called me in Italy, encouraged because he had been offered a position with a PR agency in Washington, D.C. He was convinced that he was ready to work hard. "I think I'll be in this job a long time, Mom," he said, and he explained that sobriety and returning to life were at the top of his list. He assured me that he had met with a psychologist specializing in addiction, and he liked him. Could I believe what Jeff was saying? I didn't know what to believe; I felt unsure.

At the end of July I returned to Maryland, feeling content that Jeremy's time in Italy had been perfect, and all that we had wanted it to be, yet I was anxious to see Jeff. My two sons were on very different paths and, for myself, I was ending a twenty-one-year career with no idea what the future would bring. Nevertheless, I was looking forward with curiosity, interest, and optimism. The problem was that I didn't know what the present was holding for me.

I returned from Italy and was welcomed home by Jeff and his addiction. The unease I had felt during the phone call from Italy was correct—Jeff was using again. What had happened in one month? When I left he was set with a job, Pathways outpatient sessions, AA meetings, and a sponsor. A safety net was in place. He had support.

He told me that he had been clean during most of June; however, even before I left for Italy, he had reverted, gravitating toward friends of old who were still getting high. All recovering addicts are warned to avoid the people, places, and things of their past. But even though the past was painful, it was familiar and provided a level of comfort—and an efficient return to addiction. Jeff had failed to respect the warning, yet now he had been hired by a firm in D.C., and he needed to get and stay clean. He was proud of his new job and the responsibilities it carried, and he knew that his drug use jeopardized everything.

Jeff told me that while I was away in July he was so determined to detox again that he had gone to a medical doctor in D.C. who specialized in helping people addicted to opiates, especially heroin. This doctor was rumored to have developed a relatively painless method for detox, and had given Jeff a cocktail of drugs, a mixture of eight or so pills that he was to take at specified intervals of time. This concoction supposedly worked on the neurology of the brain by stimulating some functions and suppressing others. I didn't understand much of this discussion, and my head spun as Jeff detailed what he had been told about dopamine, serotonin, and norepinephrine, and how these chemicals affect the nervous system. Although I didn't register much about the effects of the chemicals, the drugs, I did hear clearly: "When you come off heroin, your nervous system wakes up and becomes overactive. Your body feels more than it wants to. Even your skin hurts. This is one of the things that keeps heroin addicts out there for so long. It takes months to get back to a livable state. It's almost impossible." Jeff assured me that the doctor was fully certified, and although the physician had given Jeff the pills directly, without a prescription and for a fee of somewhere between three hundred and four hundred dollars, he believed this mixture of pills would help him detox. Jeff was convinced that if he followed this pill-taking regime for three months, he could live a clean, drug-free life.

It sounded so easy.

Years later, he explained.

I was always conflicted about my use. For as much stillness and warmth as heroin provides, the inevitable detox is hell. When you're carrying a habit, it's impossible to accept the drug as the source of your problems. I was convinced that life was harsh and heroin was the only thing making it bearable. Heroin was the solution, not the problem. A peaceful period lasts as long as the drugs do and if I wasn't high, I was preoccupied with getting more.

I was also trying to maintain a job and the professional obligations attached to it. Without a paycheck, I was in trouble. On top of a heroin habit, I now had rent, car payments, and bills to cover. Every week I told myself I was going to get clean. I'd set dates, contact methadone clinics, and buy detox meds from friends. I

never thought I could make heroin work forever and knew it had
to end at some point. I tried to kick once a month or so, but I
rarely lasted more than forty-eight hours. I'd start with confidence,
but as soon as withdraws got bad, I'd be out the door. Being
clean sounded great, but getting to a place where I could give up
the drug and push through a full detox was more than I could
handle.

On Friday afternoon, August 1, the week I returned from Italy,
Jeff arrived home with multiple packets of pills, all neatly organized
and meticulously rationed out in appropriate quantities, and he was
ready to start. He had detoxed at home once before, so he figured he
could do it again. "May I stay for the weekend, Mom?" he'd asked.
"Will you help me? I'll be sick soon and I want to get started."

I was desperate for him to keep this job, hoping that this position was motive enough to keep him clean, enough for him to want
to strive for something better, bigger. I wasn't certain about what
I would do, if I would help him or not, but I was certain that I
wanted to understand more thoroughly the medicines involved
with detox and recovery, so once again I called our wonderful family doctor, because I was skeptical about the mixture of drugs. I recited the names of the pills as Jeff had dictated them to me, and
our doctor questioned the uses of these medications for detox. He
couldn't offer any specific prognosis, but he explained the primary
medical purpose of each tablet and capsule; one, for instance, was
for diet suppression, one was to lower heart rate, while others had
different, unrelated effects. He advised that Jeff not begin this program, and that he return immediately to a rehab facility for at least
thirty days, or more, because Jeff needed professional care. He also
explained that there was a new drug that had been developed to
help opiate addicts, and he offered this information to us as an
option. The drug, buprenorphine hydrochloride, was developed
for the treatment of opioid dependence, and went by two names:

Subutex and Suboxone. Federal regulations required physicians to undergo specific training before prescribing it, and although our doctor was not pursuing this course of action, this drug had medical approval.

His recommendation was clear: Jeff should go to another treatment facility where he could possibly begin this new drug, which might help, but Jeff should not begin taking the pills. I explained that Jeff finally had a job, and that he didn't want to lose it. Regardless, job or not, our family doctor advised strongly that Jeff needed detox and long-term treatment.

Of course, our doctor was right. Jeff and I talked and talked about it. In the end, however, he refused this option and insisted that he would begin detoxing himself over the weekend. He wanted this job and needed to be at work on Monday. He rejected any other alternative. Reluctantly, I agreed to help him, thinking that at least this was better than nothing, and possibly it was something that might just work. He and I both took our roles in this charade, standing together in the center stage of this tragicomedy.

It was Friday, and Jeff's last use of heroin was on Thursday night. He would be sick soon, since his body would begin to react within about seventeen to twenty-four hours of his last use. Quietly I took and hid the keys to his car, another used car that my father had given him in an effort to help, in case he wanted to leave. Soon the pain started. Each time he felt sick, he'd eat another packet of the pills given to him by the doctor.

The detox didn't go well. In fact, it ended miserably. Jeff soon felt even worse and became disenchanted with the pills. He muscled through Friday night and into Saturday morning, until it was all too much for him. The sweating came, as did the pounding and thrashing. By Saturday afternoon he was uncontainable and wanted to leave. He demanded his car, but I wouldn't give him the keys and stood staunchly in his way; I was determined that he would detox. He retreated back into his room, and a short time later he went outside to smoke a cigarette, took a little walk, and returned in twenty minutes with clearer eyes and close to perfect speech. The chills were gone, and he seemed content. Obviously something had happened, but I didn't know what. After we exchanged a series of verbal assaults, he admitted, "I called a friend who's been on methadone for a long time. He had several 'take homes' [liquid doses of methadone, yet another medical alternative, to sustain opiate addicts over the weekend, when the clinics are closed], and I told him to drop off a dose. He left it in the grass by the telephone pole at the bottom of the driveway. I needed to do something, and I'm better now. I was in too much pain. I need to detox, but I can't take the pain. It doesn't stop. It's unbearable."

I felt angry, betrayed, furious, but we both continued. I'm not even sure why, but we did. Methadone, he told me, had a long half-life, so this dose would hold him for another twenty-four hours. By Sunday afternoon he was in bad shape again, and by Sunday night he was like a caged animal, yet I somehow cajoled him into staying home. By Monday morning he was a disaster, sweating, in great pain, body cramps. He was a shell of my son. He had to go. He was irrationally, adamantly, desperate to leave.

I felt beaten down and defeated by the addiction. I could see that I had no control over what he would do or to what levels he would sink. I gave him his keys, and once again his addiction was thrown in my face. I had to accept my son's addiction; I had to know that this was his reality, and therefore it must also be mine. In retrospect I now understand that I never fully understood the powerful grip of his addiction, the depths of his malady, and the intensity of the horror he was living. All those years I had wanted to save my son, and now I could see more clearly that Jeremy had struggled to save his brother, and Sophie had tried to save her love. I finally understood that with addiction there can be no savior; there can only be the addict and the illness. Maybe words like "savior" and "hero" don't belong in the same sentence with addiction. But, I also knew, if they did, Jeff would have to be his own hero; he'd have to decide to save himself.

August 4, 2003, 8:43 A.M.

I don't know what to do, what to say, so I repeat the mantras from Al-Anon: "One day at a time"; "Let go and let God." These words are the only threads to hold. I wonder when I just lock up my heart and leave Jeff out? When do I live my life without adapting it for my son? He's not grateful, and I can do nothing that will change his behavior. I must realize that what I choose to do, I do for myself. Part of me wants to run away, to escape it all; part of me stays, hoping to support his recovery. Enough is enough. I'm exhausted, but I need to go forward.

Outside I hear the kids laugh, a pure innocent laughter. I ache to hear Jeff laugh again. I ache for him to find his soul, free and clear of the demons.

Jeremy just left a voice mail: "Mom, this shit is breaking my heart."

Two days later Jeremy came home, and we had dinner together. He told me that friends of his and Jeff's in New York were calling him, saying, "We're worried about your brother." Jeremy continued, "So-and-so thinks Jeff is going to die. . . . When Jeff was last in New York, Jason tried to help him. He grabbed Jeff, emptied his pockets, and took his drugs and syringes, and he tried to keep Jeff near him." Jeff's friends in D.C. also called Jeremy, saying, "Jeff looked wasted again last night, could hardly stand up." Then I could add to Jeremy's list: "Jeff recently told me he was dizzy on a Monday morning and left his car on P Street. Then he said he had to stay at a friend's house on Tuesday night because of the weather. Jeremy, Jeff's lies fall like rain."

Concerns about Jeff were coming not only from New York and D.C., but also from friends in Maryland. My friends in Annapolis, where Jeff was living, said that Jeff often returned to the house with slurred speech and half-closed eyes, and then the next night he might look fine—bright-eyed and responsive, alert, himself, Jeff.

It was clear that Jeff needed to move out of the house in Annapolis, as he was a liability to everyone. The way I figured it, he was spending a minimum of fifty dollars a day on drugs, which was fifteen hundred dollars a month, enough for him to pay rent somewhere. (I later found out from Jeff that my calculations were off, as he told me he was buying a minimum of ten bags of heroin a day for a total of eighty dollars. Sometimes, he said, he bought and used as many as twenty bags a day.) During this time I detailed my thinking in chart form in my journal.

August 6, 2003, 6:37 A.M.

JEFF	ME
Needs AA	Detach with love
Needs therapy	Get out of the way
Time will tell the tale	Quit being a detective
Needs an apartment	Do not cosign for anything
Doesn't need a car	Wait and watch
Needs to be on his own	He'll hate me whatever I do
Needs to be out of Annapolis	Hate and love are the order of the day

I understood that Jeff would be resentful of me regardless of what I did, since I was a constant reminder, a guilt causer, of what his life had been and could be again. His feet were set in the concrete of his addiction, and although he knew that what he was doing was self destructive, the drugs and the cravings were in control. He spent all day thinking about his next fix: His focus was on heroin. Change wasn't in the cards for him—not for now.

In August, he bought a car. It was as simple as that. He visited the Audi dealership. He was working, had a paycheck, gave them his social security number, and his credit was good. He put down the necessary deposit, they worked out monthly payments, and he drove the car home. Even today I am stunned by how easily he did this, then I remind myself that this is Jeff; this is my son.

Jeff happily agreed with me that he needed to move out of Annapolis and live elsewhere. In fact, he wanted to move into a space of his own as badly as I wanted him out of my friend's home and out of Maryland, so he began looking in D.C., in areas close to metro stops, so that he could take the train from his apartment to work. One weekend we looked together, strolling through Capitol Hill, searching for signs in windows. We found a two-bedroom apartment above a dry cleaner on Pennsylvania Avenue. The owner of the shop, who was renting the apartment, liked Jeff, which was not a surprise, and after a credit check, approved him. Jeff told me that he had already made arrangements to share the apartment with a girl, a friend of his friends, who lived in our county and was now working close to the city.

He was excited about having his own space again, and he asked Jeremy to help him move. It was with pride that he later told me, "Momma, Jer's a really cool kid. If he weren't my brother, I'd want him for a friend." Jeff furnished the apartment with care, taking time to hang artwork from friends and position plants in places where they brought a feeling of warmth to his room. He was on his own, for good or for bad. His car and insurance were in his name; he had health insurance with his new company; and now he had an apartment that was his. Legally I felt extricated, although emotionally I wasn't sure what feeling extricated meant.

Jeff was settled in D.C., living his own life, so I didn't see him often. At work he received kudos for a job well done and a strong evaluation. Amazing. Even though he was an addict carrying an active habit, Jeff's work earned him recognition.

The reality of my son's addiction was clear to me, and little did I know that another reality was taking aim at my world. A month later I received a phone call from my doctor, a surgeon, an old friend whose children had been at my school.

I had breast cancer.

November 5, 2003, 5:08 A.M.

Can't sleep—just can't. I toss, turn, roll, and think. Breast cancer. I want to scream. How much misery do I need to eat before I'm left alone? Is this a walk I must make for my kids? Will this help me save Jeff? Don't know anything anymore. Certainly, don't know why.

What I do know is that I have IT. Cancer. Dad says, "You're dealt a hand of cards—now play them." No choice here. No choice really. Cut one off? Cut two off? Reconstruct? Like a mathematical formula: one breast (plus or minus) one breast = reconstruction. I wonder what formula I will use. I'm reminded of a singsong rhythm of my youth only with grown-up words this time: one breast, two breasts, three breasts, four . . . things were a lot easier when I was younger. No breasts at all, just a jump rope. What did we know about breasts?

Now I'm not a kid, and I do have breasts. My walk is singular. No one can do this for me, so there is really no need to fight it. I've fought my whole life—my life feels like one great struggle. Why not accept this? Why not just accept the cancer as mine and allow the doctors and my friends to help me.

Lib, you know you can do this. This is your walk now. Take your own hand and step forward. It's dark where you'll go, but you've been there before, in the dark and afraid. This is yours. You have no choice, so do it well.

My journal entries fell off to about once a month. I felt intense emotion and had little resilience. When my doctor called he had explained that if I had to have cancer, mine was a good cancer to have. I had in situ cancer, which meant that it had not spread to nearby tissues, and it was a noninvasive cancer confined to the ducts; however, as it could spread and become a more serious, invasive cancer, surgery was a must. When I met with him to discuss options for surgery and the prognosis for the future, I invited my sons to come with me so they would know what to expect. I didn't want them to be afraid; I wanted them to know as much as they wanted to know. Jeremy came. Jeff didn't.

> December 4, 2003, 6:30 A.M.
> Cancer. I'm less afraid than I was a month ago. The doctors aren't sure, but they feel confident that the cancer is only in my right breast. Do I believe that? I think so. Jeff always said, "Time heals all wounds, but time takes time!" And then there is Jeff.
>
> Jeff is the hardest part for me. He's still not good. I'm not sure how, but he's functioning, paying his bills, and working. I have asked him, pleaded with him to go into therapy, a treatment center, but he refuses. His voice still slurs and his reactions are slow, even on the phone. I can do nothing. I love him dearly, he is mine. Letting go of Jeff is like letting go of my soul. I must, I can, I must. But how?
>
> So much right now—cancer and Jeff and school and my dad is ill, too, dying, really, a piece at a time. I don't know what to do anymore.
>
> For today, I'll do what I'm programmed to do—I'll go to work and I'll smile.

In December my dad was in a hospital in Sarasota with Crohn's disease and a systemic infection, fighting to stay alive. Seven days before Christmas I had a bilateral mastectomy. Both boys stayed with me in the hospital and held vigil during surgery, along with my younger brother and Jeremy's girlfriend. I was in the hospital only one night. Jeff slept in a chair next to my bed, reacting and awakening with my every move. Empathy for his mother was still alive in my chameleonic son, and he was attentive and caring; he never left my side.

I wondered what Jeff remembered about my cancer and surgery.

You've always been our mainstay, strong for Jeremy and me, but now you were in the hospital with cancer and I was terrified. It's incredibly hard for a son to know that his mother is sick and there's nothing he can do about it. Although my drug use showed no regard for the family, I've always loved and cared deeply for everyone. Addicts bear a hard juxtaposition. If it weren't for the euphoria connected to the drug, we'd never be able to handle it.

Strangely, heroin provided real tranquillity during your time in the hospital. I stayed high for most of it, spending lots of time in the bathroom on the second floor of the oncology lobby. It was big and new and empty and clean. Using heroin, I became very aware of places that were good for getting high. I was always evaluating the layouts of bathrooms: Were there locks on the doors? How wide were the gaps between stall frames? Was the lighting good? How heavy was traffic? The best bathrooms were private, spacious, clean, and used infrequently. Before your surgery, I bought enough heroin to get me through the stay, but if I ran out, I could easily score in Baltimore.

I had lost both breasts, and I had only a part of my lost son.

When I returned home both Jeff and Jeremy stayed at my apartment for several days to be readily available in case I needed anything. Jeremy charged himself with helping me lift things, including myself. My chest muscles had been cut and were traumatized, so I was not permitted to lift dishes into the overhead cabinets, or even to put weight on my arms to push myself up from lying in bed. Jeremy, who was six feet six inches tall and muscular, delighted in these physical jobs—this was his way. Jeff, on the other hand, responded to my request to help me wash my hair, because it was difficult for me to do this alone without getting my incisions wet. I explained that he could wash my hair as I bent my head into the kitchen sink, and he was willing, although he was also a little timid, since he didn't know how to do this effectively. I carried from my bathroom all the necessary products and explained the procedure to him. Gently, tenderly, he did his best, trying to wash and rinse my hair under the spigot without drenching both of us. Then he set a chair in front of the bathroom mirror and positioned me so that I could see the work at hand while I talked him through the steps of how to dry and style my hair. Even in his semilucid state, my son found his humanity for his mother, as he bent this way and that, curling my hair around the circular brush, working the hair dryer, until my poker-straight hair held some wave. "What do you think, Momma? Did I do it right? Is this the way you do it?" he questioned anxiously, wanting to make sure his mother looked and felt whole—pretty, even. I could see in his face the concerted effort this task required of him, but he never gave up. My son, my chameleon son, this was the tender child I remembered, the kid I knew, and I wondered how such kindness could be contrasted with such self-destruction; the polarity, the duplicity was undeniable. But I looked at my boy who was now a young man, and I'd reply, always, with a smile, "Yes, Jeff, it's perfect. Better than my hairdresser, in fact." He'd return my smile, going along with this loving game that was played with a hair dryer and a brush.

December 22, 2003, 6:33 A.M.
My surgery is over; my breasts are gone. I wrote nothing. Why? Because I didn't want to feel. If I could keep everything sealed away, I would be fine. All I had to do was keep my head down, do as I was told, and complete my job—well, I did.

In my grief, Jeff was wonderful. He washed my hair, dried it, even styled it. He walks so many different roads. He wants to get close, to be a part, but it's as if it's too hard for him, and then he runs away and goes under.

My chest is raw and cut, but the hurt doesn't rival the perpetual state of heartache for my son.

On December 28, my oncologist called. "The surgery was 100 percent successful. The right breast had some residual tumors, the left breast was benign, and the sentinel lymph node was 100 percent clear. You're done."

The year ended. The calendar announced the close of 2003, although the difficulties weren't going to stop because the year was over. I needed to heal from the surgery; my school career was coming to a close; my dad was failing, dying; and Jeff was locked into drugs.

December 28, 2003, 4:37 P.M.
Maybe I need to begin to pray for myself—for peace, for gentleness, for an inner rebirthing of and compassion for my own humanity, my frailty.
I want rainbows, but I don't trust rainbows anymore.

Chapter 10

"Our Family Is So Fucked Up"

During the four months of January through April 2004, Jeff came home infrequently. I felt relief when I saw him, grateful that he was still alive and coming back, yet I also felt powerless and useless, unable to change what I feared was his future. I was snared in the trap of wanting to see him yet dreading to see him. During these days I had only one prayer: "Today, dear Lord, keep him alive."

When he did come home, his continuing drug use was strikingly evident, slapping me in the face. He was usually subdued and withdrawn, living in slow motion. His once extensive vocabulary was diminishing, and when he spoke he'd pause as if rummaging through his mind, searching for words. There were times when his head would tumble from side to side or back and forth, as though his neck wasn't strong enough to hold the weight steady, or his eyes would roll around in their sockets, unable to stay focused. He wore long sleeves and long pants, and now I realize that he must have been covering track marks in his arms and legs. Oftentimes, he'd

wear his sneakers untied, and when I'd tell him to lace up his shoes
(the way mothers tell their children), he'd laugh and tell me that
loose laces were the fashion; didn't I know? It wasn't until much
later that I realized that his feet would sometimes swell because of
needle use, making wearing shoes uncomfortable. In February he
and Jeremy joined my brothers and me as we moved Mom and ail-
ing Dad into a retirement village in Pittsburgh, Pennsylvania. On
their drive to Pennsylvania they stopped for gas, and while Jeremy
filled the tank, Jeff entered the restroom at the service station. After waiting twenty minutes for Jeff to reappear, Jeremy trailed into
the bathroom to check on his brother. He peered over the stall and
saw Jeff, pant leg rolled up, shooting something into his calf, probably heroin, maybe something else. Jeremy was distraught and angry, and when they finally arrived in Pittsburgh, I questioned Jeff.
Of course, he denied using anything. My father, who was now
eighty-four years old, called me out on Jeff's addictive behavior:
"What are you going to do, daughter? He's not right. I see; we all
see. You've got to do something. Tell him, goddammit. Tell him to
stop." I looked at my father with eyes that said, *Don't you think,
Dad, that I've already told him to stop, a million times over?* He said
nothing more. Jeff told me years later, "Telling an addict to stop is
as effective as telling a man without legs to stand up and do cart-
wheels."

Although I didn't see Jeff often during these four months, he
would call occasionally, and my ears became like sentinels, listening to
the minute differences in his tone and the heaviness of his tongue. I
became attuned to tracking the cadence of his voice, the way he
mumbled "Momma," and the length of the silences between utter-
ances. The distance on the phone must have allowed my senses to be
more acute, because when I saw Jeff blurry-eyed and walking unsteadily, my heart felt burdened and I wanted to turn away. One
Wednesday night in March, after the final surgery to reconstruct my
breasts, Jeff called at 1:45 A.M. to wish me happy birthday (my birthday is in November). Once every few weeks he'd recount tales of los-

ing his car, forgetting where he had parked it, or having another fender bender because someone pulled out in front of him or the traffic light changed to green but the car ahead didn't move. In fact, he once reported his car as stolen, only to find out one month later that he had, unbeknownst to him, wrecked it, left it on Columbia Road in D.C., and taken a cab to a friend's home.

He always had some story, always someone else who was causing the problems; it was never him. He mentioned new friends and new places to me, time spent in D.C.'s Columbia Heights, and some new acquaintance in particular: "The owner of a recording studio, we're working together on a project—I'm writing a marketing plan for him. We're trying to get a label off the ground." Years later I found out that this friend was a major drug dealer in D.C., and he had been funneling money into a studio in Maryland. Other names I recognized, friends with whom Jeff had used drugs before. When I asked, he assured me that he was paying rent regularly, covering bills, and keeping up with car insurance. No one called me, and I didn't want to check.

He appeased me by going to a psychiatrist in Woodley Park, who was prescribing Subutex for him, the treatment explained to us by our family doctor several months earlier, a drug that took the place of opiates and helped addicts wean off heroin. It was supposedly safer than the methadone clinic, and it allowed addicts to quit using at a gradual pace. Jeff made an appointment, was approved for the treatment, and was off and running, detoxing with yet another method. Insurance did not cover the medication, so I paid for it—what if it would work? What if it proved to be the magic bullet that would keep him off heroin? I called Jeff's therapist to talk with him, to make sure that Jeff was engaged in the process of emotional therapy and not just expecting a steady flow of pills. The physician wouldn't talk with me; the medical privacy act barred him from discussing Jeff's condition without consent. I remember feeling blocked, stopped, and cut off at every turn. Only later did I find out that Jeff took Subutex only if he didn't have the money to buy heroin.

Subutex was a safety measure used almost exclusively for emergency situations. I couldn't get high from Subutex, but it kept me well when I didn't have heroin. It's an opiate replacement drug that, much like methadone, prevents withdrawal symptoms during detox. I preferred heroin, but sometimes that wasn't an option, like when I was broke and in between paychecks, or traveling and out of town. I was always stockpiling meds for a tight spot, trying to guarantee a painless detox should something come up and keep me off the street.

Although federal regulations prevented me from talking with Jeff's doctor, I would sometimes speak with Jeff's direct supervisor at his firm, a young woman in her midthirties, pleasant, well-educated, and urbane. Oftentimes, she and Jeff would be working late at the office or somewhere on a project, and he would call me and she would ask to speak with me. She'd brag about his ability to connect with clients and to execute communication strategies. I was pleased to hear from her about Jeff's progress, and I trusted that she had his best interests at heart, but with each conversation I felt slightly disconcerted, wondering why this young woman, a senior vice president, would repeatedly want to talk with me. She and Jeff were obviously close and spent considerable time together. I couldn't quite discern the nature of their relationship, and I had doubts that it was strictly professional, so I asked Jeff about it. He said that she was just very pleased with his work and wanted me to know. Jeff had an answer for everything.

Jeff and I were both connected and separate: connected by blood and love, mother to son, yet separate, with each of us living on our own planet, unable to see inside the other's world. My life was in transition: My school career was coming to an end, and even though it was my choice to move forward, I was uncertain about my next steps. My dad, the omnipresent force that had shaped my past and the voice that set the standard for my future, was dying. My body was cleansed of cancer, but my breasts, the place that not only had fed my babies but also was a visible sign that said *woman*, were no longer there. In addition to all of this, my son was careening downward, losing himself to himself, and all I could do was watch. While I retreated inward, he chased outward after his next fix. While I needed peace, he needed a high, a feeling that he couldn't manufacture for himself. I couldn't reach past the drugs to my son, but he never left my thoughts. I didn't write about Jeff during this time. I guess I couldn't. I knew he was destroying himself. That was painful enough.

What was Jeff doing during the first half of 2004?

The party had officially ended, and drugs had become a lifestyle. Heroin was home base and getting high wasn't an option. All throughout the day I got high—I had to, my physical well-being depended on it. I hung out with kids who used like I did and either sold drugs to support themselves or barely maintained day jobs. We were all chronic addicts by this time, and when I wasn't at work, I was loaded or in the projects.

And throughout all this I excelled at work, which was unbelievable. My performance was totally inconsistent, and I would find myself in meetings nodding off, practically sleeping. I was always leaving the office to drive across town and cop, but no one knew I was nursing an addiction. To this day I'm shocked that I was able to slide by for so long. Every month or so a supervisor would pull me aside and ask about sleep and issues at home. They were more concerned than suspicious, and I always blamed the drowsiness on panic attacks, which forced me to take Xanax and other benzos. Heroin's a funny thing. Unless people are hip to the signs of opiate abuse, they don't know what to think.

In May, Jeremy achieved his goal and graduated from college with a degree in economics. He had several job offers and, in the end, he accepted a position as general manager of a nightclub and concert venue in Fort Lauderdale, Florida. He later told me, "After what I had seen and fought against at BU, I was able to keep grounded and to develop my skills as a businessman."

While Jeremy was busy with graduation and moving on with his life, May and June brought the close of Calverton's school year, and the community had planned two events to commemorate my years of service: first, a gala; and second, a picnic.

The gala was held at the end of May, and I'll forever remember that night.

My younger brother, sister-in-law, and nephew drove to Annapolis from Pittsburgh, while Ombretta and her boyfriend arrived from Italy. Jeremy couldn't come to the gala, but Jeff wanted to be with everyone and to show support for his mother. I was hopeful that he would be clean, at least for this event, so I told him that he could attend only if he was sober, not using. He swore he would be heroin free; he was adamant that he was on Subutex, and all was well. So we planned that Jeff would meet the group of five and lead them in their own car to my apartment, about forty minutes away. We would all go to the party together, arriving as a family, united.

Jeff was late.

My brother called at least five times. "Sister, just tell me the directions to your apartment," he said. "I can find it on my own. We can't wait for Jeff. He's not here, and he doesn't answer his cell phone." I pleaded with my brother to be patient, assuring him that Jeff would be there soon. I wanted to give the appearance of a family at the gala.

My brother called again. Jeff was finally there, dressed appropriately in a suit, but he was drenched with sweat and agitated. They were following Jeff in his car, and since we were already late, I was ready to walk out the door. When they arrived I took one look at my brother's face, Ombretta's face; their eyes said it all, while the others wouldn't even look at me. Jeff tumbled out of his car, plastered on a smile, and stumbled up the stairs and into the house. "Momma, are you ready?" He was trying to sound chipper.

"Jeff, come outside. I need to talk with you."

He did as he was told; he followed me while the others waited inside the apartment, silent.

I blew up. "You're a mess. You're not clean. How could you come here like this?"

He, in turn, was furious. "I am clean. I haven't used in twenty-four hours. I told you I wouldn't use on this night, and I didn't." His words came slow and thick, like molasses pouring from a cold jar.

He ranted that his last use was the previous day, and in his own jumbled thinking he felt that he hadn't used, that he hadn't used on this night, that he had kept his word.

I told him to go away. I told him he couldn't come. I told him I was done.

He pivoted and turned his back to me, walked down the stairs, sauntered to his car, fell in, started the engine, and began to pull backward out of the driveway. At the last moment he rolled down the window and yelled up at me, "I'm not a yo-yo. You tell me to come and then you tell me to leave. You need to make up your mind."

And there I was, smacked in the face once again by addiction, and by indecision, too. I was torn between wanting my son, but not wanting the drugs; between wanting Jeff, my Jeff, but not this Jeff; between wanting to have a healthy family, and knowing we weren't.

From the top of the steps, my eyes held his. I saw a boy distant and lost, but at the same time I saw my son wanting to be a part, not wanting to be abandoned and shunned.

"Do you want to come?"

"Yes."

No, he was not a yo-yo, and yes, I was his mother. The addiction had defeated me. "Then come."

With that we all silently gathered our thoughts, our purses, and our jackets, and we left for the gala, but there was little joy in our group.

That night Jeff tried hard to play his role, the son of the mother who had devoted many years to young people. There was a formal presentation, in which several alumni and faculty members spoke about my positive influence on them and the community, about my leadership. As I listened I was filled with both pride and grief, pierced by the knowledge that I had helped some children grow, yet with one of the two most important children in my world, the one who sat next to me, I was unable to make a difference.

Several people that night didn't even recognize him, and thought my nephew was Jeff. In fact, one friend, who had known Jeff for over fourteen years, said to his wife, "Too bad Jeff wasn't there tonight." She responded, "Honey, you talked with him."

The parent who organized the event in my honor e-mailed me a picture of Jeff that she had taken: an image of a shell of a young man, a skeletal form covered with skin, draped in a suit, and dressed for a gala. I forwarded the picture to Jeff, hoping that he would see for himself how he looked to the rest of the world, but he merely replied, "Why'd you send me that picture? I deleted it immediately. It was horrible."

The next event, held the following week, was a picnic organized by the parents, an event for the children, with games and music. Jeff drove his own car, greeted a few families with me, and ten minutes later, when I turned around to introduce him to someone, he was gone.

Graduation was the closing event of the school year, held a week after the picnic. This was my final opportunity to address the students and to share my thoughts. I wanted to say something meaningful, and of course Jeff, with all I had learned or thought I'd learned, was ever present in both my mind and heart as I wrote my final words. I told the graduates to "dream dreams, fight evil, make a difference, and stand tall, even if you're standing alone." I said to these young people, who were soon off to college and would later become, I hoped, leaders in the future, "You're more capable than you know, so, when you're challenged and beaten up with self-doubt, fight the impulse to give in. Move forward with the belief that you can do it.

Honor yourself and your passion—find your passion—find what makes you you and don't let go. You'll make mistakes, sure, so make them, and then do the next right thing." I advised them to most of all listen to their own inner counsel: "Believe in yourself, and go forward with confidence. Grab the next trapeze bar, but don't be afraid to hang in the darkness. That's where you'll learn. Strength comes from within." I hoped they heard my message and understood that I cared deeply for them, and for all the students who had been a part of my life.

On June 30, 2004, after twenty-one years of service and leadership, I drove off campus for the last time. That night I dreamed that Tim called to tell me that Jeff had committed suicide.

My school career ended, and within one week I moved into my parent's apartment in Pittsburgh to face another ending: Dad was dying, Mom was exhausted, and I thought I could help.

July 28, 2004, 10:00 P.M. Pittsburgh
Dad is finally at home. I've seen him in four settings in seven days: nursing center, emergency room, hospital room, and now home. He sleeps. The thin-bodied shell of my Marine Corps drill-sergeant dad sleeps with a medicine bag humming to him like a lullaby. It seeps its elixir into his blood, keeping him alive, destroying his liver as it nourishes the other parts of his dying body.

The hardest part and the saddest part is that the dying part is yet to come.

My father died on Monday morning, August 9, at 4:45 A.M. Sunday, the day before he died, he lay in the hospital bed surrounded by his wife of fifty-eight years, all three of his children, and my brothers' wives. One after the other my younger brother called each grandchild on his cell phone and held the phone to my dad's ear as the child whispered his or her final words of love to Granddad, the rock of our family. Jeff had to be called five times. My brother, the same brother who had come to the gala, was unable to reach him, getting only his voice mail and leaving frantic messages to call Granddad because time was short. When Jeff finally returned our calls, his words were as incoherent as Dad's. Dad was dying and had little strength to speak; Jeff was a mess and had little ability to speak.

Jeff's body came to the funeral, but his spirit and mind were elsewhere. He never shed a tear. Even in my grief, it was impossible to ignore his impassivity, his lack of emotion, his empty eyes, that soulless body. What had happened to my son's love for his grandfather?

> Lots of regrets about the space I was in when Granddad died. I remember you calling me throughout the week and leaving updates on voice mail. This went on for several days, and I tried to tune them out. Maybe I thought that if I didn't take the calls, he wouldn't die. I knew that I needed to be there, but I knew that I wasn't sober enough to set foot in Pittsburgh. Then the calls started from Uncle Ted telling me that Granddad was really failing, saying that Granddad wanted to speak with me. With this news, I returned the call and he put Granddad on the phone. The conversation was brief, and all I could do was cry. I hated that he would never see me sober or be proud of the man I could become. I just sobbed. My life felt pathetic and, even in his dying state, I knew that he knew I wasn't good. He said that he loved me and told me he was tired. That was it.
>
> I was on Subutex for the funeral. It was as close as I could get to sober. I wanted to pay proper tribute, but I felt like I was watching it all through stained glass.

Then, at the end of August, only two weeks after my dad's death, Jeff was fired. This news threw me into a tailspin. Without a job he'd have no money to pay for his apartment or make car payments. In addition, I had made plans to leave for Italy on September 13, and my mom had given me her blessing to go. I wanted to go, needed to leave. But what to do with Jeff?

Tim was now living in Maryland, close to Jeff's apartment in D.C., and he and Jeff were still not on good terms. For years, Tim felt that Jeff used him, came to him only for money, lied to him, and manipulated him; he felt that Jeff couldn't be trusted. All this was true, of course, as it is true with all addicts and all addiction. Yet I didn't know what to do: I couldn't leave for another country without someone watching out for my son. I continued to refuse to involve my family, especially now after my dad's death, so I called Tim. I had no one else, and with my back against the wall I turned to Tim for help. He lived in the area; he was Jeff's father. I told him that I was leaving the country temporarily in order to heal after my cancer surgeries, my dad's death, and retirement from my school community. In my absence, I explained, Jeff and Jeremy would need a parent to turn to in times of need. Jeff was sick with his addiction and, although neither Tim nor I could fix anything, I couldn't leave the country unless Tim would be present for Jeff. Tim knew I was exhausted. He also knew that Jeff was in a bad way. Even though I'm sure Tim had many mixed emotions and severe doubts about what he would do in times of trouble, he agreed to be present.

I made an appointment for the three of us to meet with Jeff's doctor, knowing that if Jeff were present he would have to talk with us. Tim met Jeff and me in front of the office on River Road in Washington. Even though I had told Jeff that Tim would meet us, he reacted with self-righteous anger: "You and Dad are both here—what's going on? I'm OK. You're making a big deal out of nothing."

The doctor was clear: Jeff was in terrible shape, needed detox, had lost his job because of drug use, could hardly drive a car safely, and was a liability to everyone, including himself. In addition, he had no money, was in debt, had racked up large credit cards bills, and his apartment lease expired in six days. It wasn't hard to see that the pieces of his life were unglued and floating around him. The doctor unequivocally recommended a treatment center at a local hospital

center where he was an associate and could help monitor Jeff's medicines and detox progress. Jeff didn't want to go, but Tim and I were
immovable.

Jeff was admitted into a hospital in Fairfax, Virginia, but they
would keep him for only five days—insurance limits again. With Jeff
in the hospital and jobless, he gave us the keys to his apartment, and
on Labor Day Tim and I lifted, hoisted, and boxed up Jeff's belongings. In the heat of that September day, I cleaned out the bedroom
while Tim emptied the closet, finding fistfuls of syringes, whole
handfuls that he pulled from the bottoms of garment bags, the corners of drawers, and the insides of shoe boxes. I didn't want to look in
Jeff's drawers; I covered them with blankets and sheets, bound them
with tape, and stacked them carefully with all of Jeff's treasures, good
and bad, stored safely inside.

Tim and I talked together about what Jeff might do after his release from the hospital, because he no longer had an apartment or
a job or anywhere to go. We discussed this with his doctor, who recommended the outpatient program at the hospital, but we had tried
this before at Pathways, and he couldn't be counted on to follow
through with the commitment. I spoke with three other psychologists, all of whom recommended clearly that Jeff needed structure,
psychological support, and most of all a sustained period of time in
a drug-free environment. With his history of drug abuse and legal
problems, they said, his need for lengthy care was clear. He had already been in several short-term treatment facilities. In addition, he
had been arrested more than ten times, typically for possession of
narcotics and drug-related offenses, which had incurred minor
charges and involved periods of informal probation or community
service. I was convinced that Jeff needed long-term, inpatient treatment, and researched programs that kept chronic-level addicts for a
year or longer in a residential setting.

When Jeff got out of the hospital, after just five days in detox,
he was still uncomfortable in his own skin. He and I talked, and of

course he acknowledged his limited options, with no place of his own to live and no job; however, he wasn't ready to acknowledge that he needed or wanted additional treatment, which is one of the primary requirements of a rehab facility. He wouldn't go. In fact, not only would he not go, he was surly. With a cool indifference and disdain, he refused my attempts to force him into long-term care. A series of verbal battles followed between Jeff and me, until Tim offered an alternative: Tim would take him away from the D.C. area to Hilton Head, South Carolina, to his family's vacation home, where Tim would work from the house and devote one month to Jeff and his recovery. During this time in South Carolina, Jeff's responsibilities would be to go to AA meetings and outpatient services at the local hospital, stabilize himself on Subutex, which the doctor wanted Jeff to continue, and stay away from the familiar "persons, places, and things" in Washington. This was the first time that Tim had made such a bold move to help with Jeff's addiction, a giving of himself measured in time and energy. I still held strongly to the belief that Jeff needed long-term care, but Tim was trying in his own way to step forward and help his son.

So on September 14, I arrived in Florence, Italy, with plans to stay three months. My dad had died, my mom had given me the freedom to travel, Jeremy was thriving in Florida, Tim had accepted the responsibility of living with Jeff for four weeks, and Jeff had agreed to go. I figured I'd have peace at least until then.

September 13, 2004, 5:40 P.M. En route to Florence, Italy
Jeff is sick. I thought I needed to stay home and take care of him, so I offered. His eyes were hostile and angry, but I said, "Jeff, I've decided to stay home and not go to Italy." He responded incredulously, "Why, Mom?" "So I can take care of you." With that the corners of his lips curled up, but there was no smile. "That's kind, Mom, but I'm going to do what I'm going to do whether you're in Italy or the United States."

Tim and I stayed in e-mail contact during this time, and he reported that Jeff was well; in fact, he was better than well. He was eating properly, resting each night, and making progress. They walked on the beach, went to movies, cooked dinners together at home, golfed, and rode bikes. In addition, Tim said that Jeff was going to AA meetings and regularly taking Subutex, but Tim was quick to admit that he could not supervise Jeff's every move. He was pleased to report that Jeff was in better health and spirits than he had been in months, perhaps years.

At the end of the month the two returned to Washington, and Tim agreed that Jeff could live with him at his apartment in Bethesda. Tim wrote me a summary e-mail, saying, "It was a wonderful time, perhaps a once in a lifetime opportunity to spend over a month with a grown son. I cherish the memory." Sadly, however, Tim's e-mail continued, "It was all fleeting. Everything went to Hell upon our return to the District and Jeff regressed within a matter of days back into the vice of addiction and the association with those who engage and dwell in that miasma."

Like two faces of a coin, Tim and Jeff had two different interpretations of what had happened during this time.

> Using every day is hard work, and in many ways I was glad that you two were stepping in. My life was falling apart, and my desire to pick up the pieces was fading. Physically, I was in bad shape, hitting any veins I could find. My arms and hands were scarred, and I was into my feet and legs. Any place where I saw blue under the skin, I poked at. These sloppy shots led to abscesses— where the drug misses the vein and eats a slow pocket through the skin from underneath. I knew I had to detox, but I also knew I wasn't done using. I hadn't yet admitted to myself that heroin was a losing battle.
>
> The time in South Carolina could have been wonderful, but before leaving Washington I bought enough heroin for five days of heavy use. I figured that I'd get high for the first week before

starting Subutex and detoxing over the month. As planned, I finished the dope, and successfully transitioned to Subutex. But I
couldn't quiet the idea of heroin. I wrestled with it for a week and
eventually called a friend in D.C. and asked him to FedEx me
more, which he did. During this period I began to resent my drug
use.

I didn't hear from Jeff for over a month, but Tim wrote that Jeff
was now living with friends in D.C. and not staying at his apartment. Throughout this time I read voraciously and wrote daily in
my journal. I had to heal, emotionally and physically, and I now had
the time to do it. Before I left the States my parish priest had given
me books written by Henri Nouwen and Thomas Merton, the
authors of many books on living a spiritual life. One of Nouwen's
ideas became my goal: "We must find the courage to enter into the
desert of our own loneliness and to change it by gentle and persistent efforts into a garden of solitude." Loneliness and powerlessness,
I knew well. I wanted and needed to find the garden of solitude.

In late November I received an e-mail birthday message from
Jeff. His words were reserved and felt alien to me: He addressed me
as "mother" and signed his name as "Jeffrey." It was not my son's voice
I heard.

I wanted to message you, mother, and extend warm birthday wishes.
I miss you and apologize for the lapse in communication. I look for-
ward to spending time with you when you return. Love you tons.
  Jeffrey

Then, on December 10, five days before I was to leave Italy for
the States, I received an e-mail from Tim saying that Jeff had turned
up at his apartment unexpectedly and stayed with him during the
weekend. When Tim came home from work on Monday he found
blood splattered on the bathroom floor and walls and a towel
marked with red stains in the hamper. Tim confronted Jeff, who ad-

mitted flatly that he was using again. Tim told Jeff not to return to his apartment. His addiction was too big for both Tim and me, and we had to understand that Jeff didn't want sobriety.

My travel plans were set, so on December 15 I took the train from Florence to Rome for my return flight to Maryland. En route I called Jeff and left a message on his cell phone telling him that I wanted to see him when I arrived home. I needed to see my child.

He didn't come to the apartment immediately, but after several days and multiple phone calls, one afternoon he showed up. He walked sheepishly into my apartment, and as he rounded the corner into the living room the pale winter sunshine filtering through the skylight brightened his hair and outlined his gaunt face. He instinctively tried to add a little skip to his step, a kind of familiar Jeff skip from when he was just a child, but he didn't get it right. The skip was off, his smile was shallow, his skin was mottled, and his eyes were timid. Without hesitation I wrapped my arms around what was left of my son; I hugged bones, but I was grateful that he was still alive, walking, and remembering that once he did skip. I took him in my arms with all the tenderness of a mother with a newborn child. To me he felt afraid, vulnerable to my every word and movement. He needed to feel accepted and loved; he needed to feel safe. As he moved I could see puncture wounds tracing veins in his neck. Shooting into his neck; I wanted to vomit.

Where had he been since Hilton Head?

For a few weeks I stayed with Dad, but it was messy. Being around him made me feel bad about myself, and I hated looking at my lifestyle through his eyes. It was obvious that I wasn't clean, and I could only assume that he knew I was out chasing drugs and money all day. Without an income, getting high is a scramble: a collage of little schemes, borrowed money, pawn shops, and sold possessions. As Dad would leave for work, I'd be coming home strung out, or I'd be around and nodding off in the apartment. He never really confronted me, and the environment was always tense.

When I left Dad's I moved into a friend's hotel room in Logan Circle—a career crystal dealer who would shuffle between hotels every month or two. He knew things were bad with me, but we trusted each other, and he was sympathetic to my heroin situation. He made sure I had money to stay well. He'd also give me crystal, which I'd either do with friends or sell for extra cash. I was gone most of the time, but I'd surface every day or two, and we would hang out and drive around town. Eventually, he started switching hotels more frequently. He was a pretty successful dealer and the rooms were always hectic and highly trafficked. He'd think hotel employees were suspicious and we'd take off—and most of the time he was right. It became this manic race around the city, convinced that people were on to him. That's when I left.

But on that December afternoon, all I knew was that he was home; a good sign, I thought. He admitted that he knew he was a disaster, needed to detox, start back on Subutex, and go to another halfway house or treatment facility to get clean. Jeff stayed for the rest of the afternoon, and that night he fell asleep on the couch. I entirely understood that my son was now twenty-six, and he was no longer a boy but a man with a serious drug addiction. His feet, arms, hands, and neck were marked from syringe use. A raw and intensely red abscess wound from a misaligned injection marred his left foot near the ankle, clearly infected. He wanted to get clean, he said, and he knew he needed long-term care: "Getting sober is a hard process, stutter-stepped almost. I know I need help." For years Jeff had tried desperately to conceal his drug use, but that afternoon his long history with addiction was clear, his using was no secret, and he spoke honestly about it all. We talked about the cravings and his inability to stop using, and he said that although he knew he was in trouble, and that heroin was commanding his life, he was stuck, frozen in place. He was afraid to stop using, but he was also afraid of what his life had become and would become if he didn't. We talked about him returning to the halfway house in Florida. It had helped once before; maybe it could help again.

Meanwhile, it was December 22, and we were facing the first Christmas since my dad's death. I asked both boys to join me in Pittsburgh to bring a sense of family to my mom, their grandmother. Jeff chose to drive with me from Maryland, and Jeremy was to arrive from Florida. Jeff began a new regimen of Subutex in order to be off heroin for Christmas, and he said that he wanted to take control of his life once more. Jeremy was conflicted about coming, but Christmas was Christmas, and he wanted to be with the family. I don't think he wanted to see Jeff.

Our reunion was not easy. Jeff was pale, thin, and cranky as he replaced heroin with Subutex. Jeremy watched his brother's every move, registered it, and held his feelings in his gut. Nothing had changed with Jeremy. I tried to keep peace among all of us. We each played our family roles well, and all was calm—that is, until the last day of the trip.

After all the festivities, dinners, and even a Christmas Eve Mass, Jeremy was getting ready to leave Pittsburgh to return to Florida. He and Jeff had shared a bedroom during their short three-day stay, one big room with a king-size bed and an adjoining bathroom. Jeremy was waiting to use the bathroom while hurriedly packing, but Jeff wouldn't come out. Jeremy banged on the door; he knew that Jeff was taking too much time and deduced that his brother was using some drug, again. We found out later that Jeff was shooting his Subutex into his muscles, which gave him quicker relief from withdrawal symptoms.

Finally Jeff emerged from the bathroom, aggravated and unsteady. Jeremy hated drugs, hated needles, hated addiction, and he exploded. "You're a fucking junkie," he bellowed. I heard the commotion and ran into the bedroom, fearing that my mother would get involved, and that her neighbors in the retirement village could hear my sons fighting. My presence was of no use. Jeffrey and Jeremy were face-to-face, screaming at one another, the younger crying out the truth while the older, defending himself, roared back about Subutex and detox. Then my mother was standing between the boys who were now men, and she braced one hand against each grandson's chest. "Please, stop," she pleaded softly. "Please."

It ended. They looked with sad eyes at their grandmother's frail figure and walked away from each other. Jeremy shot Jeff a hostile glance as he went into the bathroom and slammed the door. Jeff looked down, not wanting to make eye contact. I put my arm around my mother and led her from the bedroom. She had seen enough.

The destruction that Jeff's addiction caused was like the flow of a river during a flood. No one and nothing could stop it. Jeremy left for Florida and Jeffrey returned to his world in Washington. Within hours of returning to the D.C. area, he was gone. He was at home on the streets, in his web of darkness.

Three days later Jeff called me to apologize for being in such bad shape during the holidays, explaining, "I was detoxing and I felt awful; the Subutex is only so effective. I've decided to go back to Florida, to the halfway house, and get sober. I have to get my life back. I don't want to lose you and Jer. I have friends, but I need family. It killed me to see Jeremy step in with such disgust. He hates the person I've become, and so do I. I've already called the halfway house, and a bed is available on January 15. I'm going to take it."

December 29, 2004, 8:10 A.M. Pittsburgh

So, how do I feel? Cautious. Jeff has said things over and over and the result has always been drug continuation. My heart has been broken a million times by Jeff and I'm worn out. "I'll do what I'll do whether you're in the United States or Italy." Famous words from Jeff. It's Jeff's walk—all I can do is watch. No one can heal Jeff but Jeff.

I'm also angry with him, and I feel little sympathy. Maybe I just have to declare him dead to me, and if he resurrects, so be it. His use of heroin abuses everyone who loves him, especially

Jeremy and me. Maybe it's too late for Jeff. Seeing him this time was different—I saw him as a user of people and drugs, a liar, and an abuser. A user and an abuser—I guess they go hand in hand.

My dad always said that you never give up on your kids, but I don't know. I just don't know anymore. When am I allowed to quit?

We ended the year with Jeff saying he would return to Florida and the halfway house. Words. He was always full of words.

Jeremy summed up the year: "Our family is so fucked up."

Chapter 11

The Gravity of Roller Coasters

There followed months, nine months, of frightening descents and hopeful rises, of sudden curves and disorienting stops. I never knew what any day would bring to me, or require of me. As the *Big Book* of AA states, "This is the most baffling feature of alcoholism as we know it—this utter inability to leave it alone, no matter how great the necessity or the wish." This is the way with addiction—it is a roller coaster, and Jeff couldn't get off.

Jeff made the decision to return to the halfway house. He made the phone call himself, just as he had when he was nineteen years old; now he was twenty-six. A bed would be available on January 15, and his verbal commitment held the spot. Although Jeff had good intentions to regain control of his life, he was obviously ambivalent about returning to treatment, because he kept talking about a change of date. Maybe he would stay in Maryland until January 20, he'd conjecture, or maybe he would leave for Florida on January 25; he shifted every day, sometimes two and three times a day. Finally, Tim and I put a halt to the indecision and made the final arrangements ourselves. Tim needed to plan his work schedule around driving Jeff to Florida in Jeff's car and then flying back to D.C., leaving the car, since Jeff would need it for work while he lived at the house. From Jeff's earlier time spent there, he understood clearly the rules: He would be required to work during the day while the house provided, for an affordable price, a secure and drug-free environment: half-time working and half-time supervised living. In addition, he would have to comply with strict rules about drug testing and daily attendance at AA meetings. The house further demanded that he arrive drug free and clean, because it is a sober living environment designed for people who are recovering; halfway houses are not medical facilities licensed to oversee detox.

Jeff's move to Florida brought a subsequent problem. Jeremy was advancing in his career, living and working in Fort Lauderdale, within fifteen minutes of Jeff's halfway house. When I explained the plans to Jeremy, his reaction was quick and revealed the deep wounds inflicted by addiction, wounds that were still raw. He was severely conflicted and he broke his silence by voicing the fear we all had: the possibility of Jeff's death. "I love Jeff, Momma, and I want to be there for him, but when you told me Jeff was coming to Florida, so close to my home and to my work, I felt sick to my stomach. I ached. Jeff's like Superman with kryptonite around his neck. What do I do if he dies here? He'll be so close to me. What do I do if he needs help, if he's hurt? What'll I do? I have a life, a job, responsibilities now. I can't get dragged into all this again, but he's my brother."

I should have anticipated Jeremy's response, but I hadn't. I was so intent and focused on supporting Jeff's return to recovery that my mind was single tracked. Of course, by this time, I understood clearly that drug addiction is a family disease, destroying a system from the inside out, and I couldn't and wouldn't sacrifice one child for another.

I needed to protect Jeremy from the chaos of Jeff's problems, while Jeff pursued sobriety once more. Sure, there were many halfway houses throughout the United States, but Jeff felt comfortable returning to the Boca House, and he had succeeded there before, at least for a time. Tim and I discussed the situation at length, and we decided that since Jeff was willing to enter a program in Florida, he should go, but Jeremy could not be a part of the equation, and he would need insulation from the drama. Our position was clear: Jeff would be in Florida, but he could not contact his brother.

When we explained this boundary to Jeff, he was both angry and hurt: "Yeah, I get it. Jeremy doesn't have to worry about me. I'll get clean without him. He won't see me until I'm healthy."

My sons loved each other deeply, yet they could not find a place of peace between them, not now at least, because that space was infected and clogged with the consequences of addiction. Too much had happened—there had been too much grief. I prayed that one day they would find their connection, their solidarity, but I knew they would have to do it on their own, when they were ready.

Jeff didn't sleep at my home the night before he left for Florida, calling me around 11:00 P.M. to say that he was with friends in D.C. and wanted to stay out, because he wouldn't be with them for a long time. I felt that familiar dread that signals a problem, knowing that this was not a good idea, but I could hear in his voice that he was not asking permission; he was calling to give me information. When he arrived early the next morning around 7:30 he was highly emotional, almost shaking, and he stood at the kitchen counter, lowered his head into his arms, sobbing, "I've fucked up my whole life. I'm twenty-six and going back to a halfway house. I've nothing to show for my life. I know this is the last time before I lose everyone. I have to do it this time." He ended by mumbling through tears, "Remember, Mom, I'm your miracle."

I answered calmly, "I'll always remember," but in the same instant my mind thought about this word, "miracle." If miracles happened, we surely needed one, although maybe we'd already been blessed: Jeff had had a blood test recently, and our family doctor called to report, "Jeff has no HIV, hepatitis C, or liver damage. He'll have to have the tests repeated in six months, but God must have something special planned for your son." I considered this one miracle, and I prayed and hoped for another.

Jeff and I packed the car with the belongings that he'd need in Florida, but before we left for Tim's apartment, Jeff gave me his stash of syringes, three bags of crystal meth, and a handful of Xanax tablets, in an effort to guarantee that he would be free of temptation during the trip south. Holding these drugs in my hands brought on a visceral response: My skin bristled, my stomach lurched, and I felt as though I were holding serpents, alive and twisting and saying in a devil voice, *We control your son, not you, not him. We own his soul and there's nothing anyone can do.* As we were driving to Tim's I threw the syringes, crystal meth, and Xanax out of the window of the car; I couldn't keep them in my possession. I did notice that he hadn't given me any heroin, and I wondered if he had kept that back, although I couldn't have done anything about it if he had. In Tim's apartment two hours later, before he and Tim were scheduled to leave, Jeff became agitated and anxious, almost uncontrollable, so much so that he demanded something to take to calm his nerves. He rummaged through his luggage but could find no drug. In his heightened emotional state I was afraid that we'd lose him, and that he'd walk out on us before he ever left for Florida, but he didn't. He got into the passenger side of his car, resigned to make this trip, and he left.

Jeff explained his reaction before leaving.

> Getting clean is terrifying. With nothing but failed attempts to reference, sobriety felt impossible. It's far easier to want to change your life than to actually do it. Following through with the process takes total courage, and I was scared to my core. Drugs were destroying me, but the destruction was familiar: the arrests, the

car crashes, the loss, the violence, the scattered and insincere relationships—all became very predictable. There's a certain comfort in knowing what to expect. Drugs were my comfort zone. Heroin's a lifestyle.

I spent the night before I left getting high with friends, people I thought I'd especially miss. Although most of my relationships were based on drugs, some real connections existed underneath the chaos. I have a lifetime of love for Washington and the corners of that city, years of history with certain people. That night I used crystal and GHB, and that morning, heroin and Xanax. By the time I left D.C. I was really high and had a hard time even getting home. The combination of drugs made me really sentimental, and I was on the verge of tears for hours. Everything in my life was changing and I was scared.

Is it any wonder that Jeff failed his urine test when he arrived in Florida at the halfway house? The first and most inflexible condition required for intake into the facility was that clients must be clean. Admission is contingent on the results of a panel test for opiates, amphetamines, benzodiazepines, and cocaine. While Jeff negotiated his entrance into the halfway house, Tim returned to Maryland. He had delivered Jeff and could do nothing more. Although I was furious with Jeff, I was also angry with myself, because I had suspected that his emotional outburst the morning he left for Florida was drug based, but I hadn't confronted him. Granted, there was nothing I could have done, and in retrospect I know why I said nothing: I didn't want to risk another battle that would end badly, with him refusing to leave for treatment. I also knew that he had friends in D.C. who were supporting his drug use, and I wanted him out of the area and in a recovery community—whatever it took.

Jeff was ineligible for admission, and he called me from the intake office, insisting that he hadn't used in days, and that his urine results, which were positive for opiates, benzos, and amphetamines, were only from traces of the last weeks' use, remnants of drugs still lodged in his tissue. Of course, the staff members at the house worked with people like Jeff routinely, and I assumed they knew the truth, but Jeff had made the decision to return to a facility, and this was the most important part. Jeff drank water for hours in an attempt to flush the drugs out of his system, and three times he still flunked. By the end of the day, however, he passed, and was admitted and assigned a bed. Much later Jeff told me he was so desperate to give a clean sample that when the staff member administering the test turned his head, Jeff, an expert at manipulation, reached down, scooped water from the toilet into the cup, and handed that in for examination.

January 15, 2005, 9:35 P.M.
Jeff's redemption is critical to our health as a family. His disease debilitates all of us. Every second of every minute of every hour of every day my heart breaks and tears against its walls. Jer was right. "Jeff's like Superman with kryptonite around his neck." No one can remove the kryptonite except Jeff, but will he? Dear Lord, please save my son.

I delayed my return to Italy so that I could visit both boys in Florida, to make certain for myself that all was well. Jeff had been at the halfway house for only a few days, and when he met me at the airport he greeted me with a thin, plastic smile, one that said, *I'm glad you're here, but I'm in a lot of discomfort. Let's not talk about it, though.* He was sweating and looked sick, and I knew this sick: He was detoxing from heroin. Jeff's faulty drug test got him in the door of the halfway house, but now he was a resident with a body full of drugs from D.C. I stayed in Florida for three days, during which time Jeff was given permission by the house to be with me from 9:00 A.M. until 6:00 P.M., when he had to return to the property to attend AA and group meetings. Jeremy refused to see his brother, so I arranged to spend the days with Jeff and the evenings with Jeremy.

During my time in Florida, my heart was conflicted by this life split between my sons. I understood Jeremy's fears and supported him. He was resolute and determined, and he'd told me, even before I came, "I won't see Jeff until he's my brother again. I love him too much, and seeing him like this breaks my heart. He needs to know that he'll lose me if he doesn't get clean. I have to do this." In many respects I thought Jeremy's decision was the right one, but I couldn't do it. How does a mother refuse to see her son? I didn't know.

Jeff was trying to recover, trying to find his health and sobriety, and I was often distressed, wondering how much time he had left before he lost himself permanently. One day, while we were walking on the beach, he turned abruptly and told me he was returning to my hotel room. Later, when I checked on him, I found him curled into a fetal position, lying on the bed under a heap of blankets that were tucked high under his chin. Eyes closed, he shivered. He was suffering from the effects of detoxing; his body swung unpredictably between chills and sweats, and his limbs ached. We spent all of our time in the room or in the hotel complex, because he was irritable and miserable, and I could do nothing but watch and pray that he'd reach the other side. He refused to go to a detox center, because the halfway house thought he was clean. He was determined to ride this out on his own (hadn't we tried this before?). I prayed he'd have the resolve to stay the course.

My evenings with Jeremy were delightful, and his life was full. He loved his job, his colleagues, and he was happy. He drove me around Fort Lauderdale, pointing out all the highlights, and we enjoyed dinners at his favorite restaurants, visited both the house where he was living and the nightclubs that he managed, and he introduced me to his friends. He seemed to have all the earmarks of an entrepreneur, and he had already started a file of business plans for projects he hoped to expedite in the future. The only part of Jeremy's life that was draining for him was his relationship with Jeff. As usual, he wouldn't talk about it, but I could see how this weighed on him in his deliberate efforts not to discuss his brother or the topic of addiction.

The night before I left Florida I walked Jeff to the doorway of my hotel room. As he stood on one side of the threshold and I stood on the other, my mind jumped back to 1999, when we stood inside the entrance at the airport, the previous time he had left for Florida and the halfway house. Now, six years later, a door was about to separate us again. We said our good-byes, and then his eyes searched mine in an attempt to hold on, to feel connected, to know he would not be abandoned. His face was thin and almost translucent, and his voice whispered in quiet pleading, "Momma, don't quit believing. Please, don't quit believing in me."

"I won't, Jeff," I answered lovingly. "I won't ever quit believing."

With this I reached up to his sweaty brow and made the sign of the cross three times on his forehead. I hoped that he could feel the love and prayers that this touch represented, from three generations of women—from Nonna to my mother to me. He nodded his head up and down, as if in agreement with his own private thought, sighed heavily, turned, and walked away, head lowered, and he never looked back.

The next morning, as Jeremy drove me to the airport for my return flight to Pittsburgh to visit my mother, I realized that the landscape of Jeff's support was changing: Jeremy had cut him off; Tim was in Maryland; and I was leaving to return to Italy. As predicted in the *Big Book* of AA, each relapse was becoming more devastating. The roller coaster of his addiction was picking up speed.

Seven days after I left Florida, just ten days after he was admitted to the halfway house, Jeff tested positive for opiates and was thrown out. The director called Tim and said that Jeff was not serious about the program or about his recovery and was back on heroin. Later that day Jeff tried to call me, but this time I refused to talk with him; this time I had had enough. Jeff called Tim and asked his father to have me call him, but I told Tim to relay a message: "Jeff, I love you more than you'll ever know. I'll continue to believe that one day my son will return whole, but until that time do not call me or get in touch with me." Jeff told Tim that he had no money, needed to detox, and was sleeping on the beach and in the back of his car.

With a sense of foreboding and uncertainty, I followed through on my plans to return to Florence, but I did not follow through on my plans to stop communicating with Jeff. On February 1, the night before I was to leave Pittsburgh and my mother's home for Italy, I received a text message:

Call me. I've been jumped in Miami and need medical insurance info. Love u.

I called the number from which the text message had been sent, a number I'd never seen before. How could I not call when his health was at stake and he needed medical attention?

He told me that he had been jumped in Opalocka, a neighborhood in North Miami, and that he needed to get to the hospital. The muggers, he recounted angrily, stole his cell phone and wallet with his driver's license, passport, and health insurance information. He and a friend had driven to Miami just for the fun of it; they had nothing else to do, he said. There they were supposedly randomly accosted in a bad neighborhood, thrown to the ground, and kicked. The assailants stole the clothes in the back of his car, but they fled the scene prematurely when they heard police sirens. Jeff had then driven himself to another friend's house, a guy who worked at Boca House, and he would take Jeff to the emergency room and then let Jeff live with him at his apartment until he had detoxed fully, cleaned up, and secured space at another halfway house.

After I told him that I didn't have his insurance information with me in Pittsburgh, I asked myself what I was supposed to do with this story, this big and dangerous story. I decided that I was not in this with him, and that he was lying about being jumped, reasoning that this was a drug deal gone bad. It was now time for him to deal with consequences without his mother's help. Jeff always wanted sobriety on his terms, his way: He wanted to feel no pain during detox, he wanted treatment to be an easy process, and he wanted help when his choices led him into disaster. All this had to stop. I wrote in my journal on February 2, 2005, "It's time for Jeff to take matters into his own hands, and I need to let go. This is the hardest thing I've ever done, letting go of my son. But I have little choice, he must set himself free. HE must do it."

I knew I had to quit enabling him, saving him, bailing him out time and time again. I had to accept that my son was an addict and all that meant. Addiction is a progressive, repetitive illness, and with each occurrence he fell deeper into trouble, made a more profound descent. This is the nature of addiction, and I understood this, but getting this knowledge into my heart was like pounding on steel. I didn't know how to disengage my emotions, my soul. I wanted to protect him, but I needed to learn to love him from a distance and allow him to feel the pain his actions had created.

Before I left Pittsburgh, I told my mother, "I'm afraid we're losing Jeff, Mom."

She responded, "Honey, we lost Jeff a long time ago."

I arrived in Italy on February 3, determined to grow stronger, to find some sense of peace, and to learn to trust my inner counsel. With every breath I thought about Jeff, but I knew it was time for me to get out of his way. My Jeff wasn't my Jeff anymore, and when I talked with him I talked to the drugs, through the drugs, with the drugs. It was now time for him to find his own way home to his family, and to himself. It didn't matter what I wanted, and my wishing things to be different wouldn't make it so. Jeff had bounced from detox centers to halfway houses to county jails, and the three haunting guarantees of

active addiction continued to ring true: jails, institutions, or death.
There didn't seem much left for my son and, at this point, Jeff's patterns of behavior were lethal. Death was not uncommon within his
circle of friends. These kids used hard drugs in hard ways, and for
many of them, including my son, it had become a lifestyle. Jeff
silently identified himself as a drug user, a junkie, and a heroin addict,
and he seemed filled with both boldness and a profound sense of
guilt, existing in a space of constant emotional conflict. He saw the
destruction caused by his addiction, felt the isolation from family and
friends, yet he continued on his path of self-abuse, killing himself
little by little. My son existed in this duality of needing drugs and
feeling shame about using them. My chameleon son: When he was at
home with Jeremy and me he wanted to be one thing, but when he
was on the streets he was another. I wondered where he would ultimately stand.

February 6, 2005, 9:25 P.M. Florence
Jeff e-mailed me and asked me to call him. I e-mailed him back, "I
won't call. I'll call you when you are my son again. It's up to you."
His response, "That's fine. I just wanted to ask a quick question . . .
it can wait though."
My son—what will become of him? I have pictures in my
apartment of him in better days, in good days, in happy days.
How can I feel complete when I am not—when I am without
one son, it's like missing a piece of my heart. I can do nothing but
wait for him to return.

Waiting for Jeff to return home to his true self sounded like
something I could do, but it was almost impossible. I could hear the
cries of my mother's heart as it battled against my woman's brain,
each struggling to decide what needed to be done. Even in the dark,
as I tried to find solace in sleep, my body twisted one way and the
other. I could find no peace.

Tim was in Maryland, and he continued to talk with Jeff after the mugging in North Miami (if that's what it was), and he reported that Jeff sounded positive and upbeat. Jeff had been living for ten days with the young man from the halfway house who was helping him detox so that he might enter another facility. On several occasions Tim talked with both Jeff and his friend, and he felt confident that Jeff sounded committed to staying clean.

On February 12, 2005, Jeff passed his urine test and was readmitted to the Boca House. On Valentine's Day, two days later, my mind went back to six years ago, and I remembered our conversation around Valentine's Day 1999.

"Last year I sent you a dozen red roses, Momma."

"Yes, Jeff, you did."

"I don't have money to send you roses this year, so I thought I'd send you twelve Valentine cards."

"That would be nice."

"I don't have money for stamps. Will you send me money for stamps?"

"No, Jeff, I won't."

"I didn't think so."

I wondered if and when the addiction would be defeated, but for now Jeff was safe in the halfway house, for the third time. Jeff started applying for jobs, and was even considering joining the Navy reserves. Maybe this, the third time, would be the turning point for Jeff.

However, two weeks later Jeff called Tim to confess that he had started using again in the halfway house, and was in another downward spiral. The director of the house called Tim and explained clearly and without a shadow of a doubt that Jeff had been using heroin since being readmitted, needed inpatient treatment, and was not even close to being well. They could not do anything more, and he recommended that Jeff enter a sixty-day combined detox and rehab program at a nearby state-run facility called the Drug Abuse Foundation (DAF). They would make immediate arrangements, and even provide transportation, but Jeff would have to agree to a full lockdown for sixty days. Jeff acknowledged that he needed and wanted help. He agreed to go.

Five days at the Drug Abuse Foundation, five days of detox, five days of supervision, and Jeff sprung himself, left, walked out, and was on the streets again. He called Tim and said that the facility was a sham, no good, and the kids were not serious about recovery and were using there. He explained that he needed to leave for his own safety and would go to another center. Within hours of Jeff's release the director of the halfway house called Tim again with the truth: Jeff and another boy were caught shooting heroin in the bathroom of the detox center. Jeff had been thrown out of yet another institution.

In five weeks, from the end of January when Jeff was admitted to the Boca House until early March, the roller coaster of his addiction continued to twist and turn, jolting us forward and then throwing us back: He was dismissed twice from the halfway house, beaten up, and expelled from a state-subsidized detox center. Things had gone from bad to worse, and I feared where it would stop.

Two days later I received an e-mail message sent from Jeff's cell phone.

Call me please—need your thoughts around some decisions. Please call me, Mom. In exactly twenty minutes if you can—that way I'll know it's you. xo, me

I called. I'm not sure why; I just did.

March 6, 2005, 9:05 P.M. Florence
I talked with Jeff, and he said that he's angry, ashamed, and can't show himself anywhere; he's still carrying a habit, is afraid of being arrested, promised to stay twenty-eight days at another recovery facility called The Watershed, has no place to live, has

pawned everything except his watch, has no money for food (but he is still buying drugs!), and needs to get his life together.

He says one thing, does another—how to make sense of it all? How many phone calls, how many sleepless nights, how many people do you tell before you hate hearing your own words from your own mouth? How many times do hearts break and tears run before you suffocate on your own grief? I'm so tired of it all. I'm so tired of thinking about it. I'm ready for life to stay calm for a little while—if even for a moment. When can a parent really say, "I've done all I can do"? I want to see the line on which the words are written, "OK, you've crossed this line. Now, Lib, you're finished."

I called Tim, and after much discussion we agreed that if Jeff earnestly wanted help and would commit to staying for the full twenty-eight days in a residential program, then we would support this effort.

The next day I received a three-sentence e-mail from Tim: "Jeff checked into The Watershed about 10:30 P.M. last night. They called me to confirm his arrival. Let's pray for the best."

Jeff did stay at The Watershed for the entire twenty-eight days. There he detoxed completely and was becoming Jeff once more, slowly. Toward the end of his stay he worked with his counselor to determine his next step. Everyone agreed, especially Jeff, that he was not ready to be on his own, and that he needed to transfer to a long-term recovery facility.

Jeff and I talked on the phone, and he sounded strong, and the lilt in his voice was returning. He explained that he and his counselor from The Watershed had decided that his next choice should be Burning Tree Recovery Ranch in Texas, an extended-care facility specializing in chronic relapse. I did Internet research about this program and it seemed rigorous, so I supported this decision. In truth, I was simply grateful that he had agreed to long-term care, and that he was willing to focus on his habitual relapses.

Jeff left The Watershed on April 5, my nonna's birthday (I prayed that this was a good sign), and he celebrated twenty-eight days of sobriety. He explained to me that instead of leaving directly from The Watershed and flying to Texas, he needed one day to pack his clothes and to find a safe place to leave his car for at least three to nine months. He would leave on the second day after his discharge from The Watershed. This made sense.

Jeff entered the Burning Tree ranch on April 7, two days after leaving The Watershed and Florida, as he had planned. Burning Tree sent both Tim and me information packets, including program goals, orientation materials, daily schedules, and a family program overview. Also included was an assignment for us to write an intervention letter to Jeff, explaining that if he walked out against treatment advice we would not be in the wings to offer help and support.

Jeff's counselor contacted both Tim and me once a week to give us an update on Jeff's progress. During our first conversation, he wanted us to know that on entry Jeff had tested positive for opiates, and when they confronted him with the results of his failed test, he admitted having used twice in the time between facilities. My son had been clean for twenty-eight days, and still he used again as soon as he was discharged. This news was distressing enough, but during the counselor's second call he raised a concern about a possible liaison between Jeff and a young woman, a recovering alcoholic who also had been a client at The Watershed. They had both applied to Burning Tree, he said, because they had formed a strong interest in each other, and although she had not been accepted into their facility and was now in a recovery center in California, Jeff's counselor saw this connection as a continuing and potentially dangerous situation. In fact, Jeff had used his "one phone call a week" privilege to call and talk with her.

So now I had received two phone calls from the counselor, each yielding distressing and perilous news: Not only had Jeff used heroin after getting clean and preparing to enter long-term care, but a girl was now in the picture.

As Tim and I were drafting the intervention letter, Tim received, on April 25, 2005, a text message from Jeff's cell phone.

I've left Brng Tree & am on way back to Florida. Going to enroll in a halfway house there & continue this journey. Call ltr.

Jeff had walked out of another institution. This was unbelievable, yet totally believable. I felt as though I had been punched simultaneously on both sides of my face; one jolt for believing that Jeff would stay in treatment and one jab for being so stupid. Jeff had a list of reasons why he had left, but I could hear no more. I quit listening.

> May 2, 2005, 12:09 P.M. Florence
> My God, what will happen to my son? What will be next—prison? Death?
>
> What am I supposed to do? All the experts tell me that it's not all my fault, but look at the man that Jeff has become. I talked always to my students at Calverton about making a difference in life, contributing to life, and they've told me on many occasions that I've been a role model for them. Then I look at my own son. Was I not there when he needed me, or maybe I didn't step out of the way when I should have? This grief is mine—it's the grief, the despair that only a mother, a parent, can feel.
>
> The experts tell me that when he reaches bottom he'll take control of his life. And a mother is supposed to watch her son die?

Silence. Jeff became silent; he quit calling both Tim and me. We didn't know where he was, what he was doing, or how he was. He was on my mind constantly, and I prayed that he was taking his recovery into his own hands, although I feared, more realistically, that he was using drugs and lost somewhere.

Three weeks later, on May 26, the silence was broken; Jeff's addiction reached across the ocean, and the freedom that I longed for was tested. I received another text message from Jeff:

all court charges are dropped pending completion at a halfway house . . . very grateful. j.

I had no idea what this message meant, what the court charges were all about, or even where Jeff was, so I called him. He sounded good. He told me that he was sober again; had recently gotten out of DAF, the government-run detox center; and had reported to court to address a prior arrest. His story went like this:

It was a minor arrest, really. A friend and I were at a gas station across the street from the Boca House. We were talking with some people we knew from our time there. The night manager recognized us, knew we'd both been kicked out for using, and thought we looked suspicious. He called the police and told them we were selling drugs to the residents. The cops came and asked us to leave, said we couldn't hang out at the gas station, and we had to go. We left, but they followed us, and after a few blocks pulled us over and searched my car. Syringes and spoons were under the driver's seat, and we were arrested for paraphernalia.

Now it made sense. His arrests always seemed to follow this shape: never any violence, but always drugs and reckless behavior. The judge ordered him to complete four months at another halfway house, to be tested regularly to make certain that he stayed sober, and to report back to the court on September 29. If he completed his 120 days while remaining clean, all charges would be expunged. Jeff applied to a house called Integrity Way, and the director accepted him.

May 29, 2005, noon. Florence
Jeff called—what a disaster. He says the same thing each time,
"I'm going to get it this time, Momma. I won't be thirty and like

this. You'll see. I know what I need to do." I'm always stunned that this pattern occurs again and again. My son. Do I think he'll get it? In my heart of hearts, I think yes. Why? Because his root system is firm in love, family, and God, but I don't know if he has the time before he destroys himself.

This time Jeff stayed clean. His sobriety began on May 23, when he entered detox at the Drug Abuse Foundation again. Sure, he was living in another institution, but I chronicled his clean dates in my journal as I had done so many times before, somehow believing that if I wrote down the dates, if they were indelible and in ink, maybe, just maybe, they would hold. Although I knew well that words like "forever" and "always" were not part of the vocabulary of addiction, I marked the dates anyhow, just as a mother might mark the days from the birth of her child. I wanted it to last.

> May 30, 2005. Jeff has 7 days clean.
> June 6, 2005. Jeff—14 days clean.
> June 14, 2005. Jeff is 3 weeks sober.
> June 19, 2005. Jeff is 30 days sober; he earns a 30-day chip at
> AA today!

Along with these notations, I received e-mail messages from Jeff, little messages that gave me hope, and I hung on to each word as if it were a promise.

> June 5, 2005. Today's a good day!
> June 6, 2005. Got a new sponsor today. He has 6 years and
> works an awesome program.

The weekend of June 11, Tim flew to Florida to visit the boys. Upon Tim's return to D.C. he called me, and his voice was filled with both joy and relief, explaining that our sons were terrific and they exuded energy and spirit. Jeremy was thriving, producing concerts for globally recognized entertainers and developing into a strong businessman. Tim said that Jeff was healthy and full in the face, and his hair was cut short; he had introduced his father to the residents of his new halfway house. Jeff also told Tim about the girl in California. "Eva is a recovering alcoholic," Tim narrated, "and Jeff says she is a great person with a kind heart and close to God. Jeff seems smitten with her." Tim summarized his visit in an e-mail.

> Suffice it to say that you would be proud of our sons. I am. While we've had much despair and sorrow with Jeff's tragic state of affairs, and we question his ability and strength to ever turn it around, there's still something in him that glows and tells me he wants to do it and can do it. As you well know, his smile is infectious, and he has such polish, charm, and charisma. I know that we will see the flight of the Phoenix.

The flight of the Phoenix. I cherished those words and held them close, as if our believing could make it true. Jeff summarized it also.

> I had just ended a pretty ugly run that left me homeless, sick, and in jail. Like someone knocked to the ground by heavy punches, those relapses grounded me. I've always responded to consequences. I think most addicts do. When the judge ordered me to a halfway house, I decided to comply. I was exhausted and glad to have a place to call home. For months before this I had been living out of my car with a friend I knew from treatment. We were both into heroin and spent our days organizing drug deals and trying to stay high.
>
> Once I resigned myself to completing the court order, I started going to AA meetings. I worked steps with a sponsor and began hanging out with sober guys, many of whom I'm still tight with today. I was finally clean and committed to giving sobriety a shot.

Meanwhile Jeff's e-mail messages continued:

June 16, 2005. Today I'm good for myself and those who love me.
June 17, 2005. I'm free in mind and body today.
June 19, 2005. 30 days, Mom!

On July 27 I left Italy to return to the States. Jeff, who had traveled to Maryland for the weekend, and Tim planned to be at the airport to greet me, and I knew that seeing Jeff healthy would make my homecoming complete.

Upon arrival at Washington's Dulles airport, I collected my luggage and exited customs, wheeling my bags behind me. The international arrival corridor was jammed with people waiting for family and friends, drivers standing with name cards waiting for their passengers, and porters situated strategically to help travelers with their belongings. I couldn't see Jeff or Tim. I scanned the crowds, searching for my son, my eyes glued to every passing face, hoping to find the one that was mine. I jostled through the crowds and noticed a tall young man who had his back to me; he was slim but muscular, dressed in a white polo shirt with short sleeves and jeans, and he was leaning, legs crossed, left elbow bent, and resting against a metal column, talking to someone. I leaned my head a bit to the right to get a clearer view; Tim saw me first, and the realization hit me like a hammer that this young body was Jeff's. I paused, stared, and as Jeff followed Tim's gaze, he whipped around quickly, fluidly. "Momma," he yelped. "You're here. Welcome home." He had that Jeff skip, that kind of leap he had had as a child, the lightness of step, a kind of physical giggle, that told me in one sweeping movement that he was well. His eyes and face radiated a happiness that I hadn't seen in years. All I could do was hug him, hold him close, never saying a word. What was there to say? My son was alive, whole, and with me. This had been my prayer, and my prayer had been answered in the flesh. Jeff finally pulled away from me, stunned with my tears, and whispered, "Don't cry, Mom. I'm OK. Don't cry." I got that part; I understood, but my heart was full with my son's whole being, the all of it. I wasn't sure what would become of him in the future; I didn't even know what tomorrow might bring, but for today, for this moment, all I could do was look at him, touch his face, and quietly thank God.

Jeff and I spent three days together, doing all kinds of things, especially replacing his lost driver's license and passport. We visited old acquaintances, and we stayed with my dearest friend and her husband, the man who had talked with Jeff the night of the gala but who hadn't recognized him. When he saw Jeff looking bright and capable again, his eyes filled with tears, and he hugged Jeff in a kind of fatherly, rough embrace, patting his back and welcoming him into their home. We all wanted to celebrate his newly achieved sobriety.

During this visit Jeff gave me a mix CD of songs he selected for my homecoming, ones that were important to him. Music has always been a great passion in his life and giving music was his way of showing his softness and his love; it was the way he said things. The first song was particularly moving, and I played it so many times that it's now cut deep in my memory. The band is Sparklehorse and the song is "Gold Day."

> *Good morning my child*
> *stay with me awhile*
> *you not got anyplace to be*
> *won't you sit a spell with me . . .*
> *May all your days be gold my child.*

Even yet, each time I travel, whether to the United States or back to Italy, I carry the CD with me, a reminder of Jeff and his good days, his days of gold.

After our three days together, Jeff returned to Florida and to the halfway house. During my seven weeks at home I scheduled a flight to southern California, where Jeff would meet me and introduce me to Eva, whom he had met at The Watershed. They were still very close, and he said that it was important to him that I know her. Jeff was already in California when I arrived, and I met Eva immediately at the airport. She was a cute blonde with gentle eyes, and she looked dreamily at Jeff. She was sober, she shared, and was working in a rehab center in Laguna Beach. At lunches and dinners she sat close to Jeff, and often whispered things to him that I couldn't hear. She hung on to his arm while we walked together, and held his hand at every opportunity, like glue. In my mind it was clear: She was needy, he was needy, and in their neediness they were bonded, all of which spelled trouble. I knew perfectly well that Jeff was not ready for a relationship, especially an intense one, but I also knew that no matter what I thought, in matters of the heart my opinion would not count to any great extent. It was not until the morning of my departure, when Jeff and I were having breakfast together, that I expressed my concerns. His response was calm and noncommittal: "I hear you, Momma. I hear you."

After two more days in California, Jeff returned to Florida and the halfway house, and the following day I traveled to Fort Lauderdale, where both Jeff and Jeremy met me at the airport. They were talking now that Jeff was sober, but Jeremy was still cautious. Even though we did things together during my four days there, the boys were different. They didn't talk like they used to, or laugh or trip each other when they walked, or roll their eyes when they saw a pretty girl stroll past, but they were brothers, and even in their silence, in their separate lives and periods of distress, their connection was almost palpable and could not be denied. Toward the end of my visit Jeremy told me that he needed more professional clothes for work. Jeff took the lead and organized a shopping expedition, much like a maestro directs the orchestra. With his eyes instead of a baton, he had sales clerks scurrying to find his little brother just the right textured pants, the perfectly colored shirt, the coolest jacket. Jeff never held back an ounce of energy as he made certain that everything was just right for Jeremy. I couldn't help but think that Jeff did it as an unspoken amends: *I'm sorry, Jer, for all I've put you through. You're important to me, you're my little bro. Please forgive me.* Late that night Jeremy called and said softly, "You and Jeff took care of me today. The Team is back. Thank you." I tucked his words into my heart, although I wondered silently if the Team was back for good.

I ended my time in the States in happiness. Jeff was off all medications and healing, and Jeremy was leading a staff of more than sixty people: My sons were well. I knew I had no control over what Jeff would do, but for today he was making good choices. I left the States on Wednesday, September 21, when Jeff was almost four months sober.

One day I leave, and the very next day it starts again:

I was in D.C., spending the weekend at Dad's apartment. It was Friday afternoon and I was due back in Florida on Sunday. I was alone in Chinatown with time to kill. Standing on familiar city blocks and surrounded by memories of drugs, I instantly wanted to get high. I told myself that I was clean, but the impulse snowballed, and four months of sobriety buckled under the weight of what was now an obsession. I realized that I wasn't strong enough on my own, especially not in Washington.

Within seconds, I was on the metro, heading east. I got off at Benning Road, and walked over to Lincoln Heights. I bought five bags of heroin from a local kid I recognized, but waited until I got back to Dad's house to use. I was stunned that I acted so quickly and afraid of my sudden decision. Once I locked on the idea, though, getting high was all I could think about.

I fixed in Dad's bathroom, but it was too much. I could hardly stand up. I stumbled into the living room leaving syringes, a spoon, and dime bags on top of the toilet. I nodded off on his couch for what seemed like hours. The whole time Dad was there, at home. When I woke up, he was furious.

For Saturday and Sunday, Jeff stayed in the apartment with Tim. Disgusted and fed up with the continuing chaos of Jeff's addiction, Tim put Jeff on a flight back to Florida on Monday, Tim's birthday. Tim was done, finished.

On September 26, I received an e-mail message via Jeff's cell phone.

I refuse to let this sink me. I'll dig in & recalibrate. Trust & believe in me. Meeting my sponsor for dinner. I'll make it.

On Tuesday, September 27, I talked with Jeff from Italy. In two days he was scheduled to report to a Palm Beach county courthouse to give the judge his completion paperwork from the halfway house, to prove that he had completed the court-ordered sobriety program of 120 days in recovery. He swore that he had used drugs only that one time in Tim's apartment, met with his sponsor, and also admitted his transgression at an AA meeting. He would get it right, he assured me, and he explained that after settling the legal situation in West Palm Beach he intended to get out of Florida, leaving all his drug connections behind, and to move to California to be with Eva. There, he was certain, he could start a new life.

On September 28, 2005, the roller coaster of Jeff's addiction came to a jolting stop. Tim called me in Italy because Jeff couldn't make an international phone call from jail.

Chapter 12

Stagli Vicino, Stay Close to Him

Jeff had been arrested late the prior night: There was a felony charge for heroin possession and a misdemeanor charge for the drug paraphernalia found in the car. My son was in Miami-Dade County jail.

Jeff had been allowed one direct call from central booking; he'd telephoned Tim. After an abrupt conversation, Tim called me in Italy and he sounded both furious and incredulous. "He wants me to post bond." Tim paused as if he was trying to wrap his head around this ludicrous idea. "I'm done; I told him that he got himself into this mess, he can get himself out." Tim relayed the facts as he knew them from Jeff about what had happened: Supposedly Jeff was in a neighborhood called the Triangle, in Opalocka, with a friend, and the police surrounded their car, searched the boys, found a small bag of heroin in his friend's wallet, and arrested both of them. The details were yet to be sorted out; however, Jeff swore to Tim that he had no drugs on him at the time of the arrest. What to believe? What was true?

Our family was under assault once again, and we each reacted in our own and different ways. Tim wanted Jeff to sit in jail and told me, "He needs to feel what it's like to be cut off from family and not to be rescued continually from his bad decisions. He needs to see the bars day and night and feel the lack of freedom. He needs to understand where his choices have finally left him, the gravity of his situation, and the uncertainty of his future." Jeremy, in Florida near to Jeff, was tormented. "This is such bullshit. I want to get him out, but I don't know what to do with him when he's out." And me? I started to write this book. Just as I had immersed myself in my work at school, I immersed myself in the writing of this story. I needed to do something to help me cope with the constant and un-relenting grief; I didn't know what else to do.

The following days collided into one another while Jeff was transferred to Turner Gilford Knight, one of Miami's three county facilities, and processed into the prisoner population. I needed advice and help, so I called two young men, both recovering addicts, since they could speak from a personal point of view, from addiction. First I telephoned a friend of Jeff's who was about the same age, a kid with whom Jeff had spent a lot of time in Florida, and he warned me severely, "Your son's gonna die if you keep enabling him. I know you don't want to hear this, you're his mother, but he's going to die. You need to stop. He needs to get serious about sobriety." Next I called an old friend who had spent five years in prison for drug use and distribution and was now clean and sober, and his response was similar: "I agree that you should do nothing, but yes and no. Yes, you're enabling him, but you're his mother and you don't want your son in jail. Pray."

I joined Tim in the decision to leave Jeff in jail. At least, I rea-soned, while he was there he was safe from drugs, although I was not convinced he was physically safe. I was drowning in all my imagined fears for my son.

October 1, 2005, 11:00 A.M. Florence
I want to write this book, but maybe it is just a book of a
mother's angst and tears, and crazy lives. The disease of
addiction, a family disease, a disease that corrodes all of life,
suffocates all its members, eliminating the ability to even see the
sun. Blue skies become gray, and children's laughter becomes
impossible to hear. Yes, one foot in front of the other, but each
step becomes heavier and heavier. Like wearing a heavy coat that
you can't take off. Like going underwater for the last time
and knowing that you will stay under, gasping for air, struggling,
finding no peace. An eternal struggle. I want to quit writing,
but I don't know what else to do with my mind, my heart. My
firstborn son, what will become of him? When will he learn? Will
he ever learn?

On October 6 Jeff had been in jail for more than a week, and my
mind was a maelstrom. I tried to reach him, but it was not permitted
for Jeff to receive incoming calls. He was only allowed to make collect
calls to State-side landline phone numbers, so he called Tim, pleading
for him and me to post bond, reiterating that he had no heroin on him
at the time of arrest (which turned out to be true). From what I understood, Jeff's felony charge was for heroin possession, and I needed to
understand the full impact of what would happen if he were con-
victed. This was uncharted territory for Tim and me. As far as I knew,
Jeff's previous charges had always been misdemeanors, and I had only
heard the word "felony" used for high crimes, such as kidnapping, rape,
murder, extortion, or burglary. I was worried and Tim was concerned.
We wanted to make sure that the charges against Jeff were true, so
during that time I researched criminal attorneys through the American Bar Association in the Miami region, contacted them by e-mail
and phone, and at last identified an experienced lawyer who I thought
could check things out, make sure that Jeff was OK, and determine if
the charges, especially the felony charge, were legal and binding. Tim
and I both talked with him, and I followed up with an e-mail.

We want to do what is best for our son; however, what that means is difficult to state clearly at this point. If love were the answer, there would be no problem, but with addiction, love is never enough. I trust that you will advise us.

Jeff had been in jail for almost two weeks before the attorney could visit him, on October 9. Following their conversation the lawyer wrote an e-mail to Tim and me.

Jeff has enough money in the property room to pay the $600 (10%) premium. He told me that if he bonds out, he would reside at Integrity Way. Please advise if you believe it is OK for me to arrange bail for him. If not, he'll remain in custody, at a minimum, until the 18th.

In the end, Jeff posted his own bond arranged by his attorney, and on October 12, 2005, at 3:30 P.M., Jeff returned to Integrity Way, the halfway house. When we finally talked, he was angry with me. He felt abandoned. He couldn't understand why I hadn't responded sooner. He shouted, "Why would you leave me there? How could you leave me there?" It was a choice, it was my choice. I tried to tell him, "You've been jumped, beaten, hospitalized, institutionalized, arrested, and homeless. What's it going to take for you to stop your drug use? Maybe this is it. I don't know."

Jeff said nothing. After a long pause I told him not to call again until he had a job, a paycheck, and his life together. I didn't hear from him for the next two weeks.

Jeff's arraignment, the attorney explained, was scheduled for October 27, when his case would be brought before a judge and the arresting officers would be present. Within two days of hearing this news, Hurricane Wilma hit the west coast of Florida. Jeff and Jeremy and millions of Floridians were without electricity or running water, and South Florida was blacked out, under curfew, and declared a disaster area. Jeff had recently started a part-time job in a clothing store, Tim told me, and had an interview scheduled for a full-time position, but now he couldn't get to either one.

On October 25, two days before Jeff's scheduled hearing, I received an e-mail from Tim.

> The attorney called. The State has decided to no-action the case and will not proceed with filing of charges. Therefore, at the arraignment, the case will be dismissed. The attorney will let us know the outcome as soon as he knows, and he will then proceed with what he needs to do in West Palm.

Although Jeff was now clear of legal problems in Miami-Dade County, the West Palm Beach court appearance was still pending, because he had been in jail during the September 29 hearing that was to complete the earlier misdemeanor charge. A bench warrant had been issued, and the case would remain open until Jeff appeared in court with his lawyer, who recommended that Jeff attend to this as soon as possible.

During the next ten days, I thought I heard nothing from Jeff because I had told him not to call me until he had earned a paycheck. On November 6 Jeff telephoned me in Italy. "Mom, I wanted to let you know that I've left Florida."

"Where are you, Jeff?"

"California."

Jeff was in California, and it was predictable that his life of chaos would continue unless he chose to change. But if events got worse, this time I knew what I would do. My mind was set—I would rein in my emotions and set a bit in my heart. I had heard clearly what the young men, the recovering addicts, had told me about my son's future unless he got serious about his own recovery.

On November 9, 2005, three days after Jeff had called me to tell me he was in California, I received a text message.

Things are becoming complicated out here.

Even now, as I write, I remember feeling caught in the gap between aching to believe that Jeff could get his life together after his time in jail and dreading what seemed to be the more obvious conclusion: He would lose himself even more deeply into his addiction. The fact that I loved my son was beyond question, but feelings of anger at being used were also taking a strong hold in me.

On November 12, at 1:45 in the morning, Jeff telephoned. "Momma," he said, "I'm sorry I woke you." He had been in California for only seven days and his voice sounded wound like a top as he continued, "I'm in this beautiful apartment on the Pacific, but I can't sleep. I'm mad anxious. I keep fighting with my girlfriend. Coming here might have been a bad idea. All my support is on the East Coast. I've gotta get out of here." He swore that he was drug free and even had a sponsor, "a good guy, a little strict."

I wondered if he thought that I really believed this comment about his sponsor, but I continued by asking him if he was ill. No, he was feeling OK and, in fact, he told me, he didn't have HIV or hepatitis C. This was new information to me, so he explained that he had been required to have a blood test in jail and that they had to take blood from his neck because they couldn't find suitable veins in his arms. He had destroyed much of his superficial venous system.

Our conversation continued, and it became clear to me that he was calling for one reason: He wanted to get out of California, and to do that he needed money. I did not send any.

November 12, 2005, 2:15 A.M.
My relationship with my son has become an escape and a continuing bank account. I need to acknowledge, to admit that Jeff is

gone. Maybe I have only one son, not two. Maybe Jeff, my first-born, is lost, dead to me. This is the first time I've ever written these words. God help me.

Jeff called sporadically, and I never knew what to expect. One day he'd sound good and make sense, saying that he was looking for a job, attending AA meetings, and working with his attorney to resolve his outstanding legal issue in Florida. In our next conversation he'd sound tight, almost frantic, with his words running together like one continuous gulp. At other times he'd speak slowly, tongue thick and thoughts disconnected. However, one theme was clear: He was unhappy living in Laguna Beach with the girl he had met in treatment, and he wanted out—out to the East Coast or out to Italy. I wouldn't send him the money necessary to do either. This time, he would have to find his own way out of his problems. I responded to Jeff's phone call with an e-mail message, November 12, 2005, 9:14 P.M.:

Jeff, you've gotta find your strength. The answer is not in money; it's in you. Other people, including me, cannot keep bailing you out. You need to bail yourself out. You need to get strong. If you need money to help your situation, get a job, work, earn money, and then do what you need to do. Look at yourself in the mirror and say "Enough—the time is NOW." I love you, but love is not the color of money.

What had happened in such a short time, in a little less than a week?

The move to Laguna was a bad decision, but I could only blame myself. I met Eva in treatment and we thought we were right for each other. Relationships in rehab are common and we were both looking for someone to fill the spaces drugs had left. Throughout the spring and summer we stayed in touch, visited each other and

talked often on the phone. Per the court's request, I was in another
halfway house in Florida and Eva had moved back to California.
When I got out of jail that fall, she was there for me and made
Orange County sound ideal.

By the time I arrived in Laguna, Eva had been drinking for
weeks and I was already back into heroin. Laguna's a small community and the drug scene is made up mostly of relapsing addicts
who had either left or been thrown out of local rehab programs.
We hung out with people who partied all the time and, within a
few days of looking, we found syringes and started shooting crystal. In California, crystal's everywhere, and by this time I injected
any drug that could be cooked down with water. There were
some amazing moments initially, but they were short-lived.

I knew that my son needed long-term care, so I made one final effort and offered Jeff an alternative: a program in Italy called San Patrignano. This recovery community requires a three- to five-year
commitment, and Ombretta and I did online research, talked with
people we knew in Italy about the program, and then visited the Florence branch of the center. We talked with both the director in Florence and by phone with the central office in Rimini; we even went so
far as to fill out Jeff's application in Italian and English, making it
ready for his signature. This seemed to me to be a life-saving opportunity, and one that would give Jeff a chance to get out of the States,
start a new life in a different culture, and take his recovery seriously for
an extended period. But when I explained this option, Jeff balked. Although coming to Italy sounded great to him, he absolutely would not
agree to a three-to-five-year commitment. What was I thinking, he
seemed to ask. Was this a joke?

Jeff rejected San Patrignano, but the director did not reject him.
The Italian patriarch of this office, a recovering alcoholic himself,
struggling with his English, steadfastly tried to help me understand
the concept behind two words: *stagli vicino*, stay close to him. He

repeated these two words over and over again as he drove the point home to me, as if pounding it into my head, that Jeff needed to know that he was loved even when he was unlovable, even when he was closed away from us, and especially when he was at his sickest. He pleaded with me to *stagli vicino*, to stay close to Jeff and give him love, compassion, and support. I thought of our beloved family doctor, who had continually, and years earlier, told me, "Give Jeff love, compassion, and support, but no money." Although I had heard his words, I hadn't heard his advice. But now I understood in a different way, because, of course, I was different; I was beaten down and ready to listen, and learn.

This thinking of *stagli vicino* was contrary to much of the advice I had heard from other experts in the United States, who had encouraged me to "use tough love, let him hit his bottom, make him leave the house, don't answer his calls, bury him in your head, have a funeral for him." These responses hadn't worked for our family doctor, hadn't worked for me, and hadn't worked for Jeff.

With the concept of *stagli vicino* I had a tentative road map for my continuing trials with Jeff. I made the conscious decision to *stagli vicino*: I resolved to stay close to my son, even when he was at his worst. I resolved that I would do the opposite of cutting him off. I would not abandon him, and I would be constant. Jeff and I continued to talk, and he told me that he needed, again, to get into a treatment center, and argued that he couldn't get into any facility without money, begging me to send cash, a credit card number, a certified check made out to a facility—anything that was negotiable—and my response was clear: "I love you, and you'll have to find someplace that will accept you because you're sick and have no money."

"I hate this shit and am willing to take it seriously," he was almost screaming at me, "I want to get into another program, but no place will take me without money!" E-mail message to Jeff, November 14, 2005:

My dearest son, I checked on the Internet, and there are hundreds of rehab centers in California. You must get into one. You are immersed in a terrible situation that only YOU can change. Change, please, my son. Your family is here, waiting for your return. I love you and can only pray.

I continued to talk with him, *stagli vicino*, but I refused to send money to help him get into another program. We had been down this road many, many times before, and over the past two years he'd either walked out of or was thrown out of seven programs; he had even left free state-run centers. He'd sober up a little, feel better, and decide he could manage his own addiction. My decision not to pay for another treatment center was agonizing, but I knew that this time I could do nothing else. I stopped fighting the addiction; I was whipped. I had tried everything possible, and there was no end in sight. I would change my own patterns of behavior. I would *stagli vicino*: I answered his phone calls and e-mails and text messages; I didn't move away from him; I didn't close communication. I became implacable.

In California Jeff was isolated from family and friends, and this was the first time my son had placed himself in a position where he could not maneuver well, didn't know the terrain, the streets, didn't know how to exit and appear, or how to be his chameleon self. Throughout all the years of Jeff's drug addiction, he always had a way out, somewhere to go, someone to help. He was that guy who could make things happen, and people had always been quick to support him. Now the game had changed and he was alone with Eva, caged up with no way to escape, nowhere to run. This was a new twist for my son.

Jeff explained his situation.

We did crystal constantly and I hated the way I felt. After the first few weeks of daily use, getting high on amphetamines is no fun.

Whereas heroin quieted things, crystal confused them. This was a different world and I was starting to feel insane. I knew the only way out was to get into treatment, but without money or insurance, doors to most rehabs are closed. I looked for help, but state-run programs are tough to negotiate, especially if you're not carrying a habit that necessitates medical detox, like opiates or benzos or alcohol. My mind was a mess, and trying to get accepted somewhere without money was more than I could handle. Between my shaky emotional state and the administrative hurdles surrounding most state-run centers, I'd essentially locked myself out of subsidized treatment.

Looking back on these events, I realize that the move to California set the stage for his quick and profound descent. He was without his community or the systems that had supported him. His life became horrific, and my son finally broke, body and soul. I can write these words now with a sense of distance, because looking back allows a different perspective and objectivity. When it was happening, however, when I read his e-mails and listened to his voice, I knew Jeff's end was coming as surely as I knew when he was about to be born. I was afraid for him, but I also knew that the only way for him to change was for him to choose. My instincts as well as my experience with his addiction told me that things would get worse if he didn't find a way out, if he didn't get into recovery. The addiction was in charge unless Jeff could find his strength in himself and fight it. He was losing his grip, and I knew that all I could do for him, the very best thing that I could do for him, was to *stagli vicino.*

I continued to hear from Jeff, mostly in e-mails. November 17, 2005, 9:11 P.M.:

Things are deteriorating and I'm entirely uncomfortable. Issues are heavy and complex. This situation's a firecracker. I need some help.

November 18, 2005, 1:33 A.M.:

You've gotta help me out of this—things are tense and about to get crazy.

E-mail message to Jeff, November 18, 2005:

I'm sorry that your life is the way it is. Although I won't send you money, I will always offer you love and compassion. The days of me paying for the consequences of your addiction are over. I can offer you something else in San Patrignano—I know you don't want to stay three to five years, but you know what you need to do, and I'm begging you to do it. Fight, my son, you have it in you. Find your strength; find your way back to yourself. I love you, always and forever.

November 24, 7:37 P.M.:

Mother, life will be different soon—it has to be. I'm powerless and my rash decision making continues to leave me upside down. Not sure where to turn at this point. I am feeling paralyzed. You're a good mom and I've let you down repeatedly. That sucks and I apologize.

Words like "I've let you down repeatedly" whispered to me that my Jeff, the real Jeff, was still alive somewhere down deep. This gave me hope, because even within his desperation, I saw a patch of feeling and sensitivity, of his humanity. This division between the insanity he was living and his ability to reflect on his bad decision making caught me in a kind of emotional vise. I read the words "paralyzed," "rash," and "powerless," but I also recognized my son in phrases like "things will be different soon" and "I apologize." The constant pain and depression of those weeks are still vivid for me.

The sequence of events was caustic.

We'd been doing crystal, practically every day, for weeks on end, and the drug was turning me into someone I didn't know. We became entirely antisocial, and stayed in the apartment and got high by ourselves. Even going to the liquor store was a project. It took us half a day to get out of the house, and we'd fumble around the market for hours. Meeting drug dealers was a major ordeal, and trips to Tijuana for benzos took sometimes two and three days, punctuated by nervous breakdowns and hotel rooms and violent fights. It seemed like I wasn't even getting high from the drug anymore, just terrifically paranoid. Like an extended panic attack, I was anxious to the point of paralysis, and pains stabbed constantly at my chest. We were strung out to the gills, and I would sit in front of Eva's bathroom mirror and shoot crystal into my neck. Our eyeballs looked like they were popping out of their sockets and our teeth clattered. Our mouths mumbled words that didn't even form sentences. We didn't sleep for days, and our bodies became sticklike. The weight loss was gross. We were skeletons.

Between shots of crystal we'd drink vodka. We'd get high and try to come down with the alcohol. Often, however, it felt like we were way too wired for the liquor to have any effect. Eva and I were disconnected and had created this intensely sick little ecosystem in her apartment. I had no money and was trapped—miles away from home, in an unfamiliar environment.

Remember, I was a heroin addict because it softened the world around me. Crystal did just the opposite, and I couldn't handle it. But I couldn't stop using it, either. It was the craziest juxtaposition. I was falling apart.

Jeff fell lower than I could have ever imagined. He was imploding, careening into himself, and I prayed that some part of the old Jeff, the child we had raised, the good Jeff, would rise up and take over. It was obvious that he knew he was losing himself, and he despised his addiction, but he was locked into place.

November 24, 2005, 12:30 P.M. Florence
Jeff is sicker than he's ever been. He called, and in a fit of desperation said, "I've been using everything I can find. My neck is tracked from my collarbone to my ear, and my hands are entirely swollen from shooting crystal. I haven't eaten or slept in six days. I look worse than I've ever looked and am having trouble breathing."

Jeremy once asked me, years ago, when one of his fourteen-year-old friends was struggling with how to live with his alcoholic father, "Mom, can my friend love his father too much?" I remember saying something like "No, you can never love somebody too much, but sometimes you have to love someone enough to let him go." Now I'm faced with the same answer, only this time it's my son.

Stagli vicino. I stayed close to Jeff, offering him verbal support, encouragement, and love. I continued to talk with him whenever he called or asked me to call, I listened, and I repeatedly answered his messages. With Jeff, money had always been the answer to everything, but that hadn't helped. He was an earthquake happening inside himself. His plates were shifting, cracking, smashing into each other. I hated to see him in such pain, but I stood by and watched. I finally knew that love was not the answer, I was not the answer, money was not the answer. The answer was in Jeff.

On November 29, 2004 at 1:52 P.M., Tim forwarded me an e-mail message.

Dad,

Sorry about my absence on Thanksgiving. Trying to stop this craziness on my own is impossible. I'm trying to put options together before approaching you and mom. I know this is something I've gotta do for me, by myself—it's just tough being so far from the east coast.

Love you,
Jeff

That same day, I received an e-mail from Jeff, November 29, 2005, 7:12 p.m.:

> Mom, I don't know what I need. I've never felt so powerless and unable to activate change. I'm paralyzed. Truly. I'm miserable and just need to get out of this situation. I love you. Today's your birthday—happy birthday.

Jeff's words pierced me: "powerless," "unable to activate change," and "paralyzed." In California with no support system of friends and family, Jeff was coming face-to-face with himself. E-mail message to Jeff, November 30, 2005:

> Jeff, there IS a better way of life for you—in the States or in Italy. You have a family that loves you—we support you and your recovery. You MUST do your part. You must fight harder. What if I had given up on my cancer? What would that have said to you and Jeremy? What if I had just let the cancer eat me up? Life IS tough; your life is traumatic. But YOU are the only one who can change it. First things first—get clean, then you can make a decision more clearly. You must quit using crystal meth. You are killing yourself— but I think you know that. I love you—so does Dad, so does Jer.

Jeff's shattered state confused and confounded me because, ironically, when he used heroin he was functional. For years Jeff managed to hide his daily heroin use from me, and from many people. He carried himself with composure. He had attended university classes and managed to earn good grades, worked for large multinational companies, and was productive, even got raises and good evaluations. I had watched him converse with family and friends at the dinner table and other gatherings, carrying on intelligent conversations on substantive topics, and if he nodded off, he assured us that he was merely tired after a long workday. But now he sounded cracked and unraveled. His intense use of crystal, along with all the other drugs he found, had stripped away his ability to operate. He was a mess and he was scared. He was staying in touch with Tim and me more often than ever before because he had no one else. We were all he had.

I called Tim, and we talked and argued about what we should do, what we should have done years ago, and whether we should do anything now. Again and again I'm reminded that addiction is a family disease that infects everyone, and no one is immune. Even if there were a vacuum that allowed no communication with the addict, the addiction would still find you, reach out and grasp you by the throat.

A little over a week later Jeff sent a message that I could not ignore, from California to Italy, over six thousand miles. December 9, 2005, 11:51 P.M.:

Momma, I've been awake for what seems like weeks. I'm completely shattered. The paranoia's so intense, as is the inability to concentrate. Everything in my life feels all wrong, all of the time. I'm miserable and feel myself on the verge of a breakdown. My nerves are shot & I'm dying to shed this skin. I love you, Mom, & will be in a better space come the end of the month. I promise.

His words lacerated my heart. He was "dying to shed this skin." He sounded absolutely desperate, and again I was reminded of the three promises of continued drug addiction—jails, institutions, and death—but this time I saw what could be the final outcome, death. I forwarded this message to one of the recovering addicts with whom I had talked when Jeff was in jail. He responded immediately, "I read the message, and I felt a very strange feeling in my body and mind, and I remembered the times I used for days at a time. What can I do to help him? I'll continue to pray, but he needs help. He's in trouble."

This was confirmation of what I had known from the first moment I read Jeff's e-mail. I felt his extreme need as never before. I would leave Italy as soon as possible, and Tim and I would fly together to California. We would not send money, but we would send ourselves. Maybe this was the greatest gift we could give our son. Maybe we should have done this long ago. We would *stagli vicino.*

December 13, 2005, 9:00 A.M. Rome—New York—Pittsburgh

I think my deep and profound anxiety is because I've tried so many things in the past and they've all failed. I feel I've failed, failed to save my son, failed. I've failed at the most important role in my life—being a mother. I'm in intense pain because my first-born son is worse than ever. He's crying out for help. I must help.

I arrived in Pittsburgh late Tuesday night, December 13. I called Jeff to let him know that his dad couldn't leave work until Thursday evening and that we would arrive in California on Friday at 10:00 A.M. He said he didn't want us to see him in his current state: His body was tracked with puncture marks and abscesses, and he was weakened by a thirty-pound weight loss. He had attempted to get into a state-run inpatient program the previous day, but they wouldn't accept him (I don't remember why), but he swore he'd do something else. He wasn't sure what he would do, but he was sure he didn't want us to come.

One day I talked with Jeff, and on the very next day events exploded. This is the way with addiction. All my concerns, plans, and mental machinations were useless. Tim and I hadn't even yet paid for our airline tickets, but we weren't in control. The addiction was in charge.

On Wednesday, December 14, at 10:30 A.M., less than twelve hours after my phone call, I received a text message from Jeff that he had made an appointment for Thursday at 10:00 A.M., to meet a guy named Dexter from an inpatient treatment center called 10 Acre Ranch in Riverside. He had heard about Dexter from a friend who was in recovery. Jeff intended to enter treatment, and with this call, it seemed that Jeff had taken his recovery into his own hands.

However, this time Jeff's and Eva's addictions had taken on lives of their own, and when Jeff told Eva he was leaving for a residential facility she locked herself in her bedroom and wouldn't allow him to enter so that he could pack his things. Jeff called me frantically from the living room, asking me to ring her cell phone and explain to her that she needed to unlock the door so that he could get his clothes, and I did so reluctantly. When she heard my voice she began weeping uncontrollably in what sounded to me like alcohol-induced despair, saying, "You don't know what's happening here." I was certain she was right. She continued hysterically, "All day long, he drinks and takes Xanax to calm his nerves, and then, all night long, he shoots crystal meth into his neck and groin. He never sleeps; he never spends time with me. I love him, but he has used me, used my credit cards. He uses everyone, and I have enabled him. He won't put me first. He won't make me a priority. I love him." I hung up—sick, sick to my stomach, sick with both of them—but I was determined to *stagli vicino*. I would not back away from my son. I would not abandon him.

Around 2:00 P.M., Jeff called, even more hyper this time. "Mom," he said. "I've tried to get into the bedroom but she's calling the police, saying that I'm trying to break into her home." I didn't hear from him again until 5:00 P.M., when he called and spewed, "Six cops showed up. They asked me if I hit her. She had no marks on her, and I have scratch marks on my face and a bite on my arm. They searched the house and found syringes and prescription meds. They left one police officer here to supervise my leaving. I'm packing. I gotta get out of here. I'm going to the ranch."

Jeff had given me Dexter's cell phone number, so I called him to make certain that the ranch would take Jeff right off the streets, without waiting for detox, interviews, or signed forms. He assured me that they were prepared to help, and would accept him as is, but they needed a check for his first month's care. I knew that Jeff was sick and probably dying, and I knew, in my heart of hearts and from his e-mails, that he had been pleading for over a month for help and recovery. I had to help; I was his mother. I knew who Jeff was, I knew the son I had birthed, and I knew that this was not my Jeff but the drug-sick Jeff. I finally understood more clearly than ever before that we were fighting one of the most powerful conditions on the face of the earth, and I wasn't willing to watch my son die without trying again. I couldn't even imagine what his life was like, and I had no guidebook to follow, so I had to figure this out on my own. Tim and I talked. We would not give up on Jeff; we would *stagli vicino*.

About 7:30 P.M. that same night, a call came to my cell phone from Eva's phone number. I heard mumbling, like a drunken brawl, screams, shouts. Then the phone went dead. I heard nothing more. I tried to call back, but no one answered. I called Dexter, explained the situation, and he told me calmly, "I don't know where your son is. Call me when you find him." By 10:00 P.M., neither Tim nor I had heard from Jeff, so I called the police station. They told me that Jeff was in jail for possession of narcotics, and Eva was in jail for domestic violence. An hour later I received a collect call from Jeff. "I don't think they're going to hold me," he said. "All I had on me were Xanax pills. Once I see the judge, I should be released. She threw a print encased in glass at my face. My head's cut pretty badly. The police came. I'll call you when something happens here." Thursday morning, December 15, I called the jail, since neither Tim nor I had heard anything from Jeff. The police officer told me that he had been released late the prior night. They didn't know where he was. "Maybe he's on his way home, ma'am," he said. Home, I thought, home.

I talked with Jeremy and gave him an update, because he wanted to know what was happening. He never quit loving his brother. He listened. Torn between disgust and heartbreak, he wept.

We heard nothing from Jeff. Dead silence. Help was waiting for him at a small program in the desert, but he was nowhere to be found. Tim and I decided not to leave for California. What was the point? We didn't know where he was. He wasn't in jail; he wasn't with Eva, because she was still incarcerated; and he wasn't in a treatment center. He was lost to us, again.

Chapter 13

Choices: Mine and Jeff's

On Friday, December 16, at 5:00 P.M. East Coast time, Jeff surfaced.

He was on Tim's toll-free office number calling from John Wayne Airport in Orange County near Laguna Beach. Jeff told Tim that his car had been impounded; he had no cell phone, no money, no nothing, and he insisted that he had just been released from some hospital, although he couldn't remember how he had gotten there. He had taken a cab from the hospital to the airport, since he didn't know where else to go. Jeff was almost incoherent, fumbling with his words, and he'd nod off for brief periods while Tim hung on the phone, waiting for Jeff to speak.

Tim called me in Pittsburgh on a second business line. "What do we do? What do I tell him?"

I had made the decision to *stagli vicino*. I knew what I would say: "Tell him to stay there, don't move. Dexter will pick him up and take him to their facility." I knew that Jeff had been try-ing to get to the ranch for several days before he was arrested. I also remembered clearly the many times Jeff had said, "Never deny an addict his pain, but when he asks for recovery, get it. Help him."

"How can Jeff make contact with Dexter?" Tim asked. "He has no phone, no money, and can hardly speak."

I had a prepaid phone card, so I gave Tim the PIN. Then I felt a familiar feeling of angst. Would Jeff use the phone card to call someone else to come and get him? A rookie mistake. Would we lose him again?

I called Dexter from the landline at my mom's home. He told me that he would leave Riverside immediately and be at the airport in about two hours. I called Tim back, and he called Jeff at the air-port pay phone. "Jeff," Tim directed, "stand in front of America West, the top deck, and *don't move*. Look for a beige station wagon–type car. Dexter is coming to get you."

Then we waited.

Because of heavy traffic Dexter arrived at the airport three hours after my initial phone call, but Jeff was finally in the car. Dexter called me on his cell phone to confirm the pick-up, and then handed it to Jeff. Our conversation was short, Jeff's tongue heavy in his mouth as he struggled to put one word after the other.

"Mom, I need my car. My clothes are in it."

"Jeff, you need nothing right now. You need to get yourself into treatment."

"Fucking shit."

The line went dead.

On December 17, Jeff was at the 10 Acre Ranch. I felt ashamed; re-lieved, too, but shame seemed to blot out all other feelings, as if my heart was unable to feel much else.

December 18, 2005, 10:30 P.M. Pittsburgh
Talked with Jeff today. I can't imagine his life. I can't imagine
what it must be like to be him—never knowing what will hap-
pen, living in a world of craving, searching, demanding the next
fix, the next needle. It's unimaginable to me. Our conversation
was sad. "I needed you weeks ago. Where were you? Why didn't
you help me?" I don't know how best to help him anymore, and I
didn't answer his questions. I told him that Tim and I were com-
ing, and that he needed to stay at the ranch, to get himself
cleaned up and thinking straight.

His words "I needed you weeks ago" haunted me, but I had not
been convinced that he really wanted help weeks ago. Yes, he had
e-mailed me, telling me that he was shattered, broken, sick, but I
had never been sure when to move in, when to offer assistance,
when to try to help. How do you know the right time? This time I
had waited until I heard desperation in his voice, until I felt certain
he was serious about wanting help, needing recovery; this time I
waited until he clearly asked and put the process into motion himself.

What had actually happened? Jeff told me later.

In those weeks, Eva and I were manic and fought constantly. Like,
screamed and swore and threw things fights. We terrorized each
other. I kept threatening to leave, but she knew I was broke and
had nowhere to go. On the day of our arrests, it was clear that I
was serious about leaving and had finally lined something up. She
got really drunk, collapsing on the floor, and locked herself in the
bedroom. When I tried pushing my way into the room, she called
the police, telling them that I was trying to break into her place.

The cops came and told me to pack my clothes and leave the
apartment. Which I did, but I only made it onto the landing of the

building. I had so much stuff—it was everywhere. When the police left she came out and pleaded with me to come inside. And I did.

We talked some and drank vodka. I had ketamine stashed, and we decided to get more crystal. Within an hour we hated each other all over again. We argued, and she started throwing my CD books off her balcony, so I wrestled her to the ground. When she got up she pulled a framed picture from the wall and smashed it into my face. Neighbors called the police, and they returned to the apartment. It was a messy scene. My head was bleeding and there were drugs scattered about, in plain view, around the apartment.

Eva was arrested for domestic violence and me for the pills in my pocket. I got out of jail that night and went back to her place, gathered my stuff, and left for good. I drove to one of our friend's homes and got high on crystal, opiates, and assorted benzos. The next morning, still wasted and incoherent, I left his house for L.A. Within a few miles I got pulled over, and from what I remember, was unable to find my license or speak straight. The police pulled me out of the car and called medics to the scene. I woke up the next morning in Western Medical Center, a local hospital, with my car impounded and IVs in my feet.

The director of the ranch recommended that Tim and I not come to California until after Christmas, which was about ten days off. Jeff was safe, and although he was in bad shape and anxious, he was without a car, without friends who could help him leave, without anything to interfere. The director argued that Jeff needed time to think and to face himself in a sober and supportive environment. We agreed.

Jeff and I talked on the pay phone, which he told me was located in the center of the living space at the ranch. He said that the day he arrived he was required to attend an AA meeting with the seven guys who were there. When it was his turn to speak, he rambled about his history with recovery and his inability to stay sober. Harry, an alcoholic and a die-hard proponent of the steps, was leading the meeting.

He nodded, listened to Jeff's story, and said flatly, "Yep, some people have to die from this disease," then moved on to the next person. My son was perched on a precipice where he would either choose to fight for his health and life or choose to continue his descent into drugs and death.

I asked him how he felt when he entered the ranch.

My body was eating itself from the inside out, and I felt hollow. My eyes were sunken, and my frame was fragile. Even my hair looked too big for my head. It was hard to breathe through my anxiety, and I was shaking constantly. I was completely unable to make a decision. People would ask me questions and I'd just stare. I've never been so stripped by a drug before—every inch of composure was lost. That was the first turning point. I've never been so grateful to be that broken.

The night I arrived and heard Harry respond to my share, I remember thinking, "Unreal. Has it really come to that? Is death my final option?" It was heavy, but Harry was honest, and I need-ed to hear exactly that. He spoke plainly, and his words settled into me in a very different way, a clearer way. It was like, "Yeah, he's right, and that's just the fact of the matter." Harry, twenty-plus years sober, was still coming to the ranch to work with addicts. He was sincere, and I had to respect him for what he was doing. This message wasn't delivered by a therapist or psy-chologist, just an old alcoholic in this shit ranch in the desert telling me, in simple words, that countless people die from the lifestyle I was living.

I was scared, but I understood. I'd long since entered chronic stages of addiction and was comfortable using the way any addict on the verge of death uses. I went for obliteration. When I got high, I wanted blackness. Not using wasn't an option, and I chalked death up to an unfortunate outcome, not a deterrent. I couldn't imagine my life without drugs in it. I didn't want to die, but I didn't want to stop using, either. They say that addicts aren't afraid to die, they're afraid to live without drugs. I was there. It wasn't until I started praying that things turned around.

Tim and I arrived in Los Angeles on December 27. We rented a car and made our way through the haze and traffic to a town called Riverside and the 10 Acre Ranch. In the car we talked some about Jeff, but mostly about other things, like golf, weather, family, and world affairs.

We found the facility easily—a one-story wooden structure, a worn and torn house surrounded by a lot of dirt and some grass and a white fence, and protected by two large barking dogs, who, it turned out, didn't protect much, but who did herald our arrival. We parked the car and scanned the area for Jeff. He wasn't waiting for us, so we made our way toward the house.

We entered through the front door and saw a group of boys, who stopped talking and looked at us as if to say, *And who are you?* I spoke first. "We're Jeff's parents. Is he here?"

A good-looking, dark-haired boy with a young face, wearing a blue baseball cap, stood quickly and said, "I'll get him. I think he's in the garage using the weights."

We waited anxiously, not speaking, examining every corner from our position by the door. The living space was filled with musty dark furniture, a beaten-up coffee table, a fireplace that had been used recently, and the pay phone, my link to Jeff. My eyes drifted to the open country-style kitchen that had a table large enough for group meals. The sliding-glass door on the back wall opened to a concrete slab where a young boy was seated, alone, head down, back rounded, and shoulders bent into himself, smoking. One narrow hallway led off the common space, and was the passageway to the bedrooms, which had twin beds and wooden chests of five drawers each, and shared bathrooms. Shared everything, with nowhere to hide, I understood, but I also felt a certain sense of community, of care, of commitment. Maybe, just maybe, this strange little place with only eight boys who were in pain, led by a few men who were long-term recovering addicts and hard-core believers in the steps, maybe this was the place where our son could find sobriety.

Jeff rounded the corner, tentatively. His eyes held not only sorrow and shame, but also boldness, almost belligerence. He would take his cues from us. He must be like this on the streets, I thought, ready to react, my chameleon son.

I studied my child: His skin was the kind of translucent, pale gray color that I'd come to recognize as his in times of trouble. His movements were slow and measured, no skip, no Jeff skip. His feet were swollen, red and wounded, and were slid into plastic flip-flops that protect just the soles. Because of the mild weather, his neck was bare, a row of syringe marks and scarred skin exposed. He was gaunt, a skeleton. His eyes—here I saw something different from what I had seen during his past bad times. In his eyes I saw my son, who still cared that we were here, and who searched our eyes for connection. I saw Jeff under all the hard use of drugs, and I knew he was still alive to us.

We hugged him, big hugs embracing his beaten-up body, and then we sat and talked. He explained that he didn't remember clearly what had happened or how he had gotten to the ranch. He remembered shadows of events. Looking at me, at Tim, his eyes filled with confusion, he said, "I don't understand why you didn't come earlier. I wrote you e-mails, you never came. I had no one."

Tim and I were silent.

"It was all such a big mistake," he continued, "coming to California, leaving the East Coast. I take responsibility for my bad decisions, but I was so scattered, and it all turned so bad."

I was sad, this was troubling, but still I wondered if all this needed to happen to bring my son into recovery and face-to-face with himself.

Jeff became our guide as we walked from room to room, and then outside into the fenced-in dirt field around the house. He introduced us to the kids and staff with a mixture of pride and regret, that kind of *these are my folks*, with a tilt of the head and that smile that said, *Yeah, they came, holidays and all. Glad they're here, but too bad, huh?* All the boys were in the same situation, and they knew the feeling of seeing their parents again. At least Jeff was in a place where others had walked his walk and would make no judgments, but could offer support. Here everyone had a story.

I had made photo albums of their history as Christmas gifts for both boys, from great-grandparents to recent good times. I thought maybe if Jeff saw pictures of family and friends it would stir something inside him that would encourage him, that would make him want to stop. I prayed that the pictures would remind him that he had much to live for, that he had people who loved him, and that his life was worth living. He turned the pages without saying a word, but tears dripped down his face. He didn't look up, lost somewhere in his own thoughts, his own memories, of better times, of times of love. He never made a sound and never wiped his face, and the tears formed streams that washed down his cheeks, paused at his chin, dropped, and were lost in the blue of his jeans.

He later told me:

> The album reminded me of all the very real relationships I once had in my life. I wanted to be back in the world, but the idea of rebuilding seemed impossible. When you're out there and using, you think your friends are with you, and the dealers have your back. When I saw the album I saw the difference between forever things and the world in which I was living.

During our time in California, Tim and I spent as much time with Jeff as we were allowed. He came down with the flu, and we brought him chicken soup made in a little family restaurant. We added to the house kitchen with canned soups, cereals, and cookies for all the boys, bought a pillow and an extra blanket for Jeff's bed, and read every label on over-the-counter flu medications to find one with no alcohol content. Before we were allowed to bring our purchases into the house, Dexter checked everything to make sure they were drug free.

It was while we were there that Jeff agreed to see Dr. Patrick

MacAfee, a psychologist and family addiction therapist, who was the clinical director at several recovery facilities in the area and on the faculty at a local university. As soon as Jeff gave his consent, Dexter scheduled an appointment for him the following week.

After our three days, Tim returned to Maryland and I returned to Pittsburgh.

December 30, 2005, 10:17 A.M. Flight back to Pittsburgh
Jeff has to fight for his life. No one can do this for him—no one.
Were mistakes made in his growing up years? Sure. Mistakes are
made with all kids, but with Jeff it just ended up so bad. So self-
destructive. Now he needs to examine, tear down, and rebuild in
a stronger way. All this is academic—facts. Hearts and lives are
lost every day. I just don't want to lose my kid. I'm sure every
mother has the same prayer when her sons and daughters are in
danger. No one wants his child to suffer. Jeff has so much to give,
so much to live for. Dear Lord, let him live. Let him live.

Before I had left 10 Acre Ranch, I had asked the director if I could visit Jeff again before I returned to Italy. "Of course," he said, "you're his mother. You can't stay long, but come." I returned to Riverside on January 18, alone this time. Jeff was permitted to spend time with me, and we walked, talked, and ate in restaurants together before he returned each night to sleep at the ranch. He admitted that he had only actually stopped using drugs as of December 26, since when he first got to 10 Acre, one of the kids had shared his stash of marijuana and vodka. I was not surprised to learn that even at a rehab center, under such close supervision, drugs were available. All addicts know how to get around systems. Jeff told me, "On Christmas Day, I decided that I was done."

I asked him to explain more fully why he had made this decision.

It was finally clear that I wasn't going to make using work. For years leading up to this, I tried to deny addiction and blame the consequences on bad luck. I was determined to use differently, moderately, more successfully. In Riverside things came into focus, and I looked back on the arrests, car crashes, overdoses, fistfights, ruined relationships, debt, detoxes, treatment centers, and halfway houses that represented my twenties. The chaos was consistent, and unless things changed, a future full of the same or worse was ahead.

In California, I was stranded, stripped of all support. I'd wanted to get clean for years, but when you're using, all you can think about are the drugs. You're entirely preoccupied with the procurement, the chase, the money, and the high. There's a saying in AA: "Just when I hit bottom, the floor fell out from under me." That happened to me; when I was at my lowest, things got even worse.

Harry used to tell us that a lot of guys got clean at 10 Acre. "There's something spiritual in these walls," he'd say. I remember looking around the room and thinking about the guys who found sobriety in this old, dusty place. Every Friday night all the alumni returned for a group AA meeting, and the ranch overflowed with people. I remember everyone looking genuinely happy, like they were living these awesome and peaceful sober lives. I'd think, "Wow, all these guys come back to this ranch in Riverside. There must be something about it." There was lots of warmth at those meetings, and our little community came together in compassion.

It all worked together to bring me to a place where I chose sobriety.

Jeff spent his days at the ranch focusing on his recovery. He had organized a schedule for himself that seemed to ground him and give him an added sense of purpose. Each morning he read the *Big Book* and he prayed. Then he'd write in his journal and meditate on what he'd read, maybe take a walk, alone, to the ends of the property to think. Chores were next, and then group therapy. He'd exercise on the worn weight bench in the garage, wind down with a group dinner, and end with an AA meeting.

Jeff's legal problems in Orange County were still pending resolution, so during my January visit we drove together to the courthouse in Laguna Beach, where he had to appear for a charge of possession of a controlled substance. The director of the ranch accompanied us to confirm for the court that Jeff was in rehab. Jeff addressed the bench, admitting honestly that he was a heroin addict and was now living in a recovery facility. Since Jeff was addressing his problems, the judge dropped the charges, but said that Jeff would have to provide proof to the court that he had stayed in rehab for at least thirty days, and to pay a fine.

Two days later Jeff met with Dr. MacAfee for the third time since his arrival in Riverside. I waited for him in the reception area, content writing in my journal, but at the end of his appointment Jeff invited me to join them.

Dr. MacAfee, a slight, scholarly-looking man with gray hair and a gentle smile, greeted me kindly. As the three of us spoke together, he and Jeff were clearly united, and I realized that Jeff trusted him. Trust was something Jeff didn't give easily, and I felt that something important would happen with the work between MacAfee and Jeff. The doctor began by telling me that he was grateful that Jeff had chosen to work with him. He also said that since sobriety was now Jeff's choice, he was optimistic about his recovery. Jeff, he said, would need to learn how to surrender his will, because no one can control an addiction, and he pointed out that Jeff knew how to comply but not to surrender. Jeff would need to set goals, not expectations. "We know a lot about addiction," MacAfee said. "What we don't know much about is how addicts learn to live in sobriety. Jeff will have to learn how to live a sober life."

Jeff and Dr. MacAfee had already discussed his possible course of action for the next few months, and Jeff explained his plan to me. He expected to stay at the ranch for at least two or three months, and after he left there, his desire was to stay near this recovering community for seven months. He'd work with Dr. MacAfee, go to meetings, get a little apartment, settle down, and put his recovery first. The doctor then asked him, "Jeff, when did you ever put your recovery first?" Jeff replied with a single word: "Never."

I thanked Dr. MacAfee for all he had done for Jeff already. His response was clear: "I'm honored to do this work. I believe that addicts are saints in the making."

As I prepared to leave California, I felt hopeful for my son's recovery. I was grateful that Jeff had made the decision to live a sober life. I realized that we were both choosing. He was choosing sobriety. I was choosing to believe him.

Jeff was at the ranch for the next two months and, while he was safe, I returned to Italy—with Jeremy. My younger son stayed only a week, but I felt that this was the time to make him my priority. We cooked pasta and beefsteak in my apartment as we listened to Italian music, and talked late into the night about his dreams for his career. We walked through the medieval city of Florence, the stone streets sparkling through a haze of rainy mist during the cold January nights. I introduced him to the merchants on my street, who greeted him with a comfortable familiarity. They spoke directly to him, and I'd translate into English for Jeremy to reply. Jeremy stood next to me while I answered their questions in Italian and he smiled, charming them all, in the same way they were charming him. We dined with cousins and told old funny stories, the kind that grow more extravagant with time.

We also talked about Jeff. Jeremy said, "I love Jeff. I hate heroin. It took my brother. All I want is him back."

When Jeremy left, I settled into my life in Florence, volunteering one day a week at the international school to work with teachers on teaching writing. I had also joined the Florence Dragon Ladies, a rowing team of twenty-two breast cancer survivors who had joined together in order to rebuild our strength after surgery, and to support each other through the various effects of the illness. Twice a week at sunset we rowed on the Arno, while oranges and reds blistered the sky.

Jeff and I continued to talk on the pay phone, the one I'd seen in the center of the common space at the ranch. Often I'd call around 7:00 A.M. my time, which was 10:00 P.M. his time. At that time of his night he could talk without interruption, and he'd ramble on about all kinds of things, the type of talk that signaled to me that a tentative shift was occurring in him: He was beginning to recognize and accept his own feelings, and he was beginning to trust me with those feelings. As I listened intently to my son I was learning that addicts, the young men there with Jeff, were just kids trying to get life right. They wanted a normal life, they wanted to be like other people with regular problems, but they didn't know how to control the disease and craving of their addiction. They were caught in the suffocating web of their illness, and society loathed them. The addict, I knew from Jeff, feels self-loathing, but they live in terror of facing the world without drugs—and the suffering, of both the addict and society, continues.

During one conversation he told me about the guys who were there with him in recovery.

Devin relapsed constantly, and had been in and out of the ranch for years, but he was persistent. He'd get it right for a while, and then, without fail, end up in Mexico with another heroin habit. When things bottomed out, he'd return to the ranch.

Scott was an auto mechanic from Michigan, in his thirties and generally beaten up by alcohol. He just wanted to stop drinking but didn't know what that looked like. He was quick to embrace AA; this was his first rehab and he was determined to get it right. He couldn't understand why he drank the way he did, and he knew that he needed to get sober. His marriage depended on it.

Another guy, Victor, he was cool, in total denial of his addiction, but nice to have around. He blamed the turmoil on tough luck. Bad things just happened when he was high. He left, and we all knew he'd be back.

Most addicts genuinely want to stop hurting the people that

care about them. For many of us, though, the idea of rebuilding is just too much.

I noted in my journals, many times after talking with Jeff, that he sounded irritable and distracted. I knew he was in the midst of transition: fighting the cravings; adjusting to a life of sobriety; accepting how drugs affected him; recognizing who he had become; and hoping that life could be different. I used to believe that Jeff recovered when he was in treatment centers, that when he walked out of a facility he was healed, he was Jeff. I was finally learning that recovery didn't work like that. An institution merely puts space between the addict and the drug. The real recovery, the real transformation of becoming Jeff again, would take time. I thought about cancer, and how my healing hadn't begun until the cancer was removed—after I left the hospital. Healing takes time; healing takes more time than a thirty-day stay in a recovery center, or a four-hour operation in a hospital. I needed to be patient with Jeff, and he needed to be patient with himself.

In mid-March, after completing two and a half months of residential treatment at the ranch, Jeff found a little apartment in Newport Beach and enrolled himself in an outpatient program at Sober Living by the Sea. Here he could live independently while he was meeting the clear requirements of their program: urine tests twice a week, participation in daily group sessions that were led by an assigned case manager, daily attendance at AA meetings, and educational group sessions offered by specialists in the field of addiction. During this time Jeff also began working at a local department store. He hadn't had a steady job in almost two years, and this new position signified for him that he was getting his life back on track. He was to report for training during the following week.

It was at this time, in mid-March, that Jeff called to ask me to fly to California to help him set up the apartment and to see the life he was building for himself. He was excited and proud and he said he wanted to share the progress with me. The longer his time away from drugs, the more Jeff was becoming like my son, more compassionate and more empathetic. He was rediscovering who he was and following the thread back to his Jeff-ness, and he risked inviting me into this process. It was his gift to me, and while I wanted to believe that this metamorphosis would continue forever, my reaction was mixed. I was afraid.

March 12, 2006, 9:11 P.M. Pisa—Paris—Los Angeles

I'm filled with emotion. Last time I saw Jeff, he was a resident in 10 Acre Ranch, and now he's stepping out on his own. He has a job, he has his car, and he has an apartment. The truth is, as happy as I am for him, I feel safer when he is in a rehab center. How terrible is that—that when my son is in an institution, I feel safer. Sure it makes sense, but I feel like a terrible mother for writing these words. I should be thrilled that he's sober and making a life for himself, but I'm afraid.

So I go to L.A. with joy and trepidation. Joy to see my son alive and well. Trepidation because I fear what the future might hold.

When I arrived in L.A., Jeff was full of smiles. He was tanned and a little heavier, fuller in the face, healthy looking; his eyes were clear; his voice was strong. When he took my suitcase I saw that his hands were still swollen, but I noticed that they weren't as gray as they had been when I last saw him. I wondered if the veins in his arms would ever heal, and if his hands would ever return to their normal size, or if he would always bear these scars of addiction. But he was alive and I was grateful.

We drove to his new apartment, one large, wood-framed room that was bathed in the sunlight streaming in from several large windows and two skylights. The apartment was sparsely furnished, but it was home for Jeff. On the refrigerator he had placed pictures of his friends and our family, of Jeremy and him laughing together. After two months of residential living, he was embarking on a new life of sobriety.

Jeff had obligations during the week I was there, one of which was a meeting with his case manager from Sober Living. I sat at a nearby coffee shop while they met and wrote in my journal, trying to document all that was happening. One worrying thing was that Eva was back. Jeff told me that several weeks ago, when he was walking across the campus of Sober Living with a buddy and one of the directors, he heard someone call his name. "I turned and it was Eva," he had said. "She came from across the street, saying, 'I can't believe it's you.' It was bizarre; I was stunned. I felt disbelief, and a thumping anxiety. She told me that she was in treatment and had recently gotten out of jail. We spoke briefly. I was with a director who knew our history, so she couldn't stick around."

After her release from jail, he explained, Eva had entered Sober Living, since her use of crystal meth and alcohol were destroying her. Of course, I wondered if she had come to Sober Living because it was a good treatment center or because she knew that Jeff would be there. He had seen her several times since that initial meeting; she was familiar, he said, but after spending some time with her their relationship felt unnatural. I was unhappy that she had resurfaced; I was concerned about her presence at the recovery facility and in Jeff's life, but I knew that I couldn't control this or any other of Jeff's relationships. I could do nothing but stay close and trust Jeff and his support system to negotiate the problems that he would surely continue to face from old relationships and past patterns of behavior.

Jeff started his training program for work during the next days and went to meetings and attended to his requirements at Sober Living. He and I had good days, happy days, but I was still struggling with my fears.

March 16, 2006, 2:00 P.M. Jeff's apartment in Newport Beach
I'm tired. I'm tired of the constant threat of addiction. I'm
exhausted from the worry, but it's my own making. I take full
responsibility for my worry. I'm sure some parents can turn it off,

tune it out, but I can't. It's like a slow leak in my heart, like a drip that can't be stopped. Jeff and his addiction are always with me. I try to stop worrying; I know it does no good but to wear me down. Maybe one day I'll stop, but I doubt it. My child—any parent would understand.

Last night, Jeff was on the deck and came in to tell me he saw a shooting star. How incongruous—a heroin addict finding his mom to tell her he saw a wishing star. Amazing—innocence and addiction together. Maybe he feels the same things I feel. Maybe he's exhausted by his own addiction and aches to be young and innocent again.

Jeff had another meeting with Dr. MacAfee, and once again, near the end of their time together, they invited me to join them. As if the doctor knew the fears and anxieties that haunted me, and understood that practical reality was what I needed, he explained to me in his gentle way what I would need to understand as Jeff reentered life:

Addicts know how to live in addiction—in chaos, with court systems and legal problems. They know how to lie, deceive, and manipulate. What they need to learn how to do is live a transparent life—how to live clean and honest, how to live with serenity. Everyday problems present difficulties for the addict, since the addict spent most of his life going under, finding comfort in the euphoria of drugs. This euphoria is predictable, and the addict is sure that the feeling is there for him, just waiting. It happens every time. Not like reality, where things are never the same. Like a kiss. In reality a kiss, even with the same person, feels different, sometimes disappoints. The euphoria from drugs never disappoints. *That* feeling is incredible. The problem is that the euphoria doesn't last and is followed by real destruction. The consequences of the addiction then become the reality. The mind wants the euphoria, but the memory of the consequences needs to screen out and stop the addict at that initial step.

Dr. MacAfee also said that grief would come to Jeff, a period when he would grieve for all the lost time, the years gone by, the people hurt, the trail of destruction. He said, "The grief will overtake you, Jeff, and it will be hard. But it's also a sweet time. Savor it."

I was beginning to understand in theory, and in my son's life, what Dr. MacAfee was teaching me: Addiction is the loss of self, and that the recovery of self is a transformative process. In a way, everything was new to Jeff as he reentered life without drugs. Recovery offered Jeff the freedom to rediscover his identity and, in time, a real and authentic young man would emerge. This he would have to do alone, and I realized more clearly the enormity of the fight that Jeff had to face in order to win this battle. His would be a victory that he would have to win for himself.

Later in the day, while we were in Jeff's apartment, I was thinking about all that Dr. MacAfee had said, and I told him, "You have a lot of courage to do this again, Jeff." He paused, and then said quietly, almost to himself, "Courage? That's a word rarely used with me. Yeah, it takes courage."

His words shocked me, and my heart swelled with feelings of sadness as my mind reeled in the opposite direction, trying to make logical sense of it. I wondered why it seems easier for us to believe the bad things in life. Why does it seem people are quicker to say the critical things? And why do we remember so deeply the bad things that others say about us? Sometimes we seem to believe the words of others more than we believe our own thoughts. Jeff did get praise, that's true, but he also heard many comments directed at him or about him, comments such as "Quit screwing up, Jeff," or "How many times do you need to be in rehab before you get it right?" or even "OK, you're in rehab again. Goddammit, Jeff, don't blow it this time." I wondered what Jeff sees when he looks at himself in the mirror. I wondered if he could ever see a man of courage who is rebuilding his life, or if he sees only a screwup, a man who has accumulated years of failure. I wondered how he was finding the strength to continue. How do people go forward when others, even those who love you, give voice to all

the negative things that are lurking in the shadows of your own mind?
Words like strength, courage, and hope are seldom used in the same
sentence with addicts.

My time in California ended with these questions unanswered.
My son and I were both embarking on journeys of self-discovery.
Courage: We would both need courage as we made decisions that
would lead to our better choices. My son had chosen to fight his addiction. I was choosing to fight my anxiety; I was choosing to change.

By the end of March, I had returned to Italy; Jeff's legal problems
continued. He appeared in court for his DUI arrest from the night
his car was impounded and he was taken to the hospital. Jeff represented himself while one of the staff at Sober Living accompanied
him to vouch for his continued sobriety. The judge listened. Since
Jeff had already completed over two months of inpatient rehabilitation, and since the judge knew the programs at both 10 Acre Ranch
and Sober Living, he accepted a total of ninety days in treatment in
lieu of ninety days in jail. Jeff would, however, have to reenter Sober
Living's inpatient program to satisfy the court's full demand of
ninety days in a sanctioned facility. In this way sixty days at 10 Acre
plus thirty days at Sober Living would clearly complete the court
order. In addition, Jeff had to attend both a six-month DUI program and sessions sponsored by Mothers Against Drunk Driving;
he also had to pay a fine. The judge held the staff of Sober Living
responsible for alerting the court if Jeff relapsed. Jeff packed some
things in his apartment and moved into Sober Living's housing,
grateful that he did not have to spend time in jail and, more important, grateful that he was sober.

Jeff continued working at the department store while living on
Sober Living's property, was tested for drugs twice a week, and attended AA meetings and lectures. In addition, he attended services
at a local church and started to think about the existence of God,
and what he was meant to accomplish. Thus, many factors were at

work in Jeff's life: AA, a sponsor, spirituality, sober friends, a job, and individual therapy. He was allowing others to support him and his walk; he was finding his strength. At the end of April Jeff had completed his month at Sober Living and was able to move back into his apartment. As required by the court, he had successfully completed three months in approved treatment centers.

On June 11, Jeff and I talked on the phone, one of our many conversations during my morning hours in Italy and his evening hours in California. We talked about family, about life on two continents, and about what he was learning in recovery. Near the end of our conversation he told me that Will, his roommate from Sober Living, had relapsed after eight months of being clean. Will's girlfriend had broken up with him, and he was off and missing.

> I know that place. He was in pain, and it was too much. He used to kill it. Then he needs to keep using because the addiction has kicked in. When the drugs are reintroduced, addicts lose their sense of free will and are thrown back into obsession, always needing something more. I'm sure he's scared and confused. I'm sure he's running. Sober Living had to call the police because he's on parole. This will be a violation, and he'll have to go back to jail. That's what addiction does. Whole systems fall apart—within days they crumble. There's no stopping it once it takes over.

Jeff was speaking about addiction as if it were a living thing, a kind of demon that takes over your body. He admitted that there is a space of active thought before you use, a space when you have time to decide, but if your life feels unbearable and you give in once—it's done. Pain subsides when you use, but the devil of addiction has you by the throat, and the shame starts and the cycle continues. The pain is now the original compounded by the guilt that follows, along with self-disrespect, fear, knowledge that you've let people down again, that you fucked up again, that you are sinking again, and again, and again.

As I listened to him I thought that defeating addiction must be like moving mountains, one grain of earth at a time. How does an addict stop? He needs support, but the people who love him get sick and tired of supporting him, sick and tired of paying for recovery, because they get sick and tired of sending money down that rat hole. Thirty-day programs are limited; the addict has to choose to change, but change is hard. How do you give up the one elixir that salves you, that quells the pain, and that brings you peace every time, if only for a moment? An addict lives a tortured life, and society despises him. Choices are made from day to day, sometimes hour to hour, or even minute to minute. Will was in pain and chose to return to the place he knew best, his familiar world of drugs.

As I listened to Jeff I recognized that recovery is forever and doesn't end looking like a beautiful present tied up with a bow. Will had been clean for eight months, but he was back on the streets, desperate again. What did this mean for Jeff, for us? Life often has a tagline. Life is ambiguous. Sometimes like cancer, the disease comes back. It was June when my son told me about Will and I thought Jeff was living a sober life. He wasn't, and later, one year later, he told me the truth.

Alcoholics Anonymous says that the program of sobriety is one of rigorous honesty. MacAfee had said many times that Jeff needed to live a transparent life. Jeff was learning that his sobriety was at risk if honesty was compromised. But old patterns of behavior are hard to break, and the double-sided mirror, the split-screen movie of our past was once again active in our present. Jeff knew and I did not. Jeff didn't tell me, letting me operate under false assumptions. But a layer at a time, a day at a time, Jeff's higher self was kicking in. This time Jeff chose honesty, because he hadn't given up his hope of a better tomorrow, a future without drugs.

Jeff had told us that his clean date (the date from which he counted his days of sobriety) was December 26, 2005, the day after Christmas, the occasion he had described to me. However, I know now that his clean date is really seven months later, July 21, 2006. After one year of sobriety, on July 21, 2007, Jeff called me. He told me how his relapse happened, which might explain why it happened.

The first night out of treatment, I was with a girl from work, and we were bored. We were driving around Newport, and she suggested that we get drinks somewhere. All she knew was that I used to have a drug problem—in her mind alcohol was never part of it. Her request was an innocent one, and I was too insecure to say no. I wanted to be social, and drinking was what social people did. Just out of treatment and trying to figure out what an exciting weekend without drugs and alcohol looks like is tough. And being sober feels completely unnatural, especially in social settings. In rehab, lots of obvious barriers block using, but when you're out, nothing concrete stands between you and the life you left a month earlier. So we bought a bottle of vodka and had drinks at my apartment.

He told me that they made cocktails and drank heavily, that he felt guilt and fear about what was happening, but that he tried to convince himself that if he used alcohol only, it would be different, and not have the same consequences. He drank that night and the next night and every night that week. His drinking seemed social. Everything was fine, for a time.

I wanted to stay clean, but I also wanted life to be exciting like it used to be exciting. I had very little experience with sobriety outside of treatment, certainly not enough to handle the transition with a level head. I wasn't yet plugged into AA outside of rehab, and my old social patterns were still familiar and in place.

Once I started, I was drinking most every night, either at home by myself or out with friends. I drank to get drunk, to feel the alcohol affect my body. Then, two months later, on July 18, I went to a friend's house to celebrate our birthdays. We had been roommates in treatment and, besides sharing the same birth date, were both recently out of Sober Living. After dinner we got drunk and decided to find crystal meth. We wanted to get high and had been talking about it for weeks. We called everyone we knew in Orange County but couldn't track anything down. Some people were sober, others were in jail; a few numbers were disconnected and others rang without an answer. We left messages where we could, and after an hour of nothing gave up and fell asleep. The next morning I awoke on his couch to several voice mails from people we had called during the night. While my friend slept I got dressed and went to meet some people I knew from my time with Eva. They had crystal—we only smoked it, but we smoked it all day. Overall, it was a tortured high. I was in my head the whole time and had no peace about using. The fun and the carelessness had vanished. It was all so much heavier than I remembered, and I couldn't get thoughts of AA out of my mind.

That night I was miserable and drank alone at my apartment. Short of driving to Mexico for pharmaceuticals, alcohol was the only thing I could easily find to kill the anxiety. I couldn't sleep, and I didn't even try. I don't think I was able to get drunk, either. I had to be at work the next morning, and I was a disaster. On the way to my job I bought another bottle of vodka and drank in my car in the parking lot. I shuffled through the day, drinking at lunch, again after work, and into the night.

The next morning I woke with an unexplained sense of peace. In spite of all the alcohol, I felt at ease. As I slept, somehow a decision had been made for me, almost without my making it. I was done using, and I knew it. Even my bones knew it. I was done fighting to keep drugs in my life, and I felt myself acknowledge this final lost battle. My obsession to use with restraint had disappeared. I saw clearly where things were going and knew that if I didn't stop, I was inches away from another serious run. All of a sudden I could breathe again. Before getting out of bed, I called a friend from Sober Living who was still clean and active in the program. I explained my situation and he understood. Things changed that day.

Then he stopped his narration. After a lengthy pause, he asked me, "What do you think, Mom? How do you feel knowing that my clean date is not December, but really later? I've really been clean for one year today, and I wanted to make it to one year before telling you."

I closed my eyes as I held the phone. I thought about the many times I had been the one to say the wrong thing, do the wrong thing, speak the words that pierced his soul. I remembered taking away his college tuition, and I remembered Jeremy's anger that I cut Jeff loose without help. I remembered picking Jeff up at the police station and telling him I wished he weren't my son.

But we had come a long way since those years, my son and I. I knew what to say this time. I understood now that recovery was a painstaking process, a time of transformation, when he'd shift from the person he was and become the person he wanted to be. He was following his road home, but the road wasn't easy, wasn't trouble free. So I replied honestly, "I'm grateful that you're sober today, one year. Addiction—this thing will kill you, and I'm thankful you've not given up. I know you feel darkness and shame, because you tell me you feel these things. I learn a lot from you. Thank you, Jeff, for telling me the truth. I'm glad you found your hope."

For all of us, life is a matter of choices. I was grateful to know that my son had arrived in a place where he could make choices. He had stopped himself before he lost his ability to do the next right thing. He had decided that he would not go back to his addict's life. My son had chosen honesty, and I was choosing to trust him.

After all that had happened, how could I trust him?

Somehow I can.

Chapter 14

Never Giving Up Hope

There is no happily-ever-after ending to our story. With addiction, there can never be. It infected Jeff when he was just fourteen years old and possessed him until 2006, when at age twenty-eight he chose to fight and to live a sober life.

Jeff wasn't born this way, or maybe he was and the addiction was there, hiding, all through his childhood years. That's the thing with addiction—no one knows the cause, not for sure. I've spent a lot of time trying to ferret out the answer to why one son is an addict and the other isn't, but I've given that up. I now spend my time learning about how best to support my son in his recovery.

I began writing this story because I didn't know what else to do with the heartache, the devastation, and the perpetual chaos. I never wanted to write our story about addiction and my son and my family. I never wanted to expose our raw pain. I never wanted to reveal the shame that I worked so diligently to keep hidden. But if I didn't, our anguish and our learning would stop there, and it would help no one else. At Jeff's first rehab center, the counselors told me that for every one addict at least four other people are affected. Addiction attacks the family first, then moves outward, engulfing extended family and close friends: an uncle, a cousin, a coworker, a roommate, team members—none of their lives will ever be the same. The *Big Book* of AA states, "We think that each family that has been relieved owes something to those who have not, and when the occasion requires, each member of it should be only too willing to bring former mistakes, no matter how grievous, out of their hiding places. . . . With it you can avert death and misery for them." So what started as a journey for self and family became an occasion to give back.

Our family knows that there are many stories far worse than ours, those that have ended in death. There are other stories that continue with no end in sight, with loved ones who are homeless, sick, and destroyed. I now understand that we, families of addicts, have similar experiences, and that's why groups like Alcoholics Anonymous and Al-Anon work. In our stories we see each other, but our torment, our denial, and our trauma are our own. Just as our hands are common among us, our fingerprints are individual.

Through the writing of this book Jeff and I discovered that with honesty and hard work we could learn together about addiction. We know that only when addiction is brought out of the shadows, where it does its best work, and into the light can we conquer the shame of it, the manipulation of it, and the deceit it feeds on.

Our conversations have not been easy. Nothing is easy with addiction. During July 2007, after Jeff read a draft of the manuscript, he stopped and stared at me. Stunned, angry, and hurt, he said, "You've stripped me naked in this book. Have I no dignity?"

Of course I promised him, "We'll stop, Jeff. We won't write it. Your recovery is more important than the book."

He hesitated, as if weighing my words, eyes looking away, and in the next moment he said with determination, "No, I need to give back, and the story's my contribution—I've learned from my past, and maybe it will help someone else."

Our work continues.

The book reads like a split-screen movie, like double-sided mirrors spliced together, distorting the images as they come and go. I tell what I was allowed to know or what I discovered on my own, and he tells what really happened. That's the way it is with addiction, a breakdown caused by information and disinformation. As long as Jeff kept the lie, he kept the addiction, and our family lived in the world of deception where all families of addicts and alcoholics are trapped. None of us wants to learn to distrust the people we love, but with an addict there are always lies.

Much of what happened I discovered later, often much later. Jeff deceived me, and the truth of what was really happening eventually found its way home. I felt assaulted by my constant and unrelenting ignorance, unable to believe anything he said or anything I thought.

I've spent lots of valuable time asking myself what I did wrong, blaming myself, fighting good advice, hating my shortcomings, trying to decide what I should do or what I should have done. It was easy for me to feel blocked, to focus on my limitations, problems, and mistakes. Within the blame I felt extreme guilt, and although the experts told me that Jeff's addiction was not my fault, I didn't have much luck believing them. I felt the weight of every misstep as I pummeled myself with questions such as, "Why my son?" "What did I miss?" "What could I have done differently?" I wish I had accepted the validity of all my diverse feelings sooner, instead of hiding them from myself, isolating myself, and keeping the secret and the shame. I hated the addiction, but before I could do anything constructive I had to stop feeling that I had failed my firstborn son.

I enabled, we enabled, and although we should have stopped, we were also locked in place, a parent's place, a brother's place. I, his mother, never really wanted to believe that this horror could be happening. We bailed him out of jail, offered him a home in which to detox, fed him when he was hungry, gave him a bed when he couldn't afford a place to live, and paid his bills. When Jeff was so messed up he couldn't even walk, Jeremy carried him to bed and sat by the door of his college apartment so he wouldn't awake and leave again.

A heroin addict of twenty years from Philadelphia once told Jeff, "Never deny an addict his pain." I didn't understand what this meant for a long time; however, I understand better now: Jeff needed to feel the effects, the consequences of his choices, his addiction. We all felt great pain, Jeremy, Tim, Sophie, his grandparents, other family members, and his friends. By getting in the way of the consequences, by trying to protect him, we all suffered more, including Jeff. He needed to endure the reality of his decisions and the starkness of life on and in the streets. Only when he felt loneliness, misery, fear, cold, hunger, panic, paralysis—only when he was desperate, depleted, and broken—only then did he choose a different life.

I never truly realized the depths of his illness. As I write this today I am both shocked and not shocked. I had no experience with addiction or drugs, so how could I have imagined his life, his suffering, or his feelings of self-loathing as he chased his next fix? Sure, I saw the signs: I saw the track marks, the sallow skin, and the syringe wounds, but I couldn't see inside to the heart of my son's torment. We can't—we mothers, we fathers. Sometimes I think our children think we can, as when Jeremy told me, "You're my mother. You should be able to look into my eyes and know how I feel." I wished then, and I wish now, that I had this power. Even though I can trace most of Jeff's story, I don't know his malady. Even though I can read his words, I don't know his agony.

When I was finishing this manuscript I asked Jeff some questions that I had been wondering about for a long time: "Didn't you see how you were hurting yourself and the people who love you? Didn't you want to stop all the chaos, like arrests and near death? Jeff, why didn't you stop?" He looked at me, weary, and sighed, "You still don't get it, do you? After writing this entire book, you still don't understand that I never wanted to hurt you—I wanted to protect you from all of it, to keep you to the side. You've written about me at my worst, my most vulnerable, my most desperate. I'm an addict. I was addicted. An addict doesn't want to hurt those he loves, but he can't stop using—oftentimes until death."

What do I say to the people who ask, "Why is Jeff an addict? What went wrong?" What do I say to the people who know nothing of an addict's life, who look at the addict as a derelict, an abyss of moral failure, or who look at the addiction as an ethical malfunction, a deficiency of will? What do I say to people who I think look at me with eyes that say *It has to be your fault—you and Tim obviously screwed up and failed your son.* I don't even answer these questions, because I don't think they're questions. I think the people who make these statements (or are they veiled accusations?) often have their minds made up. Why should they have compassion for Jeff? Why should they believe that he can live a drug-free life and contribute to society? Jeff and I talked about these feelings, these perceptions. He says, "These are the chains of addiction."

I myself struggle with this paradox, of how to trust again. Do I worry that my son might go back to the world of drugs? I want to write "No. I've given it to God. It's Jeff's walk with his higher power." I want to, but I can't. I still have a catch in my heart, and remembrance. Even today, when Jeff and I talk, especially on the phone, I listen to the sound of his words, the roll of his tongue in his mouth. When we're together I search his eyes to see if they are clear and alert. I feel relieved when I see his little skip, the characteristics that are so distinctively Jeff. I hate the fact that I don't rest, but Dr. MacAfee clarified this for me: "It's OK. You've been vigilant a long time. It's a pattern, and it might not change, ever. It's normal. You're a parent. Be patient with yourself." I need to have compassion for my son; I also need to have compassion for myself. But I can report that every day I'm getting better at letting go, and I'm learning to release Jeff—to himself and his God.

Then I think that maybe it's important to remember so we don't become complacent and forget. Addiction isn't going away, not for Jeff, not for others who are addicted, and not in society. In our home, addiction took on the characteristics of another family member, demanded attention, caused anguish, concealed itself, never went away, and never will go away. My son will always be an addict. There is no finish line.

Every addict has a mom and dad, and we parents suffer as we see our children dying a little at a time. We want to save them, jump into the fire, grab hold and bring them to safety, but we can't. Tell that to a parent, that he or she can't save their child—the pain is incomprehensible. But as Jeff said, "I know that writing the book was hard, Mom, but living it was harder."

My family knows well the hell of addiction, but we know only our own hell. Those who love addicts suffer. The addict suffers. No one is immune. In our family, we each handled our grief differently. Jeremy held things inside, caught in that gap between loving his brother and hiding the truth and loving his brother and telling the truth. How does a brother handle these conflicted loyalties? Tim and I suffered and responded in our own, divergent ways. He became quiet, withdrawn; his absence spoke for him. I whirled into action, trying anything that I thought would help, running from one possible solution to another. Grandparents, uncles, aunts, cousins, friends—no one knew what to do. During Christmas 2006, when neither son came home for our family gatherings, my brothers didn't know what to say. They didn't even know whether to invite me to the festivities. The cousins were confused: Could they ask about Jeff or would it be kinder to leave him out of the conversation?

When I first started attending Al-Anon meetings in 1999, I sat in on three different meetings before I found a group where there were other parents of addicted children. At that time we were in the minority; we were only four parents out of more than twenty people. These days when I attend meetings, I find that most members are parents. It seems as if the number of young people who are addicted to drugs has increased greatly. Words like heroin, crack, and crystal meth are common. Sadly, Jeff's story is not the exception.

Many experts claim that "an addict has to hit his bottom," but I could never gauge where Jeff was on his descent. Alcoholics Anonymous defines addiction as a progressive and fatal illness, and I saw that Jeff's bottoms got continually worse. Each time he fell lower and faster, until I feared he would die.

The recovery centers, the psychologists, Jeff's arrests, and all his many interventions must have made a difference, but I don't know how much of one. Jeff was in rehab programs, jails, and institutions of many kinds. He lived on the streets and the beach. He stole, had things stolen, and ultimately pawned almost everything he owned. He lost friends and destroyed his veins. At times, my articulate, ambitious son could hardly put two words together. I banished him from the house. I threatened, cajoled, pleaded, wept, and wrung my hands. I punished, screamed, fought, ached, had nightmares, stuffed my emotions into my belly, and suffered in silence. His father and I followed the advice of experts and friends and even people who knew nothing. We wrote intervention letters, paid for therapists, treatment centers, and medicines. Tim, Jeremy, and I were like starving people, ready to latch onto anything that might alleviate our pain and Jeff's hunger for drugs. I wish we had kept communication open among all of us, and not given in to the lies and deception, but at that time I would have sold my soul for his recovery, made a bargain with the Devil himself—but all this was to no avail.

Addicts live a tortured existence. Jeff has told me that he was filled with guilt, regret, and self-blame. He says that addicts, even those who can't mouth these words, hate themselves for what they are doing to the people around them, despise the destruction they are causing, but they can't imagine a life without drugs. About the final days of Jeff's last descent, he told me, "I chalked death up to an unfortunate outcome, not a deterrent. I couldn't imagine my life without drugs in it. I didn't want to die, but I didn't want to stop using, either. They say that addicts aren't afraid to die, they're afraid to live without drugs."

Jeff became a heroin addict after years of use, and his addiction wasn't going away quickly. Jeff was in several thirty-day programs, which is the typical length of stay for most treatment centers, but for Jeff this wasn't long enough, even in the beginning. I've visited two communities in Italy, and both expect a three- to five-year commitment. When I told Jeff, he was horrified: "Three years? Five years? You've got to be kidding. I can't stay that long." But Jeff's addiction needed time and attention in order for his patterns of behavior to change.

Time in treatment equals money. Until this point I've deliberately not addressed the issue of the cost of rehab centers, detoxes, hospitals, halfway houses, and inpatient and outpatient services. I did this intentionally, because I wanted to focus the book on the addiction and Jeff's story, not on our family's monetary resources. Certainly, we were fortunate that we had the capacity to pay, but our story is not about an affluent family and a spoiled child. It is about a family crushed emotionally and strapped financially in the face of addiction. The most poignant fact is that even with money, our attempts at stopping the drugs were unsuccessful.

This financial issue is of huge concern to me and to many parents. Society worldwide is faced with enormous and growing social costs from drug abuse, including prisons, rehab centers, hospital and emergency care, legal and law enforcement expenses, pharmaceuticals and research, and, ultimately, deaths. I am not an expert on the costs of all rehab facilities, and I can only report on what our family paid, but the question of cost for care is crucial and demands attention.

Jeff's care averaged, in the middle and late 1990s and early 2000s, around $5,000 to $15,000 for thirty days, although some programs were less expensive and some were more. We also found treatment centers that cost as much as $30,000 to $60,000 for twenty-eight to thirty days. In addition, before most centers accept the client, the policy for admission is clear: The money must be paid up front, or insurance must guarantee payment. If the addict leaves prematurely, which happened to us at Burning Tree and other centers, when Jeff walked out on his own and against the recommendation of the professionals, the center kept the total, with no reimbursement for the days when Jeff was not there and did not receive care. In our case, insurance paid only once, for Jeff's five-day hospital detox. Tim and I spent hundreds of thousands of dollars when we add together the cost of the treatment facilities, plane fares, hotel bills, medications and medical testing, and doctors' visits. I used Jeff's trust fund, which had been set up lovingly on the day of his birth by my father and mother for his future home or business or education, to pay off the debts that he had racked up using drugs—cash withdrawals against credit cards (Jeff sometimes spent more than $5,000 a month on drugs), legal fees, car repairs, and unpaid rent. The cost of rehabilitation is significant and heavy.

The family of one of the boys in Jeff's last rehab center took a second mortgage on their home to pay for treatment, and when their son was released after thirty days, he picked up again. Relapse is common, and adds to the financial devastation. There are many worse stories than this, when the addict dies of either violence on the streets or an overdose: The cost of a life is forever.

What I don't understand is that there are at least two centers in Italy that cost nothing: San Patrignano and Comunità Cenacolo. They are free—free for all clients, regardless of the family's financial holdings, and regardless of the addict's personal wealth. Their only requirement is that the addict or alcoholic requests care and agrees to stay for three to five years (although the person is never held against his or her will). San Patrignano has accepted over eighteen thousand people since its inception in 1978. They don't accept money from their clients, their families, or public institutions, and they provide free medical care, legal assistance, job training, and an opportunity for people to change their lives. The center is self-perpetuating, and everyone on campus works in a host of enterprises, ranging from food and furniture production to equestrian training and high-quality printing. In addition, and most important, recent studies conducted by several major universities show that after three years of independent living off campus, 72 percent of those who completed the program at San Patrignano are drug free and working.

The same is true for the Comunità Cenacolo: It is free, not subsidized by the government or any organization, requires a three- to five-year commitment, and has a strong recovery rate. It is faith-based, founded by a Catholic nun, and has over fifty houses throughout the world, but accepts young addicted people of all faiths or of no faith. In July 2008, I had the opportunity to visit the mother house in Saluzzo, Italy, for their twenty-fifth anniversary, because American friends have a son who is there, a heroin addict, and they allowed me to accompany them. Their son has been in the community for over one year, yet when he entered he never thought he'd stay longer than six months. Now he says he wants to stay: "I'm happy here. I have hope today." I was struck with the joy and health of the young men who are recovering from their addiction in this community, a word that makes sense to me.

Relapse is real, and, although it's difficult even to think about, it happens, and it happened often to us, to Jeff. Dr. Kevin McCauley, with the Institute for Addiction Study, explained to me that if, during Jeff's strong times, we had planned for relapse by working closely with Jeff and a therapist to set up a compassionate and supportive relapse plan, we might have been able to slow down or even arrest the progress of this fatal disease in our son. Dr. McCauley feels strongly that it is essential to develop a relapse program with the addict or alcoholic lasting at least the first year, better the first three to five years, and really for all of his life. Addiction is a chronic disease, he explained, and both Jeff and our family needed a plan.

Our family understands that we must stay humble in the face of addiction, because it lurks in the shadows, always taunting, biding its time, gauging just the right moment when vulnerability is high and relapse is possible. We must stay humble and stay grateful—and continue to hope. Hope is a powerful source of strength. Hope doesn't change reality. Or maybe it does. I don't know, but I do know that it fueled our spirits and helped us to hang on. There is a Tibetan expression: "Even if the rope breaks nine times, we must splice it back together a tenth time. Even if ultimately we do fail, at least there will be no feelings of regret."

Jeremy once asked, "Mom, how will you end the story about Jeff?"

I admitted, "I don't know, Jer. It's not my story to end."

His answer was clear: "But that's the point. We don't know what will happen to Jeff, but no one can ever take away our hope. You have to end the story in hope."

And we will.

On July 21, 2006, Jeff made the decision not to go back to an addicted life. With this choice of sobriety, he also decided that it was time for him to reenter his professional world of public relations. Although he knew how to obtain a job, and had done so successfully several times before, at this time in his recovery this stepping forward felt daunting to him. Dr. MacAfee had cautioned me many times: "An addict knows the world of chaos; what's tough for the addict is the world of day-to-day life. We know a lot about addiction. What we don't know a lot about is how an addict learns to live in sobriety." However, Jeff was learning to trust himself and to trust others. He applied for positions, tentatively, step by step, with courage and hope. He interviewed with several firms, and after weeks of waiting was offered a position with a public relations agency in Los Angeles. He was relieved that the strength of his résumé, combined with interviews and his education, had been recognized, and had served him well. His professional life could begin again.

After receiving his first paycheck in August, Jeff was able to sign a lease on a two-bedroom apartment in Venice, California. He and a buddy decided to live together and share expenses. Jeff knew Michael from his days working in D.C., and even though Mike has never had issues with alcohol or drug abuse, and even though he knew Jeff's history with drugs, he believed in Jeff and trusted that he would stay sober, pay rent, and be a good roommate. So now Jeff had a job, a paycheck, an apartment, and sober friends; he was rebuilding his life. I asked him how he felt during this time of transition.

I was thrilled and terrified to enter real life again. But more thrilled than terrified. It had been years since I was a part of anything professional, and I was eager to start feeling productive again. For as optimistic as I was, I'd only been sober for a few weeks and had little confidence in my ability to stay that way. My relapse history was extensive, but my attitude was different this time.

In L.A. everything was new: the people, the city, the job, the terrain. And socializing as a guy who doesn't drink, or at least smoke pot, is pretty uncommon. I found myself wanting to prove to normal people that I could be normal, too. That I could say normal things and respond in normal ways. Emotionally, I felt isolated, and I didn't know exactly how to connect with people outside of AA. To this point my life surrounded drugs almost exclusively. Even in treatment, my life revolved around them. Drugs were my identity, and now, for the first time in fourteen years, I was alone and trying to define myself by the things I did and the things I believed in. At this point, however, I didn't much know what those things were.

Some real spiritual breakthroughs were made during this time, and I began learning how to lean on something other than myself. It's hard to put into words the sensation, but I felt almost carried through this stretch.

Today, Jeff acknowledges his past and strives for a better tomorrow. Today, he works—works at his job, works at his recovery, and works with his God. I asked Jeff to help with the writing of this book, and he painstakingly advised and counseled me, all the while enhancing and clarifying his thoughts, his feelings, and his truths, because he wants to make a difference. He says this is part of his twelfth step: "Having had a spiritual awakening as the result of these steps, we tried to carry this message to alcoholics, and to practice these principles in all our affairs." This is our way of contributing, of carrying the message of hope and compassion, of reaching out a hand to help another family, another parent, maybe even another brother. AA calls recovering addicts to witness that sobriety is attainable and sustainable. Jeff knows the power of addiction and the power of cravings: He not only speaks about addiction, he speaks from addiction.

I've visited Jeff several times in L.A., wanting to stay close to him, and also to see his apartment and his office, and meet his colleagues and friends. These young people are hardworking, creative, and bright, both men and women who are good friends to him, and they laugh easily and talk seriously about jobs, music, films, fashion, politics, economy, religion, and spirituality. They represent all walks of life, from a young man building a career as a movie producer to a young woman who helps manage the medical system at the University of California at Los Angeles. Their enthusiasm is contagious and their goals are clear. They know Jeff's history because he told them; they respect him and his walk.

Jeff's days are filled with work at the PR agency, where he oversees multiple account teams. He excels in his job; I know this because he's already had promotions and pay increases. He is content in his work, proud of his contributions, and puts in long hours. Each morning Jeff has a routine that seems to stabilize his day: He reads from an assortment of spiritual and philosophical books, stretches, prays, and has a breakfast of fruit, complete with an espresso. He runs on the Venice boardwalk and, when it's too crowded and crazy, in the alleyways and next to the canals. At nights he and his friends often go to dinner, and then to concerts and shows. He has favorite authors and actors and artists. He's identified his special spots for coffees and teas, and he has developed an appreciation for diverse foods. His health is important to him, and he tries to eat well. Little things bring him increasing pleasure, like talking with his grandmother every Friday morning on his way to work, discussing a new or little-known film with his roommate, discovering an upstart band, or feeling his blood pump through his veins when he runs and skateboards. He has been accepted into a graduate program at a respected L.A. university, and he is considering pursuing a five-year Ph.D. program in clinical psychology. This is a long-term goal, but he's sober, and dreams are possible again.

Our family is finding peace and unity, and we're learning, together and independently. Jeremy has begun to break his long-held silence. He told me, "I love Jeff. He's my teammate. I never quit loving my brother; love was never the question. Did you know that I saved the message on my cell phone from December 2005, when you found Jeff and he went into treatment? I could play it for you today." He continued, "I'm OK with the way things went down. I'm more self-aware, more intuitive. I lost a big part of my brother to drugs, but I'm finding strength from it." They visit each other and spend time together. They are still brothers and friends: One moment they are discussing their careers, psychology, business opportunities, or family issues, and then in the next, Jeremy is wrapping one of his long arms around Jeff, tugging his ear or squeezing his cheek as he trips Jeff, and they tumble sideways together. I don't know if they talk much about the years of Jeff's addiction, but I don't need to know. As Jeremy tells me, "No matter what happens or what the future holds, Jeff and I are brothers. *Fratellanza*, an unspoken bond of brotherhood. Jeff will always be my heart."

Tim talks more frankly about what happened with the addiction: "Jeff and I didn't say much to each other before, but we talk openly now. He has such promise, and I hope he stays committed to his path. Sobriety is fragile. I see that now." In July 2007, twelve years after our separation and divorce, Tim planned a vacation for the four of us, and we spent one week together, golfing, cooking dinners, and walking on the beach. We didn't discuss much about the things of our past, not during that visit, but the four of us were together, and it was good. Tim and Jeff talk often these days, and they enjoy a round of golf or a fine meal as they laugh together and talk about business and life.

For me, I believe I've grown stronger as a mom: I've adopted a new motto—"Talk Less, Pray More"—and usually I remember to abide by it. I stay close to my sons, trying not to enable or interfere, and I respond with greater patience and understanding. I remind myself to stay in the present, to enjoy today, and to be grateful and hopeful. When people ask me how I am, I respond that I live in a space of gratitude. In Florence I still row with the Dragon Boat Ladies, a group united in the hope that one day all women will survive breast cancer. We know we're the lucky ones. My love of schools and children continues, and I serve on the board of an international school. But most important, my sons know that they are my priority, and I laugh when I tell them a familiar Italian expression, *la mamma e' sempre la mamma*, which means "the mother is always the mother." All over the world, this seems to be a universal truth.

When Jeff and I talk about his future and the addiction, I now understand more fully the power of a family staying close, and the words *stagli vicino* are becoming part of our family's consciousness. Jeff needed patience, tolerance, and love. Learning how to do this was difficult for me, because I had to learn how to love Jeff while watching him fall, crash, and possibly die. I wanted desperately for Jeff to know that he had a home waiting for his return, that he could trust that communication between us would be open and honest, and that we would never give up hope that he would one day be Jeff again.

I'll forever be lovingly indebted to the director of the Florence site of San Patrignano, who struggled with his English because he was determined that I must understand that Jeff needed to know that he was loved even when he was unlovable, even when he was closed away from us, and especially when he was at his sickest. This is what guided me at the end. I tried to give Jeff love, compassion, and support, and this helped me to stay close without interfering in the disastrous effects of his decision making.

During Jeff's final descent, I answered his phone calls and listened. I encouraged him to get help, but I didn't offer him a place to live, a job, or even money for rehab. I stood by and watched. Might he have died? Yes, and I lived with that knowledge and fear. Many parents have lost their children, many spouses have lost their mates, and many innocent people have lost their loved ones because of an addict, a drunk driver, a drug abuser. For all of us, there is no salve that can heal those wounds. The loss of a child is forever, beyond words.

I believe, as firmly as I believe anything, that families and people who love addicts must stay close to them, *stagli vicino*. I can now promise my son, "Jeff, if you ever feel at risk of using drugs again, trust me this time. Don't keep me in the dark. If you need help, if you're afraid of using, or if you've used, please trust that we will help. You're not alone, ever. You have AA, and you have lots of friends who love you. You have your family. Remember, we're only a phone call away."

In late August 2006, three days after Jeff started his new job, I wrote about my fears. Choice is powerful in the world of addiction, and I chose a different way to feel about Jeff's sobriety.

August 24, 2006, 4:00 p.m.
Do I want to write that obviously Jeff's different, that anyone can tell that this time is different? Sure. Will I write it, can I? I can, but I'm afraid. We've been at this juncture before, like Alice looking into the rabbit hole, not knowing if the next tunnel, the next chute, would tumble us into the land of the healed. I do know that he sounds strong, he sounds vibrant. He speaks with reflection in his voice, his words ring out with conviction, but with humility. Yep, he sounds different this time. Will it be different? I pray so.

Maybe I should write YES, it IS different. So, I will. Today I will rejoice. Even with all my hesitations, hiccups, and fears, I will say, "Hallelujah, Jeff will be different this time. Jeff will live and be productive. Yes, Jeff will live."

This book is an effort to bring addiction out of the shadows and into a place of healing. There is great shame associated with this illness, I know. However, I also know that when I was young, we didn't talk about topics like abortion or breast cancer or homosexuality. Today we talk openly about these things. We name the issues and try to face them. This kind of dialogue takes courage, and we all need courage—courage to fight, to forgive, and to live again.

Jeff and his daily choices end this story. Addiction still sits at our dining room table and in our family's collective conscious, but it's not in charge, not today. It's powerful, though, and we have to be vigilant, because it knows when to pounce—when despair and sorrow strike, when grief and anxiety suffocate him, and when fear and worry grip his soul. Jeff must always be on guard. He must understand that he'll always live with the addiction. Today Jeff looks forward, and he looks back.

Addiction has changed my life and made me a different person, a better person in many respects. Life is richer, because I was forced to confront myself. I can't change the past, and I wouldn't want to if I could. Drugs were my life, but drugs left me empty. The party ended and life got ugly. The hustle to stay high became a deadly one, and in the process I found something amazing and outside of myself.

In 2005, when I was at the ranch and trying again to get clean, I fought everything. But most of all I fought the idea of spirituality. It was in everything attached to the program, and I told my sponsor that the God thing would never work or make sense to me, that I needed to find something else. He laughed and said simply, "I don't give a damn what you believe—just pay attention to the coincidences." And with that my perspective shifted. In spite of years of cynicism and disbelief, I've seen with my own eyes something at work on this planet that's bigger than I am big.

Every day we're grateful. Every day, in the very marrow of our bones, we give thanks that today Jeff is OK, that he is alive and productive, and that he is making up for the lost years.

Our ending is in the present, in Jeff's day-to-day choice of sobriety. Can there be celebration in the everyday, in the commonplace events and rhythms of everyday life? For us, for all the families of addicts, for the addict himself, we think yes. Jeff finds hope in his daily choice of sobriety because each choice, one day at a time, signifies that he earns the right to choose again—and again, and again. There's freedom in choice. This story is not a promise for tomorrow but a celebration of today. Our story ends in hope, because it ends in beginning.

"Never quit believing, OK, Momma?"

"I won't quit believing, Jeff."

Never.

Libby with her sons, Jeff (sitting) and Jeremy, winter 2008
MICHELE BORZONI

Acknowledgments

During my writing, one thing never left my mind: the pain of all the parents who have lost their children to drug addiction. I felt then, writing, and still feel now a heaviness for all the losses, all the unremitting heartache. I continued to write for these parents and their children.

Cynthia Voigt, an accomplished writer and a friend, never left my side as she mentored me through the writing process. She and Ray Haas, my lifetime editor in chief, read many drafts and their encouragement gave me the tenacity to continue. Their careful teaching, opinions, and guidance brought this story home.

Patrick MacAfee, Ph.D., Jeff's therapist and our friend, has devoted more than forty years of his life to working with addicts, and he shared his wisdom in the afterword. He's helped me to understand my son; he's helped me to be a better mother.

I am blessed with a community of friends who have stayed close. Judy MacWilliams has helped me selflessly for over twenty years.

Thanks to George Burroughs III and Lauren Giordano, Kay Aronhalt, Laura Corwin, and Sue Apple. The Calverton School family, my Maryland family, and my Italian family supported me through many tough times.

Thanks to Victoria Skurnick and Lindsay Edgecombe at Levine Greenberg Literary Agency. Lindsay is a former student of mine, and I learned happily that I could become the student as she became the teacher. Victoria knocked on and opened publishers' doors. Thanks to Elizabeth Beier and Michelle Richter at St. Martin's Press. Michelle offered her constant assistance. Elizabeth believed in our story, and I couldn't have a better, or smarter, or more intuitive editor.

My brothers stood by me, always. My mom and her prayers gave me direction and peace; she is a woman of great strength, and it took me a long time to realize it. My dad, who died in 2004, is with me every day. I think one day that the heavens will open and I'll hear his voice, because I hear him every day in my heart.

Tim, I'm glad to know that you are as proud of our sons as I am. Here's to golden days and to staying close.

Afterword

Patrick MacAfee, Ph.D.

It is wonderful to help, said the monkey
as he saved the fish from drowning
by placing him safely in the tree.

The above fable captures the essence of dealing with the complexities of addiction and recovery, an illness that is still substantially unrecognized. The monkey puts the fish in the tree and tells him to get a grip and to stop using, and he promises the fish that the addiction will go away. Not so.

Libby and Jeff have been caught up in this miasma of addiction for years. Libby tried to do what she thought was right, what other people, even professionals, told her to do, and on the face of it she was doing the correct things, the right things—like getting Jeff therapy and into rehab and detox centers over and over again—but the struggle with addiction went on. Libby and Jeff's story is a fair cross-section of what families face. Their struggles are real and offer a human characterization of the depths of this malady.

The stories of addiction and families demand to be told because they can help to break the cycles of dysfunction and hold the light up to and expose some of the social misconceptions of addiction.

By retelling these stories and sharing the pain, others can benefit. This is the recovery process.

How do we, as professionals, deal with the addict and addiction? Because it is notoriously difficult to treat, many therapists I know do not like to work with addicts. In addition, our training as clinicians can get in our way, as noted by C. G. Jung: "If the wrong man uses the right means, the right means works in the wrong way."

The rules to deal with addiction come from history, the justice system, and the emerging recovery movement. The medical and psychological fields have become increasingly aware of addiction's serious hold and have recognized it as a legitimate—and treatable—illness, but it seems to me that few people outside these professional areas understand the addictive condition as a legitimate life-threatening illness. People often approach with disgust not only the addiction but the addicts themselves. This attitude of contempt permeates society into the level of the individual family and seeps down to the addicts, reinforcing the self-loathing that likely is already firmly established in their identity. And all conditions, from those affecting society as a whole to those affecting the person as an individual, continue to collide and worsen.

Addiction marginalizes people through its attendant criminal activity, societal repulsion, and often celebrity sensationalism, rarely showing the personal trauma of individuals and their families. These catastrophic and sometimes fatal situations with addiction might seem to be other people's problems—that is, until they enter our homes and become parts of our life stories. Addicts are real people: brothers, sisters, mothers, fathers, husbands, wives, sons, and daughters. They live among us. Those who view the illness of addiction and those who treat it determine the "right methods . . . wrong persons." As a therapist, I think it is essential that we don't overlook the real human tragedy—the tragedy that forces families to rewrite their stories, their lives, and their understanding of survival and living.

I am no apologist of drug use. I am a clinician who has worked for over forty years with countless addicts and families through difficult times, and no matter the outcome, all persons suffered and endured almost unbearable pain along the way. Libby and Jeff's story reflects the true-life drama of addiction and details the horrific effects on the family. Their story is a microcosm of isolation, fear, terror, confusion, and secrecy, all turned inward in a never-ending litany of: "What went wrong?" "Who is to blame?" "Why can't you stop?" and "Why are you doing this to us?"

As with most parents confronting the dilemma of addiction, Jeff's struggle became a part of Libby. How could it not? This is natural, a part of healthy parenthood. Parents don't stop loving their child because he is an addict, but the behavior of the addict starts to contort, distort, and make unhealthy all the best of parental love. It is addiction's way.

During Jeff's addiction, Libby both helped and enabled him—and today, she knows this is true. Enabling, however, is oftentimes a normal response. The mother-child bond is natural and deep, and her attempts to help by bailing Jeff out were acts of love. She wanted to trust her son; however, she didn't see the level of duplicity and deception that Jeff was living and perpetuating. Not initially, and not for many years.

In time, Jeff's lies and chronic betrayal created massive confusion, anger, and rage. Libby knew that much was wrong, and she wanted to fix things because, after all, aren't parents supposed to be able to save their drowning children? During Jeff's earlier years, their lives were enjoyable, but what had happened? The confusion continued, as did Libby's belief that there must be a way back to innocence.

To know their family in the throes of active addiction, in the throes of struggling with all the malfunction of Jeff's behavior, is to understand that they did what they thought was best. Libby, Tim, and Jeremy helped and supported Jeff, not understanding that embedded in this natural act of caring and loving is the chance for the addict to exploit and manipulate. Ultimately Jeff exhausted their resources and good will, leaving them in a state of psychological desperation. They, in turn, felt defeated and in desperation responded by flipping between acting with kindness to doling out punishments. This is an uneasy observation. Addiction takes the healthiest parts of love and smashes them into worry, helplessness, and hopelessness. These are not exaggerations; they are extremes, and they are the very nature of the family's dilemma. Learning to be an addict takes time, and a substantial loss of self.

The addict is drawn into a culture that calls him, welcomes him home. In fact, these are the very words Jeff wrote in an earlier chapter: Heroin felt like home. Drugs are filled with the promise of permanent soothing and offer a powerful sense of well-being.

During group therapy one afternoon, I asked a young man, "Rob, what is your drug of choice?"

He rubbed his chin as he thought for a moment before answering, and said, "More."

His answer was not an attempt at humor, and no one laughed. Instead, the group answered with a consensus of silence, affirmative head nods.

Substances drive the addict, and families grow ever more dysfunctional and stressed as they try to cope using the tools that society has given them. They are attempting to do what is right, and in doing so, they are adapting to an insane condition. They move deeper into ignorance and denial as they continue to underestimate the severity of the malady. They are shocked and angry and overreact, believing that somehow they should have known the truth from the start, but not knowing why they didn't. Feelings of betrayal run rampant. But what rules should they follow? This spiraling ordeal and shift of identity leaves the family in a state of self-blame, and they feel immense shame for themselves and for the addict in their midst. All the while, the addict is deeply absorbed in his search for drugs.

One of my patients observed, "No addict ever intends to end up where he's really going."

. . .

Jeff and I started our work together in January 2006. In our first session as he sat in my office, he said, "I can do this," almost to himself, nodding and looking up to the left. "I can do this."

He then looked straight at me and simply smiled. I felt that he wanted to be heard, though not engaged. He wanted me to listen and believe in him. His quietly affirming self-dialogue seemed a private one. I sensed that Jeff did a lot in silence. This was my first encounter with something that would characterize much of our therapy: Jeff's silence.

I came to know that Jeff spoke a lot through his silence, which makes this afterword difficult. What words can give meaning to his silence? It has been hard to explain, though perhaps it's not so difficult to describe what happens in those moments in the therapeutic encounter when all is right, when the sense of trust feels established. There were many instances in our work when Jeff set aside his vigilance, revealing innocence in this place of safety. He heard in me a willingness to learn from him as well. Maybe it was nothing more than mutual regard and my holding him in respect that forged the doctor-patient bond and made the path more tolerable for him. I don't know.

Tall, lean, angular, and handsome, Jeff has a smile that is large and bright. In public, he would divert his large brown eyes, keeping his personal space. He would frequently turn the heads of the women and girls in the waiting room as he hurried his way out of sight. I thought he was trying to make himself invisible.

Jeff carried one of the thorniest of problems found in the addict: the competence/confidence themes of pretense. His attempts to compensate for what was happening to him in his addiction threw him into elaborate cover-ups because he needed to appear to be on top of things while his life was falling down around him.

The arrests, the chaos, the deceit stacked up on one side, but they were counterbalanced by his very real accomplishments on the other side. When he was back on his feet and living without drugs, he would repeat words like, "Okay, this time I can stay sober; I've really got it." Inside the addiction, Jeff was competent and he accomplished much: He returned to university, earned high grades, got jobs, obtained internships, and even received promotions. It is as if he was saying, "See how well I can master things?" Yet all the while drugs and the addictive process were *his* masters. He showed up on time, looked good, and tried to maintain an impenetrable defense of denial, deflecting the consequences, externalizing his condition, acknowledging his part, but always going back to the same behavior.

There is an old adage around the recovery community: "The non-addict changes his behavior to meet his goals; the addict changes his goals to meet his behavior." Jeff tried his best to stay in control and to achieve in an effort to maintain the counterfeit self-assurance he needed to support his double life. He needed to be seen as capable and confident; he needed to maintain his fiction of wellness. Until, of course, the fiction bled through to his awareness and started to erode his denial. This was a slow process, but he started seeing himself in a clearer light.

Jeff was extraordinarily effective in holding up his false front, his dual lives, but he lacked the belief in himself at the most basic level. Jeff's controls were temporary tours into compliance. Following a relapse or a spin in treatment, he would try to present a renewed and solid image of himself to demonstrate that he was on the right track . . . for a while, then back, just an occasional slipup, late here, a lie there, which then becomes the norm all over again. He was well aware of his fraudulent behavior, so he created more facades. He thought, "If I can convince you that I'm OK, I can hang on to my addiction. Then I won't have to see your pain—or mine."

Addicts want to be seen as they portray themselves. It is part of the illness, again this fiction; it is their attempt at control in a delusional world. In fact, their immense depth of delusional thinking is confounding. In Jeff's mind he was portraying a sense of adeptness, projecting his well-being to the external world, which, of course, wasn't accurate, true, or even sane. When faced with the drug-related disasters, he viewed them as independent occurrences, without direct connections and external in nature. I believe that this fixed form of denial becomes habitual thinking with many addicts and family members—they all live in delusion. It is a phenomenon of addictive thinking: "You'll see me as I portray myself." But in spite of the damage, he never lost his determination.

Jeff had many real successes during this time of madness, but this made it very difficult for other people, even those closely connected to him, to see how badly, how poorly he saw himself. Living inside his skin was more than he could bear at times. The heaviness of his reality, combined with the fictitious scripts he struggled to maintain, weighed on him, but it is exactly this weight that provided early signals of his getting well.

Returning to Jeff's silence that day in my office, which was now a solace no longer accompanied by defensiveness or mute deception, Jeff was deciding to begin living his life differently. Like most addicts I have known, Jeff could accurately read people to get his way; his "bullshit meter" was well developed. He was superb at it, but in time, he grew tired of lying and getting away with it. He hated himself for perpetuating the lie, hated others for not recognizing it, and became very defensive when the lie was brought to his attention. A core pathology of addiction is in its defenses.

In recovery, the power of the therapeutic alliance is not to be underestimated. Along with the family, it's one of the primary relationships on the road to getting better. Characteristically, the therapeutic relationship between doctor and addict is both powerful and tentative. Jeff could smell insincerity from miles away and he would flee the moment he caught a whiff. Beneath the layers of manipulation, the one thing Jeff desperately needed was honest contact, respect, truth, and candidness—the very things he chased away in his life of lies.

Jeff's abstinence started to clear his mind. He was beginning to recognize his defeat by drugs; the very lifestyle that he had fought to protect had failed him entirely. He began to recognize and internalize the similarities between himself and other addicts, and he discovered that he was not unique or different. He could see himself in their lives, their defenses, and their stories. This awareness created vulnerability, a place where a real dialogue began—a place that could no longer hide his fiction.

I respected him for not giving up after having been in such difficult straits and through so many treatments for so many years. His vulnerability was real, and I have noticed this vulnerability in recovering people before. It is surrender. He could finally be silent. There was no need to explain himself, no need to be smart, intelligent, charming, or in charge. Jeff once told me, "It feels good not to have to look over my shoulder anymore."

This leg of his recovery was self-initiated and was both appealing and appalling to him. He would have to be open and to continue telling the truth. We worked closely for two years, tapering down from weekly sessions to twice a month, and then finally to once a month.

Jeff had one great advantage over addicts who find their way into therapy through the legal system or from family pressure: *He* had surrendered. When Jeff came to see me, he possessed the genuine desire to quit using drugs for good. Now, his question was: *could he?* Jeff's heroin had to go; use of all mind-altering substances had to go as well. Anyone with Jeff's drug history would have to accept complete abstinence. There was no more room for cutting back or moderating. He had lost control. He exemplified the old saying: "One is too many and a hundred is not enough." Loss of control is one of the major markers of addiction. In this loss of control, he found that real recovery and the search for a spiritual center began sinking into places made hollow by his years of using and running. He was tired, but fatigue alone does not stop an addict.

Yet hope is another thing. Jeff had hope, and he was beginning to hope in ways he had not thought possible before. He remembered that he once had a life filled with honest relationships and wholesome activities. He was starting to listen as he once had. He finally wanted recovery for himself, for his own sake, but first he had to learn to trust himself. And he did.

Jeff's progress was rapid and substantial. The first few months of our work addressed his learning to live drug-free; so did the next two years. Jeff was not sure of what he wanted to accomplish or what a drug-free life was supposed to look like. He just knew he didn't want to return to the despair of running dope-sick, trying to look for a way out with a needle in his arm. Knowing what you don't want is every bit as viable a position as knowing what you *do*, and a good place to begin.

Learning to live drug free touched every facet of his life. He had to learn to be authentic without using. He had to learn to laugh without using. He had to learn to be intimate in his friendships without using. He had to learn to feel emotional and physical pain without using. His life without using made him feel exposed, suspicious, and, again, vulnerable. Like starting over, he had only a memory of a life lived before.

We know the most important work in treatment with recovering people is rebuilding the relationships they have with themselves and their loved ones. Their relationship to their drug is also very powerful, often described as their only relationship, and from this place, making room for human contact is difficult. Early in our work, we dealt a great deal with the impact of total abstinence and total sobriety. Like a double-edged sword, abstinence is both the gateway to recovery and the largest block to maintaining it. His focus shifted from doing things that appeared to be right to doing things that were genuinely right. He began to find efficacy in his own decisions, choices, and behavior. He recognized his own growth and started to live for the truth.

Recovery, however, is not a linear process. For example, one day, about nine months into our therapy, Jeff started feeling increasingly edgy and discontented, wondering why he couldn't use alcohol or drugs the way other friends he knew could—in a kind of recreational and social way.

"You always have the right to use, Jeff. Sobriety has to be your choice, your decision."

"Doc, don't tell me that—it scares me and lets me think that maybe I don't have to quit—not totally." He paused. "And why are you bringing that up now?"

"You're changing, Jeff, and you miss using. I am relieved by the awareness of your fear; your fear in this context is a positive driver. The discomfort is your awakening. Jeff, you can't sleep in an awakening personal world. Something in you is waking up and that sounds like health to me."

Jeff had come to a place where there was nothing left to understand. Although there was much more work to do, there were no additional question marks in his head as to why he was an addict. The only thing left to do was to focus on his day-to-day behavior, the integrity of his choices, and the pact of abstinence that he made with himself—not with me and not with his family. This was a crucial time, and he had turned a critical corner. He reestablished his need to "do the next right thing." The terror in the concept of life without using was eroding and the belief in his new reality was setting in. He could acknowledge the fullness in a life without drugs. He could imagine living with freedom.

When I asked him about his years of fear and why he felt so much heaviness, even as he entered his second year of recovery, he replied, "Staying clean has always been hard; I have a long history of failure."

Today, Jeff's story is a happier one.

Many families are caught in this nightmare of active addiction and they are often advised to turn their loved ones loose or to learn to live without them. Addicts constantly abuse boundaries, and families need to learn ways to protect themselves. Self-preservation becomes the goal. This is easier said than done, and we know from research that the family has an enormous impact on the addiction and is enormously impacted by it. There are painful questions and painful answers: What to do? Where to turn?

The family remains both one of the greatest resources and one of the most troubling components in the addict's recovery. Operating in ignorance, a family can perpetuate the very condition it is attempting to help. Family members repeatedly blame themselves and try to straighten out the addict. This is a mission filled with good intentions, but unless the addict is ready to stop, good intentions are exploited. Addicts will do anything in their power to keep using, and families will do anything in their power to stop them. When the family is unable to make the addict stop, the system is infused with anger and resentment. This happens again and again, becoming an unbearable cycle.

Addiction operates by its own particular rules and when we attempt to cajole, plead, or rage, we are walking into its trap. Addiction isolates and separates strong families and once thriving social systems. When people are divided, addiction does its best and most destructive work. As things spiral out of control, the family of an addict adapts to the dysfunction, becoming conditioned to increasingly destructive behavior. No-talk rules abound and the family keeps the silence: They are ashamed and beaten down and the organizing principle in the system becomes the addict and his using. Families are crippled by their attempts to cope and the traditional tools of problem solving do not work.

Even when the addict begins to live in sobriety, family members who are used to dealing with the addict and his erratic behavior keep broken systems in place. Entire relationships need to be rebuilt and relearned. Old systems must be realigned.

With accurate information, education, and support, families can learn to address the problem. Al-Anon and other family-focused groups are superb contacts and can be found in almost every community throughout the world (http://www.al-anon.org). In Al-Anon, family members are introduced to the concepts of enabling, detaching, and caring for self and family. They can bring material and new learning home and begin to approach the addict with a better understanding, increasing their support and decreasing enabling.

The Al-Anon groups emphasize self-care and encourage talking with other families, helping to avoid feelings of isolation. Families are safe to share stories about enabling a situation and perpetuating the issues they intended to solve. As addicts become increasingly drawn into addiction, their families are drawn into the confusion. They feel alone, like they are the only family in such peril. Families polarize, moving into either/or thinking. The addict becomes the major focus for some members, while for others he becomes a target for rejection, disdain, and fury.

The ideal family group focuses upon the common characteristics of recovery. Usually, these groups run themselves, mentoring their members. The empathy and understanding that families have toward one another is heartfelt and immensely helpful. Hope is the tone.

In addition to Al-Anon and family groups, the family should turn to certified addiction specialists, many of whom are recovering addicts themselves. They are important resources and their personal experiences with addiction help establish the critical bonds of empathy, respect, and openness. Some references that I recommend include the literature from Al-Anon, Alcoholics Anonymous, Hazelden Publishing, and the PBS video series *Moyers on Addiction: Close to Home*.

I believe that *stagli vicino*—staying close but out of the way of the insanity—is best. If you are dealing with addiction, offer the addict roads to recovery, not more money or bailouts. Excuses keep people sick. The first and most necessary step, for the addict and the family, is to realize and accept that there is a problem. For the addict, inescapable accountability needs to emerge and he must feel the consequences of his behavior; the family must begin to reflect reality. In recovery, it is imperative that the addict learns to be *rigorously honest*, saying what is meant and meaning what is said. This approach does not happen all at once; it is a process. Characteristically the road to recovery has greater and greater transparency. Because addicts are defensively oriented, therapists and family members will not have the impact they desire if they attack the individual with a jack hammer. Complaining, threatening, forcing, and handwringing rarely, if ever, succeed. Instead, such approaches tend to drive the condition underground. Defensiveness must be lowered and communication must become clearer. The overall emotional environment needs to be more honest, compassionate, and less stressed. The restoration of safety slowly encourages trust; this happens with time and consistency. Safety allows connection and a sense of belonging increases.

The fear of watching a loved one failing is frightening, but don't let it cloud your realization that the natural extension of love and caring may only enable the addict's condition.

Jeff and his family are good today. Their trials have revealed their bonding and their strengths. Jeff is happy; he is well. Although he and I no longer see each other regularly for sessions, we stay in touch. He gave me his permission to write this afterword, and I think he has shown great courage. Today Jeff lives in honesty; his life is transparent and he is reclaiming his belief in his future. He is learning that dreams are possible again and he is committed to creating new ones. His years in the wilderness have taught him the value of life. His family is becoming strong at the broken places; the ruptures continue to heal and there is laughter, joy, and great comfort. It has taken time and will continue to take time— it is a slow process, and there are no short cuts or quick cures. Recovery requires knowing when to hold on and when to let go. There is no formula; it is a living and breathing way of being. Recovery is transformative. Jeff and his family have an even greater appreciation of what has gotten them here. There are happy endings . . . for today.

Resources and References

Al-Anon. *Courage to Change: One Day at a Time in Al-Anon II.* New York: Al-Anon Family Group Headquarters, 1992.

———. *Paths to Recovery: Al-Anon's Steps, Traditions, and Concepts.* New York: Al-Anon Family Group Headquarters, 1997.

———. *Hope for Today.* New York: Al-Anon Family Group Headquarters, 2007.

———. *Twelve Steps and Twelve Traditions.* Center City, MN: Hazelden, 2002.

Alcoholics Anonymous Big Book. New York: Benei Noaj, 2007.

Brown, Stephanie. *Treating Adult Children of Alcoholics.* New York: John Wiley & Sons, 1988.

———. *Treating the Alcoholic: A Developmental Model of Recovery.* New York: John Wiley & Sons, 1985.

Brown, Stephanie, and Virginia Lewis. *The Alcoholic Family in Recovery.* New York: Guilford Press, 1999.

Dalai Lama. *Ethics for the New Millennium.* New York: Riverhead Books, 1999.

———. *The Art of Happiness.* New York: Riverhead Books, 1998.

Dorris, Michael. *A Yellow Raft in Blue Water.* New York: Picador, 1987.

Frankl, Viktor. *Man's Search for Meaning.* New York: Washington Square Press, 1984.

Gendler, J. Ruth. *The Book of Qualities.* New York: Harper Perennial, 1988.

James, William. *The Varieties of Religious Experiences*. New York: American Library, 1958.

Jung, C. G. *Modern Man in Search of a Soul*. New York: Harcourt, Brace & World, 1933.

———. *Psychological Perspectives: A New Anthology of His Writings 1905 to 1951*. Jolande Jacobi, ed. Los Angeles: C. G. Jung Institute of Los Angeles, 1970.

Kaufman, Gershen. *Shame: The Power of Caring*. Cambridge, MA: Schenkman, 1980.

Levin, Jerome. *Primer for Treating Substance Abuse*. Northvale, NJ: Jason Aronson, 1999.

Lutz, William. *The New Doublespeak*. New York: HarperCollins, 1996.

May, Gerald G. *Addiction & Grace*. New York: HarperCollins, 1991.

———. *The Awakened Heart*. New York: HarperOne, 1991.

———. *Care of the Mind, Care of the Spirit*. New York: HarperOne, 1982.

———. *Will and Spirit*. New York: HarperOne, 1982.

Merton, Thomas. *New Seeds of Contemplation*. New York: New Direction, 1961.

Nouwen, Henri J. M. *Compassion*. New York: Doubleday, 1983.

O'Donohue, John. *Anam Cara: A Book of Celtic Wisdom*. New York: Harper Perennial, 1997.

White, William. *Pathways: From the Culture of Addiction to the Culture of Recovery*. Center City, MN: Hazelden, 1996.

VIDEOS/FILMS

Affliction, directed by Paul Schraeder; released January 1999.

The Disease Model of Addiction, by Kevin McCauley, M.D., produced by the Institute for Addiction Study, released 2008.

Moyers on Addiction: Close to Home, produced by, directed by Kathleen Hughes; Bill Moyers, a five-part series on addiction; PBS, 1998.

Requiem for a Dream, directed by Darren Aronofsky; released October 2000.

Trainspotting, directed by Danny Bay; released July 1996.

When a Man Loves a Woman, directed by Luis Mandoki; released May 1994.